D0205323

The Burden of the Past

THE BURDEN OF THE PAST

*Problems of Historical Perception
in Japan-Korea Relations*

Kan Kimura

University of Michigan Press
Ann Arbor

Copyright © 2014, 2019 by Kimura Kan
English translation ©2018 Japan Publishing Industry Foundation for Culture (JPIC)
Originally published in Japan by Minerva Shobo, in 2014.

Published in the United States of America by the
University of Michigan Press
Manufactured in China
Printed on acid-free paper

First published in January 2019

A CIP catalog record for this book is available from the British Library.

Library of Congress Cataloging-in-Publication data has been applied for.

ISBN: 978-0-472-07410-5 (hardcover : alk. paper)
ISBN: 978-0-472-05410-7 (paper : alk. paper)
ISBN: 978-0-472-12503-6 (ebook)

Contents

Foreword   vii

Preface to the English Edition   xi

Introduction: The Complexities of the Dispute over
    Historical Perception   1

PART I: THEORETICAL EXAMINATION

ONE A Theoretical Framework for Examining the Historical
    Perception Dispute   5
    1. The Origins and Development of the Dispute   5
    2. Historical Perception as a Standard of Value   13
    3. History and Historical Perceptions   17

TWO Three Factors in the Dispute over Historical Perceptions   21
    1. Generational Change   21
    2. Changing International Relations   32
    3. Economic Policies and the End of the Cold War   39

PART II: CASE STUDY 1: HISTORICAL DISPUTES IN THE 1980S

THREE The History Textbook Issue   49
    1. The Root of the Issue   49
    2. South Korean and Chinese Responses   53
    3. New Political Fluidity in Japan and South Korea 59

FOUR The Turning Point of the 1980s   71

1. The Closing Days of the Cold War   71
2. Changing Japan-South Korea Relations   77
3. The Second Textbook Dispute in 1987   84
4. Emergence of the Nationalistic *New Version of Japanese History*   87

PART III: HISTORICAL PERCEPTION DISPUTE: CASE STUDY 2: THE COMFORT WOMEN ISSUE

FIVE Japan-South Korea Relations at the End of the Cold War   95
1. From the Textbook Controversy to the Comfort Women Dispute   95
2. The First Katō Statement   103
3. The Miyazawa Visit   110
4. Insincere Apologies?   115
5. The Response of the Japanese Government   122
6. The Second Katō Statement   125
7. The Kōno Statement   130
8. From the Murayama Statement to the Asian Women's Fund   136

SIX Issues of Historical Perception during Japan's "Lost" Twenty Years   151
1. Changing Japanese Society   151
2. An Era of Populist Nationalism   158
3. The Historical Perception Dispute in an Era of Populist Nationalism   163
4. Deteriorating Bilateral Relations   168

SEVEN Revisiting the Japan-South Korea Historical Perception Dispute   175
1. Generational Change, Mutual Loss of Importance, Collapse of Cooperation between Ruling Elites   175
2. The Slow Collapse of the Cold War Regime   177

Afterword   179

Chronology of the Japan-South Korea Historical Perceptions Issue   183

Notes   187

Bibliography   223

Index   239

Foreword

Peace in Northeast Asia is being threatened by rising nationalism, a renewed search for national identity, and revived rivalry between Japan and China. In particular, unresolved historical and territorial issues stemming from the unfortunate past of colonialism and war raise the specter of collision between two main allies of the United States—Japan and South Korea. Written by a Japanese scholar who specializes in Korean history and politics, this book presents unique yet balanced accounts of historical disputes between the two nations since the 1980s by stressing their complex interactions at both official and civil society levels. This is a fascinating read not only for experts but also for anyone interested in the politics of memory and international relations in Northeast Asia.

In this book, the author examines two prime cases of contention over the past, history textbooks and comfort women. According to his account, the 1982 controversy on history textbooks, which triggered the so-called history problem in Northeast Asia, did not necessarily reflect Japan's turn to the right, contrary to the conventional wisdom. Rather, it was the outcome of Korean people's growing recognition that the differing views of history were significant. In Kimura's view, it reflected the concern that Korea had about the reemergence of militarism in Japan, as the rapid expansion of Japanese economic power in the 1980s thrust Japan onto the world stage. Also, the dynamics of their bilateral relationship shifted for worse as both countries gave rise to a new generation of politicians who without shared colonial experiences held different ideologies about the historical events; the end of the Cold War that removed a reason for security cooperation only exacerbated the rift. In the past before this change, the South Korean elite sought support from the Japanese right in the face of the critical stance of Japanese progressive forces that were represented by the Japanese Socialist and Communist Parties who were sympathetic to North Korea. Likewise, the Japanese elite saw the need to cooperate with the Korean elite in the Cold War era. Thus the ruling classes of Korea and Japan had worked closely together through personal ties and networks to contain disputes over their pasts. However, in this new era, all these ties and reasons for cooperation have weakened if not disappeared, providing fertile ground for historical disputes.

The comfort women issue too was the outcome of domestic politics, in this case as the result of civic activism in democratizing Korea influenced by Marxism and dependency theory. In this emerging view that saw women as victims of capitalism, when one addressed the comfort women issue, one was also dealing with the issue of women in capitalist society and, by extension, in contemporary Korea. In explaining the rise of this new discourse and movement, the author stresses the role of progressive forces in Japan, including the liberal media and "conscientious" experts who brought the issue to the forefront, showing close cooperation between Koreans and Japanese at the civil society level, who fought officially. The book details the protracted process of struggles and negotiations between the two governments, which culminated in the 1993 Kōno Statement, a landmark apology that admitted to the Japanese state's involvement in the comfort women.

This book also offers an excellent account of the rise of populist nationalism in Japan and South Korea, which has deepened the perception gap in recent years. In both countries the public became increasingly distrustful of the old elite, largely due to economic slumps and growing inequality, leading to the emergence of such populist leaders as Koizumi Junichiro and Roh Moo-Hyun. Neither were afraid of challenging the status quo including historical issues—Koizumi's open visit to the Yasukuni Shrine and Roh's public criticism of that—and thus the bilateral relationship over historical issues worsened during their tenure. More worrisome is the recent growth of anti-Korean sentiments in Japan called *Kenkanryu*, while anti-Japanese sentiments are nothing new in Korea. The author attributes this recent trend to new technology. With internet and social media, ordinary people now come into direct contact with the perception gap between Japan and South Korea over matters of territory and history, something that was previously known only to a limited group of experts. In his view, the historical perception dispute between Japan and South Korea has consequently entered a new phase of direct confrontation between public opinion in the two countries.

The author makes some arguments that can be controversial. For example, he believes that the 1993 Kōno Statement was "the product of political compromise between the Japanese and Korean governments, which meant that both governments had to bear responsibility for it." This was the same logic that Prime Minister Abe used when he was trying to revise the statement in 2014, and his attempt provoked strong reaction by Koreans. The author also contends that regarding historical and territorial issues, Koreans generally raised them and Japanese responded. Koreans may disagree.

Is time going to solve the history problem that divides the nations of Northeast Asia? Unfortunately, the answer is "no," as we witness even stronger nationalist sentiments in the new generation. The answer attests to the urgency of concerted efforts to narrow the perception gap through better understanding of how historical memories are formed and politicized on the other side. This book will make an important step forward in achieving that challenging objective.

Gi-Wook Shin (Stanford University)

Fall 2018

Preface to the English Edition

The original Japanese edition of this book was published in 2014 by Minerva Shobō, based on a series of articles entitled "Nikkan rekishi ninshiki mondai ni dō mukiau ka" (How to approach the Japan-South Korea historical perception issue) that were serialized in the Minerva magazine *Kiwameru* from April 2011 to March 2014. As a result, the content reflects to some extent the situation pertaining at that time. While in August 2010 the two countries managed to ride out the centennial of Japan's 1910 annexation of Korea relatively smoothly, this was nevertheless a period in which serious differences arose again over the comfort women and other issues of historical perception.

The rift began with the August 2011 ruling by South Korea's Constitutional Court that the government's failure to make a tangible effort to resolve the comfort women issue was unconstitutional, and calling on the government to take action. The Lee Myung-bak administration consequently abandoned its previous reluctance to foreground issues of historical perception and began to actively press the Japanese government on the comfort women issue, leading to a rapid deterioration in bilateral relations. This situation continued under the Park Geun-hye administration that came to power in February 2013. As of October 2014, when the Japanese edition of this book was published, Japan and South Korea had failed to hold so much as summit talks for the past three years.

Those summit talks finally took place a year later, in November 2015, and in December the situation took a turn for the better with an agreement reached on the comfort women issue, the most contentious among the many issues of historical perception. However, this was not to last, largely due to public negativity toward any improvement in bilateral relations. In South Korea, the public rejected from the outset the 2015 agreement on the comfort women issue as running counter to the wishes of the comfort women themselves, a criticism that only grew more vociferous over time. The Japanese public greeted the agreement much more warmly, but the erection of commemorative statues to the comfort women in South Korea and elsewhere drew considerable condemnation in Japan, and public opinion darkened. In this context, the Japanese edition of the book perhaps inevitably took a rather pessimistic stance on the historical perception issue.

Today, as I write the preface to the English edition, tensions over the issue are again rising. On December 27, 2017, a report issued by a Korean government task force examining the 2015 agreement was strongly critical that there were portions of the agreement not disclosed to the public and, above all, that it did not reflect the wishes of the actual former comfort women. The South Korean public is now pressing hard for the agreement to be renegotiated and revised, but the Japanese government appears strongly opposed to any such move.

In other words, for better or worse, more than three years since the Japanese edition of this book was published in October 2014, the state of affairs between Japan and South Korea over the historical perception issue remains unchanged, and it might even have gained gravity and importance as a result of two other developments in Northeast Asia. The first is North Korea's nuclear missile program, the threat of which has already reached as far as the United States. The other is the rise of China, which continues to joust with the United States in the South China and East China seas. Meanwhile, the international community remains actively engaged with the Korean Peninsula, including the U.S.-North Korea summit talks on June 12, 2018. As the international situation continues to evolve, cooperation between Japan and South Korea on issues such as these is more critical than ever before, but the historical perception issue is complicating the situation and souring public opinion in both countries on the prospect of cooperation.

In these circumstances, the publication of the English edition of this book seems quite timely. As I note in the introduction, the book examines the mechanisms underlying the historical perception issue and how these developed, an understanding of which will be critical in terms of considering not only the bilateral relationship but also the increasingly complex international environment in which the two countries find themselves.

At the same time, given the significant differences in prior knowledge and interest between Japanese- and English-speaking readers, I could not put out the same book in English that I wrote in Japanese for a Japanese audience. The English edition consequently features two major changes. First, I have revised numerous passages to clarify my theoretical framework and create a tone more suited to an academic work, in order to better address the needs of the majority of readers of the English edition, who are more likely to be academics with a deep interest in Japan-South Korea relations and the historical perception issue, rather than general readers. I have also added references, which were absent from the Japanese edition as the publishing company felt that it would make the book more accessible to the general reader. The English edition now contains detailed notes for readers with a more academic interest, as well as those who wish to confirm the basis for my assertions. In this sense, the English edition both reflects the original Japanese edition and incorporates major revisions that make it effectively a different work.

Publication of this English edition would not have been possible without considerable assistance. First, my deep gratitude goes to the University of Michigan Press. This is my first full-length English publication, and as such, I am not particularly familiar with English-language publishing conventions. Feedback from the University of Michigan Press has been invaluable in that regard. I was also fortunate to have strong backing from Professor Kiyoteru Tsutsui, Director of the Center for Japanese Studies at the University of Michigan, and I thank him for his recommendation, without which this English edition would not have been possible. I received various forms of support right through to publication from Keiko Yokota-Carter, research librarian for Japanese publications in the University of Michigan Library, an old friend from my Seattle research days. I hope my book repays this generous support from everyone at the university.

Even more important has been the support I have received from the Japan Publishing Industry Foundation for Culture (JPIC). I was fortunate to have this book selected for the Japan Library series, with JPIC consequently handling the whole process from translation to negotiations with publishers and even advice on publication of the English edition. I am particularly grateful to Asonuma Futsuki, who kept the negotiations moving forward. I would also like to pay my respects to Marie Speed for the excellent translation and to the Festina Lente editorial team for the high professional standard of the English edition. It was no mean feat to translate a book on such a sensitive issue with so much difficult terminology, especially given my idiosyncratic and awkward Japanese!

Finally, thank you to all the readers of this book. As a researcher on South Korean politics and Japan-South Korea relations who lives in Japan, I am eager for people to learn more about my region, and I would be delighted if my book succeeds in contributing to that end.

June 21, 2018
From my rainy season-wreathed Kobe study
Kimura Kan

Introduction

The Complexities of the Dispute over Historical Perception

Takeshima/Dokdo,[1] comfort women, history textbooks, and Yasukuni Shrine visits—Japan and South Korea have battled for years over these issues. It sometimes seems that the antagonism will continue indefinitely and grow more serious as it does.

With World War II now seventy-three years behind us, this state of affairs in bilateral relations seems extremely strange. Actually, more than strange—Japan and South Korea seem so caught up in their dispute over historical perception that they cannot even cooperate to tackle the shared challenges of China's economic and military expansion and North Korea's nuclear missile development. The dispute affects even the domestic environment in both countries. In Japan, its growing severity has spread anti-Korean sentiment to the point that some elements of the population are engaging in hate speech. Meanwhile, the South Korean government is struggling to deal with increasingly vociferous citizen movements and urgently needs to convince its people of the need for a cool-headed, future-oriented bilateral relationship.

Why do the two countries face this situation? I must point out here that the dispute over historical perception has never before impacted so heavily on bilateral relations. While the seeds of the dispute certainly existed from the 1960s through the 1980s, Japan and South Korea managed to build a stable cooperative relationship. Today, however, the situation is completely different. How did the current relationship develop? That is the issue this book attempts to address.

Aims and Structure

My aim is to reexamine the dispute over historical perception between Japan and South Korea, going beyond the descriptive emphasis of previous studies to clearly identify the various independent variables that have affected the situation. The order of that reexamination is as follows.

First, I use Japanese and South Korean newspaper databases to review discussion of the dispute over historical perceptions between the two countries from the end of World War II to the present and present a provisional hypothesis as to what brought about this situation.

In this context, I emphasize the significance of developments in the 1980s and 1990s in fixing the historical perception dispute in its current form. It was almost forty years after the end of World War II and the liberation of the Korean peninsula from colonial rule that Japan's history textbooks and the comfort women attracted attention as issues. Why did the gap between Japanese and South Korean perceptions of history that had previously remained latent suddenly become politicized during this period?

Second, I investigate my provisional hypothesis in the context of historical developments since the 1980s. Specifically, I examine the history textbook uproar of the 1980s and the comfort women issue that has become increasingly grave since the 1990s. I clarify the impact that the changing international environment of the 1980s had on the history textbook issue, as well as the factors in the comfort women issue that caused established cooperative relations between the Japanese and South Korean governments to break down.

Third, I deal with the impact that the heightened tension over the historical perception dispute has had on the bilateral relationship down to the present, focusing primarily on developments in Japan. Intensification of the dispute has stimulated Japanese nationalism, and this in turn has been used by politicians. The incorporation into policy of this rising nationalistic discourse has hardened the dispute over historical perception into the form that confronts us today.

I close with a summary of the above discussion.

PART I

Theoretical Examination

ONE

A Theoretical Framework for Examining the Historical Perception Dispute

1. The Origins and Development of the Dispute

What Databases Can Tell Us

How should we tackle the historical perception dispute? First, we need to examine how this issue has been discussed in Japan and South Korea to date, using this as the basis for laying out a theoretical framework.

Let's start with a simple exercise. Figure 1.1 uses the article database from one of South Korea's major daily papers, *Chosun ilbo*, to present comparatively simple data on the way in which the paper reported matters related to historical perception from the end of World War II and termination of Japan's colonial control over the Korean Peninsula and Taiwan to 2009. Specifically, it indicates the number of articles in the *Chosun ilbo* database that used the word "Japan" in a headline or the main body, as well as the number that also contained the various other terms noted in the table. The only exception is the term "pro-Japanese collaborator,"[1] the figures for which indicate simply the number of articles in which the term was used, as the term itself obviously already includes Japan. It should be noted, of course, that the *Chosun ilbo* is not necessarily representative of the historical perceptions discourse in South Korea, nor are article databases infallible.

At the same time, as trends in newspaper articles do reveal the movement of public opinion, albeit to a limited extent, we can use this table

Figure 1.1. Trends in the number of articles related to historical perception in *Chosun ilbo*

	Japan	Historical perceptions	Historical issue	Reparations	Pro-Japanese collaborator (see note in text)	Dokdo (Takeshima)	Forced transport	Comfort women
1945–49	1,236	0	0	47	31	0	0	0
1950–54	936	0	0	13	2	22	0	0
1955–59	3,250	0	0	24	3	9	0	0
1960–64	4,534	0	0	22	2	31	2	0
1965–69	3,535	0	0	7	3	26	3	0
1970–74	5,620	0	0	8	0	6	2	0
1975–79	4,643	0	0	5	1	44	0	0
1980–84	5,133	1	0	4	0	13	2	0
1985–89	4,748	0	0	4	2	12	11	0
1990–94	17,539	45	39	344	79	56	150	3
1995–99	28,121	113	47	357	119	550	186	459
2000–04	34,943	135	56	286	174	386	44	349
2005–09	35,867	101	141	215	217	1341	27	366

Source: Created by the author from *Chosun ilbo*, Chosen Ilbo Archive (http://srchdbl.chosun.com/pdf/i_archive/)

to assist in drawing up a theoretical framework for examining the way in which the debate on historical perception has evolved in South Korea from 1945 to the present.

What do we glean, then? First, at least in the case of this database, the number of articles concerned with historical perception climbs rapidly from the 1980s into the 1990s. However, it should be borne in mind that South Korean newspapers have tended to add pages as the country has prospered economically; moreover, the number of articles recorded in databases has also increased over time. Therefore, it would be difficult to argue from these figures alone that discussion of the historical perceptions dispute suddenly picked up pace during this period.

Yet a detailed examination of the figures does reveal certain reasons for the growing number of references. In relation to the forced transport of Korean laborers during the colonial period, for example, references first appear in any number in the 1980s, while serious discussion of the comfort women issue does not emerge until the 1990s. In other words, the data identifies a clear discontinuity in the way in which *Chosun ilbo* framed issues of historical perception between the years prior to the 1980s and 1990s and from the 1990s onward, the reason for which we need to explore.

The second observation that we can make is that, conversely, many of the key events in the dispute, as well as the related terminology, seldom appeared (at least in this newspaper) until the early 1980s. This is again exemplified by the comfort women issue. While now perceived as central to the dispute between Japan and South Korea over historical perception and presented in South Korea as the quintessence of the dark side of Japanese rule, South Korean media in fact seldom identified this issue as a major example of the harm caused by Japanese colonial rule until the early 1980s. The same can be said with regard to the textbook issue (which does not appear in the above table but is discussed later). It was 1982 when Japanese revisions of history textbooks were first foregrounded in South Korea as an issue of international magnitude. Moreover, as discussed later, this was not because of a lack of contradictory content in the respective history textbooks of the two countries.[2]

The Irony of the 1990s

From the *Chosun ilbo* article database cited above, it is clear that public interest in issues of historical perception has undergone a significant quantitative and qualitative change in the period from the early 1980s through the 1990s. What should we make of this?

First, the change in public engagement with issues of historical perception cannot be explained from the facts of the past events generally associated with the dispute. Obviously, as the past is indeed past, once it has happened, it doesn't change. If our concern with this past changes, it must be because our understanding as dwellers in the present who are interpreting the past has changed, not the past itself. Accordingly, knowledge of the past is less important to understanding the evolution of issues of historical perception than knowledge of the present as the locus of debate over these issues. In sum, issues of historical perception are more directly connected to our present lives than they are to the past.

Another interesting point in this regard is that the 1980s and 1990s were in fact a time of great optimism on the part of the media in both countries, as well as the international community, over the prospects for the historical perception dispute. Two main reasons were given: the passage of time and the increase in interaction. In other words, as time went by, the younger generation who had not experienced colonial rule and had little hesitation to talk about the issues would become the social mainstream, and if more interaction were to develop among them, historical perceptions would move naturally toward reconciliation.

Given the era, this was not an unreasonable outlook. The 1980s and 1990s were the time when the second generation of baby boomers (the second postwar generation) in Japan and South Korea was reaching adulthood, and globalization was prompting burgeoning bilateral exchange. In that climate, it must have seemed that the 1990s would be the promised time when historical disputes moved toward reconciliation.

Limits of Existing Explanations (1): The Democratization of South Korea

However, expectations were disappointed when the opposite ensued. As noted above, the historical perception dispute between Japan and South Korea rapidly intensified from the 1980s to the 1990s, a situation that continues today. Why did the initial optimistic forecast miss the mark?

A number of explanations, both general and academic, have of course been suggested. To the best of my knowledge, most have followed two patterns, the first seeking the answer in circumstances on the South Korean side, and the second drawing on the situation in Japan.

Explanations grounded in South Korea typically highlight the country's democratization.[3] The democratization movement that emerged in South Korea in 1987 generated a new political regime called the Sixth Republic that continues today. Political democratization expanded freedom of speech, spurring various citizen movements. These movements in turn opened the way for debate on various previously taboo issues.

Thus the argument is that freedom of speech in South Korea created a new discourse over historical issues, demand for which had been latent in the country from liberation onward but was forcibly constrained by South Korea's authoritarian government in order to maintain its relationship with Japan, as sought by the United States in the midst of the harsh Cold War environment. When democratization gave people the freedom to discuss the past between Japan and South Korea that had formerly been taboo, debate over issues of historical perception also increased.

However, this argument overlooks one point. The strict constraints on speech in South Korea prior to democratization—or, more specifically, prior to President Chun Doo-hwan's time in power just before democratization—did not necessarily mean that there were restrictions on the sort of debate about Japan that would have something in common with the historical perception issues of today. Unlike the Park Chung-hee administration, which was in power when the Treaty on Basic Relations between Japan and the Republic of Korea was concluded in 1965, and many key members of which, including the president himself, had so-called dark histories of cooperating with Japanese colonial rule, the Chun Doo-hwan administration that came to power in 1980 actively sought from the outset to leverage issues related to the country's past with Japan—the "special historical relationship"— including calling on Japan for a six billion dollar loan.[4] Some observers have even suggested that, having come to power through a coup d'état and then additionally burdened by the Gwangju incident, the Chun administration deliberately used issues of historical perception to enhance its own legitimacy.[5]

In fact, closer examination reveals that many of the issues that have subsequently become central to the Japan-South Korea historical perception dispute actually surfaced for the first time, not as a result of democratization, but during Chun Doo-hwan's presidency, with the administration itself sometimes playing a significant role. The prime example is of course the 1982 history textbook issue, triggered when the Japanese media reported[6] that the Ministry of Education had ordered textbook authors to change references to Japanese aggression against China. It was actually the Chun Doo-hwan administration that raised this matter with the Japanese government and demanded that corrections be made.

In other words, from around the time of President Park Chung-hee's assassination in 1979, South Korean society began to experience a major generational shift, resulting in the emergence of a new cohort of politicians who had not dirtied their hands under Japanese rule. This was exactly why the Chun Doo-hwan administration chose to mobilize nationalist sentiment by actively foregrounding issues of historical perception, in an effort to bolster the weak legitimacy that was the legacy of its emergence through a coup d'état. The intensification of the dispute over history between Japan and South Korea as of the 1980s was therefore partially the product of a paradigm shift in the debate over Japanese rule that took place in South Korea while the country was still under authoritarian rule.

These facts of course do not rule out the suggested causal relationship whereby democratization engendered greater freedom of speech in South Korea, which, as a byproduct, also led to active discussion of historical perception issues.[7] However, the existence of a prehistory behind this shift is important. In other words, there was a two-stage process, whereby the Chung Doo-hwan administration sought to bolster its weak legitimacy by raising new issues in relation to the "past," and these issues subsequently came to center stage when democratization brought with it greater freedom of speech, generating explosive debate over historical issues.

Limits of Existing Explanations (2): Investigating the "Japan-as-Cause" Argument

Next, I would like to examine the established argument that ascribes the deterioration in Japan-South Korea relations to developments in Japan. Most commonly indicated, of course, is the emergence of nationalism—

the so-called tilt to the right—in Japan, with escalation of the historical perception dispute viewed as the natural outcome of this change in Japanese society. Particularly in South Korea, this notion has become a widely accepted fact. For example, in the report of the second meeting of the Japan-ROK Joint History Research Committee, a South Korean academic insists that "contentions over history and the history textbook issue have arisen due to Japan's view of history, which supports and glorifies the invasions, wars, and colonial rule perpetrated by Japan in the past."[8]

Are the contentions over history that we currently face really due to this purported shift to the right by Japanese society? Here I must again draw attention to the circumstances surrounding the history textbook issue to which the South Korean academic was referring. As I noted earlier, Japan's history textbooks, which are now one of the central issues in the dispute between Japan and South Korea, are another prime example of an issue that did not come to prominence until the 1980s.

If, as some have suggested, issues of historical perception have emerged as a result of Japan viewing the invasions, wars, and colonial rule perpetrated by Japan in the past in an affirmative light, the status of debate over the history textbook issue must obviously be linked to changes in those history textbooks. But is that the case? Let's take another look at the actual data. Figure 1.2 shows changes since the late 1970s in references to modern Japan-South Korea history in one senior high school textbook on Japanese history.[9]

What is immediately apparent is that, at least in this textbook, references to modern Japan-South Korea history—or, in other words, to differences in perceptions of history between the two countries—cannot be said to have deteriorated since the 1980s, because references to Japan's invasion and colonial rule of the Korean Peninsula have clearly increased. As Japanese textbooks are subject to a certification system, and multiple textbooks are used for each subject in each grade, the example of this textbook alone is of course insufficient to capture trends across Japanese textbooks as a whole. However, all Japanese history textbooks for all grades that were published during this period reveal the same rise in references to colonial rule and other aspects of Japan-South Korea relations. In other words, at least from the 1970s to around 2005, all textbook series released by publishers evince a consistent upward trend in the number of references related to Japan's invasion and colonial rule of the Korean Peninsula.[10]

In addition, this means that, far from moving to the right and glorifying Japan's colonial rule and war, Japanese history textbooks during this period

Figure 1.2. Changes in references in a widely used Japanese history textbook (senior high) (Key terms that appeared in bold in textbooks are indicated by circles, and those that appeared as regular text are indicated by triangles)

	1978	1983	1990	1993	1996	2000	2004
First Japan-Korean Convention	O	△	△	△	△	O	O
Second Japan-Korean Convention		△	O	O	O	△	O
Third Japan-Korean Convention			△		△		
Hague secret emissary affair		△	△	△	△	△	O
Residents-General	△	O	O	O	O	O	O
An Jung-geun (independence activist, assassin of Ito Hirobumi)							O
Japan-Korea Annexation Treaty	O	O	O	O	O	O	O
Governor-General of Korea		O	O	O	O	O	O
Land survey		△	△	△	△	△	O
March First Movement	△	△	O	O	△	O	O
Banzai incident		O	O	△	△	△	O
Kōminka movement (Japanization of education)			△	△	△	△	O
Sōshi kaimei (Japanization of names)			△	△	△	△	O
Righteous Armies (Korean resistance before colonization)			△	△	△	O	O
Great Kantō Earthquake						O	
Comfort women						△	O
Forced transport							O
Document text (Japan-Korea Treaty of 1904)	△						
Photo: Ito Hirobumi and the Korean crown prince	△						
Photo: March First Movement							△
Photo: Koreans bowing toward the Japanese imperial palace							△
Photo: Righteous Army soldiers						△	△

Source: Jung Na-mi and Kimura Kan, "'Rekishi ninshiki' mondai to daiichiji Nikkan rekishi kyōdō kenkyū o meguru ichikōsatsu (1)" [Reflections on the historical perception issues and the First Japan-South Korea Joint History Research Committee Meeting (1)], *Kokusai kyōryoku ronshū* [Journal of International Cooperation Studies] No. 16:1-2 (2008), 72.

clearly shifted toward more detailed references to the facts of Japan's invasion of the Korean peninsula and the harm caused by colonial rule. Accordingly, it would appear almost impossible to ascribe the intensification of the history textbook dispute in the 1980s to the rightward shift of Japan's textbooks during this period.

A Life of Its Own

Nevertheless, the idea that the escalation of the history textbook issue is the natural result of Japan's move to the right remains strong not only in

South Korea but also in Japan. Where did the whole idea come from? Let us briefly examine the background.

It was 1982 when the textbook issue first emerged in relation to the historical perception dispute as we know it today. The catalyst was front-page reporting in the Japanese media to the effect that, as part of the text-book screening that year, the Japanese government had ordered the Jikkyō Shuppan publishing company to change references to the "invasion of North China" to the "advance into North China." Media and government in China and South Korea responded by protesting to the Japanese gov-ernment, and the matter escalated into an international issue.

However, as is now widely known, the reports were, strictly speaking, false. According to the account given by Shigemura Toshimitsu in the report from the second meeting of the Japan-ROK Joint History Research Committee, what happened was the following.[11]

In Japan, when the content of new textbooks has been finalized, all the new textbooks for each subject in each grade are released simultane-ously. At the time, it was standard practice in the Japanese media for this mountain of new textbooks to be divided up and assigned to press club journalists, who would individually provide a summary of the results of their analysis. Along the way, the journalist who had been assigned the new Jikkyō Shuppan history textbook heard that during the screening process, the publisher had been pressured by the Ministry of Education to change "invasion" to "advance." Although this had actually occurred in a previous year, the journalist mistakenly assumed that the publishing company had been required to make the above change during the 1982 screening pro-cess, which was what he reported to his fellow journalists. What emerged as a result was the statement that publishing companies had been forced to change "invasion" to "advance" in the 1982 screening process. Further, the Japanese media, including the reporter's own newspaper, somehow failed to check the actual text of the textbook before and after screening.

The actual facts were somewhat different. In the course of past screen-ings, the Ministry of Education had often suggested to publishers that the term "invasion" not be used in textbooks, and some parties interpreted this as pressure from the Ministry. In fact, such comments only held the status of a suggestion and had no power of compulsion, and while the term was removed from some textbooks, others continued to use it. In any case, this is the explanation given by Shigemura for the story that one of publishing companies was being "forced to change their descriptions" in the 1982 screening.

The Japanese media of course subsequently admitted their mistake and issued retractions.[12] However, these retractions reached few ears, particularly in South Korea, and the idea that the 1982 screening forced publishers to change the term "invasion" to "advance" began to evince a life of its own. Taking the original reports out of context, many people came to believe and fear that an increasingly right-leaning Japanese government was pressuring publishers to debase textbooks, creating a widening gap in historical perceptions between Japan and South Korea. And that is how the now-familiar understanding of the history textbook issue came into being.

I am not seeking to imply here that this discourse is groundless, and consequently not worth serious thought. The key issue is why many people in both Japan and South Korea came to believe it. Looking back, the reasons are clear. For example, 1979, the year in which Park Chung-hee was assassinated, also marked the publication of Ezra Vogel's book *Japan as Number One*, as the world began to notice Japan's emergence as a new economic superpower.[13]

Coinciding with this trend, alarm bells began to sound in South Korea over Japan's growing national muscle. In November 1982, the year that the textbook issue came to the fore, Nakasone Yasuhiro became prime minister. As Nakasone was known in Japan as an advocate of constitutional revision, his appointment was greeted in Japan with some concern as possibly marking a shift to the right for Japanese society. South Korea's feeling that Japan was trending rightward in fact exactly mirrored international sentiment, as well as the tenor of debate within Japanese society. This is what lent the textbook discourse a certain degree of credibility, and why it has been believed for so long since.

2. Historical Perception as a Standard of Value

The Historical Trajectory of the Issue

We can now return to a big picture discussion of the historical unfolding of the historical perception issue. In figure 1.1, I simply traced the change in the number of articles related to historical perception appearing in *Chosun ilbo*. However, as I noted, given that the number of newspaper articles published daily also changed, the change in the number of articles is not sufficient in itself to evidence change in the level of interest in phenomena related to issues of historical perception. Obviously, we need a more detailed analysis if we are to develop a more accurate understanding of the way in which the situation has developed.

Here I have employed another method to achieve a greater level of accuracy. First, the number of articles serving as my parameter has been limited to those that include a term directly related to historical perceptions in the headline rather than just the text in order to eliminate major annual variations in the processing of text caused by the particular characteristics of the database used. This method renders some events unsuitable for analysis because of the limited number of references that remain, while also capturing several other events not previously addressed. Second, I have divided the number of articles identified through this process by the number for each period that included the word "Japan" in the headline. There has been a major change in the number of articles printed by each newspaper between the end of the colonial period and today, with the greater number simply indicative of a greater number of pages in each newspaper. Consequently, I have taken the number of related articles as one standard indicating the degree of newspaper interest in Japan in each period, comparing the size so as to observe the degree of frequency of articles on the various issues. The resulting figure therefore indicates the rough degree of interest evinced by *Chosun ilbo* in historical perception issues as compared to the total number of Japan-related articles.[14]

The results are shown in figure 1.3. What is again clear is that debate over historical perceptions has picked up since the 1980s–1990s. We can see that issues such as pro-Japanese collaborators and reparations for colonial rule were more intensively discussed immediately after Korea's liberation from Japan's colonial rule than in the 1990s. Moreover, *Chosun ilbo* has consistently engaged in a certain degree of debate on the territorial issue, which suggests that it is accorded a special status amid the many diplomatic issues between Japan and South Korea.[15]

With these points in mind, let's take another look at the table, which now reveals three phases in relation to issues of historical perception between Japan and South Korea.

The first phase ensued immediately after Japan's defeat in World War II and the liberation of the Korean peninsula from colonial rule. During this phase, matters now regarded as representative of the historical perception dispute, such as history textbooks and the comfort women, as well as Yasukuni Shrine, were barely discussed. Instead the most heated issues were reparations for colonial rule and Korean collaborators with colonial rule. In other words, during this period, rather than individual incidents that occurred during colonial rule or the war, the main focus of discussion was how the Japanese government and individual Koreans were implicated in colonial rule itself, and how they should atone.

Figure I.3. Changes in the ratio of articles related to key issues of historical perception to Japan-related articles as a whole in *Chosun ilbo* (%)

	Japan + Textbooks	Comfort women	Volunteer labor corps	Yasukuni	Shrine + Worship	Dokdo (Takeshima)	Independence movement	Pro-Japanese collaborator	Japan + Compensation	Japan + Peace Line
1945–49	0	0	0.16	0	0	2.43	0.89	2.51	3.8	0
1950–54	0	0	0	0	0	8.44	0.75	0.21	1.39	1.07
1955–59	0.06	0	0	0	0	1.35	1.88	0.09	0.74	2.37
1960–64	0	0	0	0	0	1.12	1.3	0.04	0.49	2.01
1965–69	0.06	0	0	0	0	1.98	2.07	0.08	0.23	0.37
1970–74	0.05	0	0	0.11	0.12	0.50	0.77	0	0.14	0.02
1975–79	0.04	0.02	0	0.02	0.04	1.85	0.9	0.02	0.11	0
1980–84	5.55	0	0.10	0.02	0.19	0.95	0.94	0	0.08	0
1985–89	1.52	0	0.08	0.04	0.25	0.84	1.54	0.04	0.08	0
1990–94	0.68	9.8	17.57	0.34	1.8	3.27	4.84	0.56	0.79	0
1995–99	0.84	3.64	1.69	0.19	0.64	5.42	6.18	0.16	1.11	0.03
2000–04	2.33	3.32	0.58	1.25	2.9	4.57	3.71	0.34	0.29	0
2005–09	1.14	2.42	0.34	2.65	1.93	15.94	4.06	0.76	0.25	0
2010–14	1.48	7.86	0.51	2.21	1.76	10.31	1.82	0.3	0.55	0

DB Chosun, http://db.chosun.com/DBmain.html (last checked 5 March 2015). The above figures indicate the ratio of the number of articles in the *Chosun ilbo* article database that contain the above terms and the word "Japan" to the number of articles which contain only the word "Japan."

However, this changed in 1965 with the signing of the Treaty on Basic Relations and the normalization of diplomatic relations between Japan and South Korea. The key feature of this second phase—the late 1960s and 1970s—was the lack of discussion of almost all issues of historical perception. While it is not apparent from figure 1.3, discussion was similarly muted not only with regard to bilateral historical perception issues but also to domestic aspects of the past, such as war crimes in the case of Japan and pro-Japanese collaboration in South Korea.

As noted earlier, a major change occurred in the period from the 1980s to the 1990s that resulted in ongoing and extremely frequent debate on issues of historical perception from the 1990s onward, after which, as far as we can ascertain from this data, there has been no major shift down to the present.

Theoretical Framework for Analysis

How should we interpret these changing circumstances in relation to the historical perception dispute?

I find it very strange that while various debates have arisen between Japan and South Korea in relation to historical perception, and numerous issues have been raised, to my mind no sufficiently rigorous analytical framework has yet been presented for the purpose of explaining why contention over historical perceptions has become so fraught. This suggests that research to date on the relationship between the factors thought to have caused the various issues has been based on intuitive reasoning along the lines of "relations have soured because either Japan or South Korea did something bad."

Analysis based on intuitive reasoning is not necessarily without merit, nor are the results necessarily mistaken. But it is clear that we have only undertaken the roughest of analyses of a major problem that continues to exert a huge impact on Japan, South Korea, and East Asia as a whole, and this has unquestionably seriously detracted from our understanding of these issues. At the very least, intuitive reasoning needs to be verified by some means, if both an accurate understanding of issues of historical perception and the exploration of possible solutions are not to retreat beyond reach.

What preconditions must pertain for an event to develop into a dispute? There are clearly at least three. First, there must be multiple actors who attach meaning to the event. In other words, no matter how much potential significance an event might have, if its existence and significance are not "discovered" by multiple actors, it might as well have never existed.[16]

Second, those actors must have different perceptions of the same event.

Even if multiple actors find meaning in an event, to the extent that they share the same perception in relation to it—for example, which country should have possession of a certain island or how a certain historical event should be interpreted—there again will be no conflict.

Third, the multiple actors must recognize the existence of sufficient benefit to stir them to action. If, for example, multiple actors attach meaning to an event, even if that meaning is different for each actor, the actors must attach a sufficient level of importance to the meanings they have ascribed before they will take action. What is important here is that, given two actors attaching different value to the same event, when one actor launches action based on that value, a clash with the other becomes inevitable. Obviously, that clash will damage the existing relationship between the two actors and the initial actor will lose some benefit previously garnered from the relationship. Consequently, for an actor to initiate action, they must have the prior expectation of reaping benefit sufficient to outweigh the possible demerits of that action.

In other words, only in cases where multiple actors satisfy all three conditions simultaneously will they take action, accepting that they will incur demerits through the clash resulting from that action.

This extremely simple theoretical framework offers two insights. First, examining how these three conditions were satisfied in relation to individual events in the development of the historical perception dispute should enable us to understand to some extent why the events developed.

Second, conversely, we can see that many of the events related to the past shared by Japan and South Korea cannot in fact satisfy all three conditions, and must consequently have sunk into oblivion. In fact, most historical debate between the two countries today focuses on a bare handful of items—primarily the comfort women, the forced transport of workers and soldiers during the period of all-out war, history textbooks, and territory. In that sense, the historical perception dispute between Japan and South Korea clearly does not map directly to the era of colonial rule and the entire subsequent history between the two countries, given the infinite number of forgotten elements of the past contained in that period.

3. History and Historical Perceptions

Three Stages

To recapitulate, the theoretical framework that I have laid out suggests that at least three conditions must pertain before an event will develop into a conflict. First, the event and its significance must be "discovered" by multiple actors; second, these actors' perceptions of the event must clash; and third, the actors must invest sufficient importance in the matter to outweigh the demerits that they will suffer as a result of the clash.

What insights can we draw from this formula in terms of analyzing the historical perception dispute between Japan and South Korea?

Starting with the first condition, we can say that the mere fact of an event does not lead directly to conflicting historical perceptions. For a certain past event to develop into a matter of dispute, government and society in both Japan and South Korea need to "discover" that event and attach significance to it. Our task, therefore, is to observe exactly how a certain event was "discovered" and imbued with significance by both countries.

Based on the second condition, we then need to identify what perceptions the government and society in Japan and South Korea have come to hold in relation to the discovered event. Obviously, even when events have been discovered and imbued with significance, commonly held social perceptions have a particular developmental process. Moreover, it is not uncommon for social perceptions of an event to subsequently shift and recompose. It is thus important to examine what changes occur and why.

It is apparent from the third condition that we also need to observe the degree of importance that government and society in Japan and South Korea attach to the perceptions they have formed. Moreover, in examining this, we need to focus not so much on the absolute importance of an event but to its relative importance compared to the demerits likely to be suffered as a result of a dispute. For example, even if either Japan or South Korea happens to attach major importance to a certain historical event, it will still be difficult to raise the matter with the other country if the potential drawbacks clearly outweigh the potential benefits of doing so. Accordingly, in each period we need to identify the changing absolute importance to each country of individual events, as well as the extent to which the country foregrounding the issue anticipates being disadvantaged as a result.

This means that there will be three stages in the development of a dispute over historical perception: the stage at which the event and its significance are discovered; the stage at which different parties form different perceptions; and the stage at which the event takes on such importance that the benefits from foregrounding it are believed to outweigh the potential losses.

These stages of development are shaped by the social circumstances of the time. To reiterate, the historical dispute between Japan and South

Korea is not just about a shared, singular past. Rather, it is grounded in how people in their own contemporary context engage with their respective pasts in the complex shadows of contemporary experience. More specifically, the issues of historical perception between Japan and South Korea are as much issues of the experiences of war and colonial rule as they are problems of how the past has been dealt with in subsequent years.

TWO

Three Factors in the Dispute over Historical Perceptions

I. Generational Change

Here I would like to summarize the main points I have made thus far. First, I looked at how the historical perception dispute between Japan and South Korea has changed over the years, pointing to its escalation from the 1980s to the 1990s, suggesting that the dispute is not a simple reflection of the past. Second, I noted that previous frameworks for understanding the issue—the democratization of South Korea and Japan's tilt to the right—have not provided an adequate explanation, and we need to revisit our methods for engaging with this issue. Third, I laid out my own theoretical framework. I highlighted the need to identify the importance of each particular issue of historical perception to Japanese and South Korean society at various points in time. I also suggested that there were three stages in the development of issues of this kind: discovery of an event, development of social awareness, and finally attribution of importance to the event and resulting action. I also noted that issues of historical perception are rooted in the fundamental question of the nature of history.

The next question, then, is what factors have influenced the historical development of the issues of perception outlined in the previous chapter?

I have argued that the historical perception issue between Japan and South Korea has moved through several phases. The first was from 1945 through the 1950s or early 1960s; the second ran through to the early 1980s; and the third has continued from the late 1980s and the 1990s to the present. I will now examine the debate over historical perception in Japan and South Korea as it evolved in each of these phases.

First Phase: Postwar Closure

The first phase was characterized by a very different focus of debate than that of today. In South Korea, the issues most hotly debated were reparations for Japan's colonial rule, the Syngman Rhee Line (known as the Peace Line in South Korea—a boundary line established to protect South Korea's marine resources around the Sea of Japan), and how to punish South Korean citizens who cooperated with Japanese rule during the colonial period (generically known as *chinilpa*, or pro-Japanese collaborators). In Japan, the focus was on wartime responsibility for events during and prior to World War II, issues highlighted by the Tokyo War Crimes Trial (officially known as the International Military Tribunal for the Far East).

It is not surprising that in the moment immediately after the end of World War II and colonial rule, people were discussing who should take responsibility and how. While regarded now as only one part of the historical perception issue as a whole, at the time these were not issues of the past but were directly involved with the living present.

For example, in the effort to normalize diplomatic relations between Japan and South Korea, the decision of where to draw the territorial boundary between the two countries was something that needed to be discussed—and in fact emerged in the debate over the Syngman Rhee Line, even though both countries ultimately chose to push that matter under the rug rather than find a real solution. What should be done in terms of compensation for colonial rule was also an inevitable topic. In Japan, the questions of who should bear responsibility for WWII and how they should be punished were serious issues in terms of how Japan would remake itself as a nation after its defeat.

Consider the circumstances in Japan immediately after the war. Ordinary Japanese citizens were fascinated by the spectacle of individuals facing trial by the Allies as Class A war criminals who had only a few years previously ruled the country as ministers of state or commanders of the armed forces. The issue of Class B and Class C criminals was even more compelling for those involved, in that the outcome of the trials was literally a matter of life and death for family members. Watching the trials conducted by the Allied powers, individuals who had been involved in the war in other capacities could not help but feel that, given only the slightest twist of fate, they might find themselves standing before the same court.[1] It was the same with the Yasukuni Shrine issue. For people at the time, Yasukuni Shrine was where the souls of deceased family members and friends were enshrined, as well as the place where former soldiers had vowed to meet again with their comrades in arms after death, so this was viewed as a debate not about the past but rather the present, and was invested with a corresponding sense of seriousness and urgency.

It was the same for the South Koreans. The issue of reparations from Japan was closely bound to efforts to construct the essential economic foundation for rebuilding their lives after the general wartime mobilization and the turmoil following the country's liberation from colonial rule.[2] The situation was made even more pressing by the peculiar circumstances of the southern half of the Korean peninsula at the time, as Japan's defeat and the breakup of the Japanese empire led to the south being inundated by three different groups of people owning no more than the clothes on their backs.

The first comprised individuals mobilized from the Korean peninsula during the war as soldiers, civilian auxiliaries, or laborers, who began returning home en masse immediately after Japan's defeat. The second was an influx of refugees from the Soviet-occupied north. Many of these refugees, known at the time as "southern border crossers," had lost assets through the Soviet's land reforms and were consequently strongly anticommunist. Finally, there were the Manchurian returnees. Many people from Korea had settled in Manchuria before the war, most of whom lost their livelihoods following the Japanese defeat and the collapse of the Japanese puppet state of Manchukuo, prompting them to return to the Korean peninsula. Left with no way to earn a living, this group considered reparations from Japan to be essential in rebuilding their lives.

The handling of "pro-Japanese collaborators"—South Koreans who cooperated with Japanese rule during the colonial period—was an issue fraught with implications for the kind of postliberation state that South Korea planned to build. According to how widely the term was defined, a vast number of South Koreans stood at risk of being labeled as collaborators.[3] During the colonial period, many had little choice but to develop some connection with the colonial authorities in order to survive, and few came out of the war with an entirely clear conscience in this regard. To borrow the words of one politician on his return from exile immediately after liberation, everyone in the country might potentially be called a pro-Japanese collaborator.[4] The desperate defense of the Syngman Rhee Line, or Peace Line, by South Korean fishermen who put to sea with equipment woefully inadequate compared to their Japanese rivals was, in the minds of the fishermen, a matter directly linked to their livelihoods.[5]

In any case, many issues now considered past were once again urgent issues of the present. In the natural course of things, debate over these issues abated in Japan in the early 1950s, once the Tokyo War Crimes Trial was over and the San Francisco Peace Treaty had returned Japan's sovereignty, and in South Korea after 1965 and the normalization of diplomatic relations with Japan—because these agreements brought the appearance of closure to many issues and pushed them at least temporarily into the past.

The San Francisco Peace Treaty and the Treaty on Basic Relations

Debate over divergent perceptions of history therefore rapidly muted, at least temporarily, in Japan as of the late 1950s and around a decade later—the late 1960s—in South Korea. The ten-year lag between Japan and South Korea was probably due to the different significance that the normalization of bilateral relations had for the two countries, as I will explore briefly below.

Given that Japan's greatest postwar diplomatic challenge was regaining its sovereignty, the top priority was naturally placed on mending its relationship with the Allied powers who were its former enemies. The 1951 conclusion of the San Francisco Peace Treaty therefore marked a watershed moment in the debate over historical perception in Japan.[6]

However, the conclusion of the San Francisco Peace Treaty did not bring complete closure to the postwar process for Japan. Amid deepening conflict with the Western nations, the Soviet Union and other Eastern bloc nations did not sign the agreement. The United States and the United Kingdom also had different views on whether the People's Republic of China or the Republic of China should be invited to the negotiations as the legitimate government of China—so ultimately both were left off the list. Even India, which had been a key Allied nation as part of the British Empire, dropped out of the conference because of dissatisfaction with the proceedings.

In short, even after the San Francisco Peace Treaty, Japan still had many postwar diplomatic concerns. Normalization of diplomatic relations with South Korea was simply not considered as important to Japan as normalizing relations with other countries. Negotiations with the Soviet Union and China were essential in transforming the partial peace into a comprehensive peace that would normalize Japan's relations with all former Allied

Figure 2.1. Articles concerning issues of historical perception in the *Asahi shimbun* (No. of articles in each period containing the respective terms in the headline)

	Comfort women	Forced transport	Wartime responsibility	"War crime"	"War criminals"	Takeshima	Tokyo War Crime Trial	Yasukuni	Historical perception	"History issue"
1945-49	0	0	32	260	348	1	406	35	0	0
1950-54	0	0	1	182	683	63	5	35	0	0
1955-59	0	0	1	1	328	8	0	42	0	0
1960-64	0	1	1	0	0	55	1	24	0	0
1965-69	0	0	2	19	58	73	2	83	0	0
1970-74	0	5	17	11	32	8	1	138	1	0
1975-79	1	15	10	3	68	71	6	93	0	0
1980-84	1	8	17	0	57	15	17	216	3	0
1985-89	6	14	80	2	97	17	6	402	2	1
1990-94	600	275	20	23	75	15	11	151	17	1
1995-99	822	222	55	26	141	108	11	132	102	6
2000-04	126	169	27	19	152	79	6	723	43	18
2005-09	225	142	31	14	120	500	47	906	92	32
2010-14	413	57	13	8	56	371	9	324	70	31

Source: Created by the author from *Asahi shimbun*, Kikuzo II Visual (http://database.asahi.com/library2/)

powers,[7] while Japan's relationship with South Korea was no more than the construction of a new relationship with a newly independent nation that wasn't even one of the Allies.

Tracking the situation in Japan based on changes in the number of related articles in the *Asahi shimbun* at the time produces the results shown in figure 2.1. In South Korea, however, it was a different story. For contemporary Koreans, Japan was the main party in colonial rule, so dealing with that relationship was essential in putting colonial rule into the past. South Korea was not invited to the San Francisco Peace Conference because it was not recognized as an Allied nation. This caused a huge amount of dissatisfaction in the country, with the result that debate over colonial rule did not abate but rather became particularly vociferous.[8]

As a result, the end of the first phase in South Korea had to wait until the Treaty on Basic Relations in 1965 and the consequent normalization of relations. In any case—albeit with a gap of around fifteen years—this brought an end to the first phase of the dispute over historical perception between Japan and South Korea.

Second Phase: The Silent Era

The debate over World War II and Japan's colonial rule over Korea died away quickly in Japan once the San Francisco Peace Treaty was concluded in 1951 and in South Korea once the Treaty on Basic Relations was concluded in 1965. In fact, all media data for both Japan and South Korea from that time to the early 1980s shows an attenuation of discussion about the past.

What caused the historical perception dispute to die down in this way? There are a number of possibilities. One is that, as noted above, various treaties, tribunals, and legislation brought about some closure on the immediate issues. Legal solutions were found, at least temporarily, to many issues related to reparations for colonial rule, war responsibility, and the territorial boundaries between Japan and South Korea (as epitomized by the Syngman Rhee Line) that had been hotly debated immediately after the end of World War II, apart from a few exceptional issues such as Takeshima/Dokdo that were pointedly shelved.[9] As a result, debate between Japan and South Korea over the past came to focus on interpreting these international agreements and judgments and whether or not their results should be accepted.

Second, the international environment during this period was such that both Japan and South Korea had little choice but to accept the results of

Photo 1. Official signing ceremony for the Treaty on Basic Relations (June 22, 1965). South Korean Foreign Minister Lee Dong-won and Japanese Prime Minister Satō Eisaku shake hands. (Jiji Press Photo, Ltd.)

these treaties and tribunals. Forced into unconditional surrender in World War II, Japan had virtually no right to reject the will of the Allied powers with regard to choosing its domestic political regime or punishing those responsible for the war. The same could be said to a lesser extent for South Korea. As was apparent from the large-scale anti-Japanese demonstrations when the Treaty on Basic Relations was concluded, the South Korean public was deeply dissatisfied with the way in which their government was approaching the normalization of relations with Japan.[10] However, it was extremely difficult for South Korea to turn down this agreement, given its pressing economic difficulties, ongoing military tension with North Korea in the context of the Cold War, and the strong desire of the United States, then embroiled in the Vietnam War, that South Korea and Japan, both US allies, normalize their relations.

Third, both countries were also experiencing political and social circumstances unique to that period. In both Japan and South Korea, the years from the 1950s to the 1960s saw members of the pre-World War II ruling elite reinstated at the heart of society. In Japan in the 1950s, Hatoyama Ichirō and a group of other politicians who had been ousted from public office during the Occupation were gradually rehabilitated and took over the political mainstream.[11] When the first Hatoyama administration came to power in 1954, Shigemitsu Mamoru, who was convicted as a Class A war criminal at the Tokyo War Crimes Trial, was named foreign minister, while Kishi Nobusuke, also designated a Class A war criminal, became secretary-general of the ruling Democratic Party. Kishi went on to become prime minister in 1957. In 1962, Kaya Okinori, yet another convicted Class A war criminal, became head of the Japan War-Bereaved Families Association.

The same thing happened in South Korea, albeit to a lesser extent. It is common knowledge that most of the so-called pro-Japanese collaborators who had played an active role during the period of colonial rule were meted out tepid punishments immediately after the Republic of Korea was established, and then rehabilitated during the Rhee Syngman administration. In fact, in the 1950s under President Rhee, the "founding father" of the new republic, the prime minister and most other politicians in key government posts had the kind of colonial-era backgrounds that from today's perspective would appear to leave them highly vulnerable to criticism as pro-Japanese collaborators.[12] A more critical event in terms of its relation to the colonial period was of course the military coup staged by Park Chung-hee and his allies in 1961.[13] Park studied at Changchun Military Academy in the Japanese puppet state of Manchukuo and later graduated from the Imperial Japanese Army Academy in Japan and served as an officer in the Manchukuo Imperial Army. The fact that such a figure became president following a coup is a clear illustration of the convoluted relationship South Korea had with its colonial past.

Moreover, the rise of these figures in both Japan and South Korea was hardly the direct result of the abuse of political power and suppression of public sentiment. In Japan, at least at that time, politicians who had been ousted from public office were welcomed back with open arms, influenced by ambivalence over the Allies' postwar handling of Japan. This was apparent in the "Hatoyama boom" supporting the appointment of Hatoyama Ichirō as prime minister,[14] with the public hoping he would make a clean sweep of the bureaucratic atmosphere of the Yoshida Shigeru years, as well as in Kishi's achievement of the first stable absolute majority of the postwar years in the snap general elections he called immediately after taking up the prime minister's post.[15] It was the Park Chung-hee administration in South Korea that really struggled. Park had to fight hard to win the succession of presidential and National Assembly elections held after he seized power, and ultimately staged his own coup from above in 1972 to force an end to this discomfort. However, this was not necessarily the result of his record as a pro-Japanese collaborator. At the time (for example, during the presidential elections), he was attacked for the interruption to the democratic process caused by his coup d'état, along with his purported "Communist past" in the days following Korea's liberation from colonial rule, not his past collaboration with the Japanese.[16]

"I Want to Become a Shellfish"

So why were the pasts of these politicians prior to and during World War II not regarded as a major issue during this phase? Part of the reason is clear if we look at the contemporary lineup of key figures in Japanese and South Korean society in areas other than politics— for example, the media moguls in both countries. Japan's two main newspapers at the time, *Asahi shimbun* and *Yomiuri shimbun*, were owned by Murayama Nagataka and Shōriki Matsutarō, respectively, both of whom had initially been removed from public office after the war. It was the same in South Korea. The heads of South Korea's two major papers, *Chosun ilbo* and *Dong-a ilbo*, immediately after liberation were Bang Eung-mo[17] and Kim Seong-su,[18] both of whom had a history of collaboration with colonial rule.[19] The opposition parties had a similar problem. Many members of Japan's biggest opposition party, the Japanese Socialist Party (JSP), including Kawakami Jōtarō, who led a conservative faction and became JSP Chairman in 1961, had been purged from public life by the Allies.[20] In South Korea, too, many opposition party executives and presidential candidates had some history of cooperating with Japanese colonial authorities.

Clearly, many of the individuals holding key positions in both Japanese and South Korean society in the 1960s and 1970s were of the generation that had experienced Japan's harsh total-war regime and had been forced to develop more than a casual association with that regime. The same could also be said for ordinary citizens. In short, only a quarter-century after 1945, the "past" of the total-war period was still far too viscerally "present" to encourage the pursuit of wartime responsibility.

That feeling was epitomized by the smash hit television series *Watashi wa kai ni naritai* [I want to become a shellfish].[21] Remembered as one of the key programs of the infancy of Japanese television, its hero was a former soldier designated as a Class B/C war criminal and eventually sentenced to death for executing Allied pilots on the orders of his lieutenant in the closing days of World War II. The program vividly portrayed the brutality of the Japanese military system as well as people's distress at the apparent unwillingness of the Allies to take this into consideration in meting out their punishments. The hero's final words, whispered as he mounts the stairs to his execution, have become famous: "If I have to be reborn, I want to become a shellfish"—rather than relive the agony of being human. This succinctly encapsulates the wartime anguish of the many Japanese who had to suppress their thoughts and feelings and simply accept the injustice all around them.

Many individuals who played central roles in Japanese and South Korean society in the 1960s and 1970s belonged to the generation most heavily scarred by total war. Mobilized on battlefields and in mines and factories as soldiers and laborers, or inculcated with the most nationalistic of educations, their psychological wounds were so severe that they were simply unable to engage with issues related to their wartime experience.

Third Phase: Emergence of the Postwar Generation and the Rediscovery of History

There was possibly also a further reason that debate over the past was not actively addressed during the 1960s and 1970s—namely that the bulk of society at the time comprised individuals who had actually experienced the total-war period and the last days of colonial rule, and who consequently felt no need to confirm or recount the details of that time.[22] To put it another way, while they may have been in different positions, those comprising the social mainstream in Japan and South Korea at the time had actually lived the past that we debate today. As a result, there was tacit agreement among them, not as much about what should be recounted as about what did not need to be recounted.

However, the situation was to change in the 1980s, when more than thirty-five years had passed since World War II and colonization. The driver for this change was the new social dominance of the postwar generation in both countries. By "postwar generation" I mean the generation that had not directly experienced total war or colonization and whose growing social presence wrought a complete transformation in the nature of debate about the past.

This development was epitomized by the simultaneous emergence in the 1980s in both Japan and South Korea of war-related research as well as movements protesting the status quo. A prime example is what happened in relation to the comfort women. At the time when this issue was initially articulated in the 1970s by Senda Kakō and others in Japan, it attracted little interest in South Korea. The pioneer of research on this issue in South

Korea, Yun Jeong-ok, was an English literature specialist,[23] indicative of the way that the comfort women issue was almost entirely ignored at the time by scholars of Korean history, despite having been foregrounded by some Japanese academics. In fact, at least according to South Korea's main academic database, there were virtually no papers on comfort women or the volunteer labor corps prior to the 1970s, and only a handful even in the 1980s. Moreover, the few papers that were written were published not in history journals but in Christian magazines on women's issues.[24]

This situation began to change at the end of the 1980s. The first symposium in South Korea addressing the comfort women issue was held in 1988, with Yun Jeong-ok (as mentioned above) revealing the results of her research.[25] In 1990, Yun began publishing her famous series of articles entitled "In the Footsteps of the Volunteer Labor Corps" in a progressive newspaper, *The Hankyoreh*.[26] The series attracted much attention in South Korean society, and comfort women finally emerged as the most important historical perception issue between Japan and South Korea around the end of 1991.

The point here is that during this phase the historical perception issue was presented as an uncovering of hidden historical facts.[27] In other words, by this time, research and activism related to the colonial period were approached with the assumption that people would not have direct knowledge of the facts. This is most clearly indicated by the fact that one of the key initiatives in relation to the comfort women issue was the effort to seek out actual comfort women[28]—typifying the way in which memories of Japanese rule in Korea were already becoming vague. This manifested with even greater clarity in the case of the comfort women, since having been a comfort woman was regarded as shameful in South Korea. This forced many former comfort women to hide their pasts, with the result that for a time their identities were almost deliberately forgotten.[29]

The Prewar Generation and the Postwar Generation

Clearly, the change of guard from the prewar generation to the postwar generation played a major role in the development of this issue. To the prewar generation, colonial rule was a directly experienced reality that they had no wish to recall, so it was not something that they sought to speak out about. In addition, if they did screw up their courage and try to speak out about their experience, they risked hurting a lot of people, themselves included, which sometimes caused them to hesitate about causing too much of a fuss.[30]

As a result, the retreat of the prewar generation from the front lines of society brought about a major memory loss in society. The comfort women issue epitomized the new situation created by this generational change. Memory loss was followed by the discovery of facts, an order of events that made the discovery process particularly shocking to the younger generation. The comfort women issue would of course become the greatest concern between Japan and South Korea in the 1990s.

The trajectory of the comfort women issue provides a key to considering the entire issue of historical perception between Japan and South Korea. The first symposium on the comfort women issue to be held in South Korea was in 1988, and there was a reason for that timing—namely that for South Korea 1988 was the year of the Seoul Olympics. Below we turn to another element that impacted the development of the historical perception issue.

2. Changing International Relations

The Seoul Olympics, Criticism of Sex Tourism, and the Historical Perception Dispute

The focus on comfort women resulted from a coincidence of timing with the Seoul Olympics. While the two issues might at first glance seem unrelated, there was in fact a major connection.

What must be understood is the huge importance of the Olympics for South Korea at the time, and what a burden this created. In 1988, the international community was still deep in the Cold War, and South Korea's social and economic influence was a mere fraction of what it is today. The Olympics focused the eyes of the world on the country, and the nation's destiny was on the line. The situation was further complicated by a serious crisis facing the games themselves. The two Olympic Games prior to Seoul had struggled with boycotts related to the Cold War. The United States and other Western bloc nations had boycotted the 1980 Olympics in Moscow to protest the Soviet invasion of Afghanistan, reducing it to a very halfhearted affair. The Soviet Union and other Eastern bloc nations then retaliated by boycotting the Los Angeles Olympics in the United States four years later. Despite being held by two superpowers with enormous international influence, the previous two Olympic Games of that decade had failed to attract the world's athletes. It is no exaggeration to say that, in the period leading up to the Seoul Games, the very raison d'être of the Olympics was in question.[31]

Given the circumstances, it seemed reckless for a small divided Asian state like South Korea, located on the front lines of the Cold War, to hold the next games. In fact, the Eastern bloc nations had an infinite number of reasons to boycott the Seoul Games. First, of course, was the fact that South Korea was controlled until right before the Olympics by the Chun Doo-hwan administration, which had seized power through two coups d'état and the Gwangju incident. Given the state of human rights and democratization under that regime, it was almost a foregone conclusion that the Eastern bloc countries would exploit the Olympics as an opportunity to unsettle South Korea and, behind it, the United States. Not only was South Korea still locked in an extremely tense standoff with North Korea, it didn't even have diplomatic relations with the Soviet Union, China, or East Germany, all of which were major Olympic nations. In 1983, the shooting down of a Korean Airlines plane by the Soviet Union was followed by North Korea's attempted assassination of President Chun Doo-hwan in Yangon, Myanmar, and in 1987, the year immediately preceding the Olympics, North Korea blew up another Korean Airlines flight. Given the circumstances, it seemed highly unlikely—to say the least—that the Olympics would proceed as usual in South Korea.[32]

With the odds stacked against it, the Chun Doo-hwan administration threw all its resources into the games and into promoting South Korea to the world. One of the government's strategies was to attract foreign tourists, aiming to draw as many people as possible from around the world, showcase for them the charms, and also the safety, of South Korean society, and lead the games to success. The most important target for this exercise was, of course, neighboring Japan, which was riding high on an economic bubble in the 1980s, and South Korea staged a vigorous advertising campaign directed at the Japanese market. This was the era when Atsumi Jirō scored a massive hit with his cover of the song "Return to Busan Harbor," while Cho Yong-pil, who sang the Korean original, was invited to participate in the annual New Year's Eve music extravaganza "Kōhaku Uta Gassen" on NHK, the Japanese public television network. The government's efforts produced a dramatic increase in the number of Japanese visiting South Korea—the first time since the end of World War II that so many "ordinary Japanese" had traveled there.

This apparently positive phenomenon did, however, have a dark side. Most of the Japanese who visited South Korea during this period were male, and in a relatively large number of cases the purpose of their trip was to purchase sexual services. Known as "*gisaeng* (courtesan) tourism,"[33] this was enough to provoke hostility toward the Japanese among South Koreans, particularly women, who felt that the same people who had controlled Koreans with military force were now using their economic power to buy South Korean women. This also encouraged a reaction against the South Korean government and its policy of welcoming the Japanese with open arms.[34]

A single link grew into a major chain. Resentment toward *gisaeng* tourism became resentment toward Japan, and this led to criticism of Japan's past colonial rule, with the Japanese labeled a despicable people, both then and now. It was this upsurge of antipathy toward Japan that resulted in the rediscovery of the comfort women issue. In a sense, it was natural that this movement was led from the start not by historians but by female activists. Moreover, this movement also contained an element of condemnation of the current government, creating a natural connection to the democratization movement that was gathering momentum in South Korea. As a result, the comfort women issue would ultimately acquire symbolic status in three different arenas: the movement against colonial rule, the women's rights movement, and the democratization movement.

In this sense, South Korea's situation as it headed into the Seoul Olympics had crucial significance for the development of the comfort women issue as one element of the rediscovery of history by the postwar generation noted earlier.

South Korea's Changing International Position

From the evolution of the comfort women issue, it is clear that issues of historical perception were influenced not only by the domestic situation in both countries but also by changes in the bilateral relationship and the broader international context. As discussed earlier, a clash between two actors requires the actor making the initial move to expect a benefit. This expectation is shaped in turn by the extent to which the previous benefits of the relationship between the two actors will be affected as a result.

In other words, if major benefits were being derived from the relationship between Japan and South Korea, it would make little sense to foreground the historical perception issue to the extent that such benefits were damaged. Conversely, if both countries stood to reap only limited benefit from the relationship, it would be easier to risk foregrounding the issue.

Figure 2.2 presents a schematic model of this relationship. What should be noted here is the way in which the significance of the bilateral relationship changed for both countries, particularly for South Korea. For example, figure 2.3 shows the changing share of South Korea's external trade among three major trading partners: Japan, China, and the United States. The first thing we can read from the graph in terms of Japan-South Korea relations is that Japan's share has shown an almost straight-line reduction from the late 1970s to the present. As Japan has been unable to assert its presence through military force in the way of the United States, economic muscle has been its greatest source of national strength. With trade standing alongside investment as a key indicator of a country's economic presence, the rapid drop in Japan's share of South Korean trade paints a vivid picture of Japan's declining importance to South Korea. The same can be said of Japan's falling share in direct investment. In sum, Japan's importance to the South Korean economy has dwindled in a number of areas.[35]

Why did Japan's economic share in South Korea decline in this manner? Two common answers are sluggishness in the Japanese economy and the emergence of China in Japan's place.[36] According to this rather basic understanding, a rising China seized the share of a weakening Japan.

A more detailed look at the graph, however, immediately reveals this view as overly simplistic. As noted earlier, the decline in Japan's trade share began in the late 1970s. Given that the Japanese economic bubble would subsequently reach its peak in the following decade, it would seem extremely difficult to ascribe the drop in Japan's share to Japanese economic sluggishness. China, on the other hand, had virtually no direct trade with South Korea in the late 1970s, as the absence of diplomatic relations between the two countries during the Cold War, as noted above, ruled out any official direct trade.

The change in the other figure—for the United States—makes it even clearer that the fall in Japan's share cannot be explained solely by an economic slump in Japan and China's emergence. The US trade share tracks Japan's almost exactly, suggesting that declining economic share cannot be ascribed to Japanese factors alone. China's share soars as from the 1980s onward, but even in 2015 it never reaches more than just over half Japan's share at its peak. From the late 1970s to 2015, Japan and the United States together may have lost about 60 percent of their share, but China in fact absorbed only a little over 20 percent—less than half—of that.

So how should we interpret this change? We need to direct our examination along two planes: individual circumstances associated with particular issues and the larger environment in which those circumstances are situated. In our particular context, this means phenomena particular to the

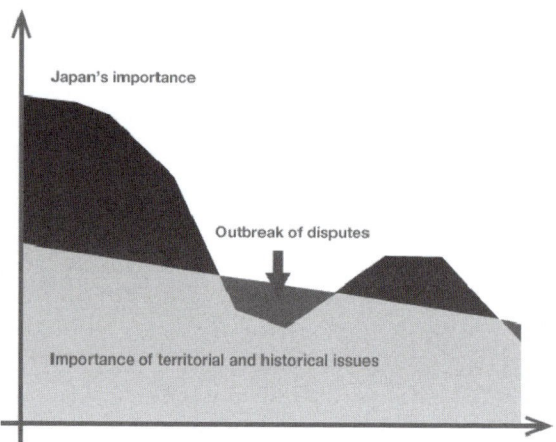

Figure 2.2.

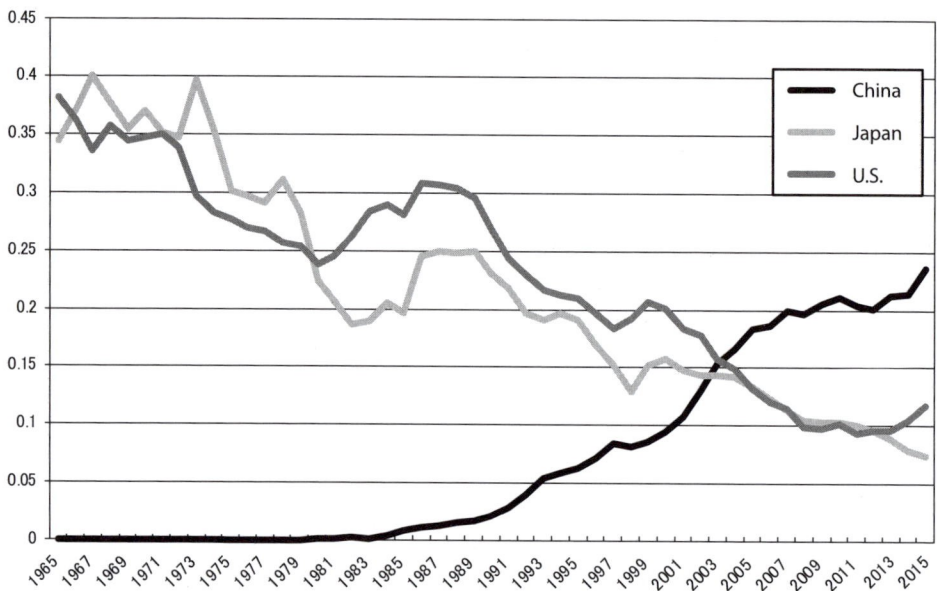

Figure 2.3. Share of South Korea's major trading partners (total imports and exports). (*Source*: Created by the author based on Korean Statistical Information Service (KOSIS) portal, http://kosis.kr, statistics.)

relationship between Japan and South Korea, and more general phenomena. Let's look first at the latter, more general phenomena.

First, we need to ascertain Japan's situation in relation to countries other than South Korea. In short, what we see happening between Japan and South Korea can also be observed in many other countries. For example, there is a similar decline in Japan's share of trade and investment in China and Southeast Asia. To go a step further, if we regard this weakening as a phenomenon whereby the economic presence of developed nations in certain developing countries—including the presence of former colonial powers—undergoes a marked drop, we can discover many similar examples around the world. We have already noted the decline in American influence in South Korea, but a similar decline in American economic influence can also be observed in China and Southeast Asia. Europe manifests a comparable pattern. Even the European Union, where economic integration has advanced so strongly, has seen its intraregional trade share continue to decline over the last decade despite currency integration and other major institutional developments.

This phenomenon can be explained by two factors. The first is the decline in the share of the developed world in the world economy. Developed and developing nations necessarily have a wage gap. Prices can obviously be set lower for developing country products manufactured with cheap labor than for products manufactured in developed countries with expensive labor, which means that as long as their products offer the same quality, developing countries have the chance to significantly boost their competitiveness. Economic development utilizing cheap labor became a worldwide trend in the late 1980s as many developing countries, spurred by the example of the economic development of South Korea and Asia's other Newly Industrializing Economies (NIEs), adopted similar export-led economic development strategies. Today, it remains quite normal that the growth rate for the developing world outstrips that of the developed world. As the weight of the developed world in the world economy continues to decline, the downward trend in Japan's share, as a developed country, in the markets of South Korea and other countries is more or less unavoidable.

This situation has had an even greater impact when coupled with a second, parallel phenomenon—the globalization of the world economy. Put simply, globalization means an increase in our international options. As I hardly need to add, Japan-South Korea relations have also been affected by globalization, not only in terms of movement of goods and money, but also human movement. A growing number of South Korean tourists are visiting Japan, as might be surmised from the frequent appearance of Hangul

Figure 2.4. Movement of people between Japan and Korea (1996–2010)

	"Japan → Korea (A) Unit: No. of people"	"Korea → Japan (B) Unit: No. of people"	"Total Unit: No. of people"	"World → Korea (C) Unit: No. of people"	"Korea → World (D) Unit: No. of people"	"Ratio of Japanese among tourists visiting Korea (A/C) Unit: %"	"Ratio of Koreans tourists visiting Japan (B/D) Unit: %"
1996	1,526,559	1,111,316	2,637,875	3,683,779	4,649,251	41.4	23.9
1997	1,676,434	1,126,573	2,803,007	3,908,140	4,542,159	42.9	24.8
1998	1,954,416	822,358	2,776,774	4,250,216	3,066,926	46	26.8
1999	2,184,121	1,053,862	3,237,983	4,659,785	4,341,546	46.9	24.3
2000	2,472,054	1,100,939	3,572,993	5,321,792	5,508,242	46.5	20
2001	2,377,321	1,169,620	3,546,941	5,147,204	6,084,476	46.2	19.2
2002	2,320,820	1,266,116	3,586,936	5,347,468	7,123,407	43.4	17.8
2003	1,802,171	1,435,959	3,238,130	4,752,762	7,086,133	37.9	20.3
2004	2,443,070	1,588,472	4,031,542	5,818,138	8,825,585	42	18
2005	2,440,139	1,739,424	4,179,563	6,022,752	10,080,143	40.5	17.3
2006	2,338,921	2,117,325	4,456,246	6,155,047	11,609,878	38	18.2
2007	2,235,963	2,600,694	4,836,657	6,448,240	13,324,977	34.7	19.5
2008	2,378,102	2,382,397	4,760,499	6,890,841	11,996,094	34.5	19.9
2009	3,053,311	1,586,772	4,640,083	7,817,533	9,494,111	39.1	16.7
2010	3,023,009	2,439,816	5,462,825	8,797,658	12,488,364	34.4	19.5
2011	3,289,051	1,658,073	4,947,124	9,794,796	12,693,733	33.5	13
2012	3,518,792	2,042,775	5,561,567	11,140,028	13,736,976	31.5	14.8
2013	2,747,750	2,456,165	5,203,915	12,175,550	14,846,485	22.5	16.5
2014	2,280,434	2,755,313	5,035,747	14,201,516	16,080,684	16	17.1
2015	1,837,782	4,002,100	5,839,882	13,231,651	19,310,430	13.8	20.7
	People	People	People	People	People	%	%

Note: Created by author from Korea Culture and Tourism Institute statistics (http://www.tour.go.kr/stat/st_inbound_view.asp).

signage around Japan these days. But this is not because South Koreans and Japanese are finding each other's countries more important tourist destinations. This is clear when we look at Japan's share as a destination for South Korean tourists in figure 2.4. Despite some major fluctuations shaped by exchange rate volatility, Japan's share as a destination for South Koreans traveling abroad continues to decline, while the ratio of Japanese tourists visiting South Korea has dramatically decreased since its peak. Given the two countries' cohosting of the FIFA World Cup in 2002, the South Korean culture boom in Japan that began in 2003, and the increase in absolute numbers of Japanese tourists taking advantage of the steep depreciation of the won precipitated by the Lehman Brothers bankruptcy, this would seem genuinely surprising.

The reason, however, is clear. Tourism shares are falling despite the increased exchange between the two countries because of the rapid growth in exchange with other regions.

Clearly, an increased amount of exchange does not necessarily lead to a closer relationship. In a globalizing world, exchange with regions where this has been limited will increase more rapidly than with those regions with which there has been considerable exchange. In both East Asia[37] and Europe,[38] shares of intraregional trade and investment, as well as human movement, are generally falling rather than increasing, again driven by globalization. Relations with neighbors who were formerly important because of their geographical proximity are on the verge of being relativized by the more rapid advance of relations with countries further away. Japan-South Korea relations are situated within this major trend. The formerly close relationship is now in danger of being relativized amidst the advance of globalization, whether we like it or not.

3. Economic Policies and the End of the Cold War

South Korea's Economic Development and Development Strategy

However, this does not mean that the decline in Japan's importance to South Korea can be ascribed purely to general phenomena such as the declining share of the developed countries in the world economy and the advance of globalization. Japan-South Korea relations have key features not seen in international relations in other regions that are having a major impact on the bilateral relationship today. Let's take a closer look.

The changing asymmetry in the bilateral relationship is telling in this regard. We have noted Japan's declining presence in South Korea from the perspective of the movement of both goods and people, yet South Korea's presence in Japan has not declined to any major extent. In fact, the share of bilateral trade in Japan's total trade, as well as South Korea's status as a destination for Japanese tourists heading abroad, has not shrunk by much at all. In other words, Japan's importance might have dwindled in South Korea, but South Korea's importance in Japan has remained much the same.[39] Some elements of South Korea's presence in Japan have even grown, as has clearly emerged on the cultural exchange front. One only has to look at the sheer number of South Korean programs on Japanese television and the volume of Hangul signage in Japanese towns.[40]

The first factor explaining the asymmetry in Japan-South Korea relations is the latter's economic growth. For example, as the scale of trade between the two countries is the same for both, if Japan's share of South Korean trade is shrinking while South Korea's share of Japanese trade evinces no major change, it must be because overall trade growth in South Korea is faster than trade growth in Japan. One factor behind South Korea's burgeoning trade is economic growth. No more than a small developing country in the Far East in the 1960s, South Korea has evolved into a world economic power and member of the G20. As a result of its dizzying economic growth, South Korea has expanded its markets to countries with which it had previously limited relations, so that Japan as an old customer has inevitably become less important.

Economic Policies Accelerate Globalization

I have identified three factors implicated in the decline in Japan's economic status in South Korea. One has been the universal phenomenon of the developed countries losing their share in the world economy, and the decline in the economic status of Japan as one of the developed countries has been shown to be congruent with that trend. The second factor has been globalization. Because globalization brings more international choices into our lifestyles, it was inevitable that it would relativize the former overwhelming dominance of neighboring Japan's status in the South Korean economy. The same trend can be observed across all bilateral relations of this nature—former relationships between geographically close developed and developing countries. So in this sense, the change in Japan-South Korea relations is explicable by patterns also seen elsewhere.

However, this is not to say that other aspects unique to the Japan-South Korea relationship can be ignored. I have identified one such aspect,

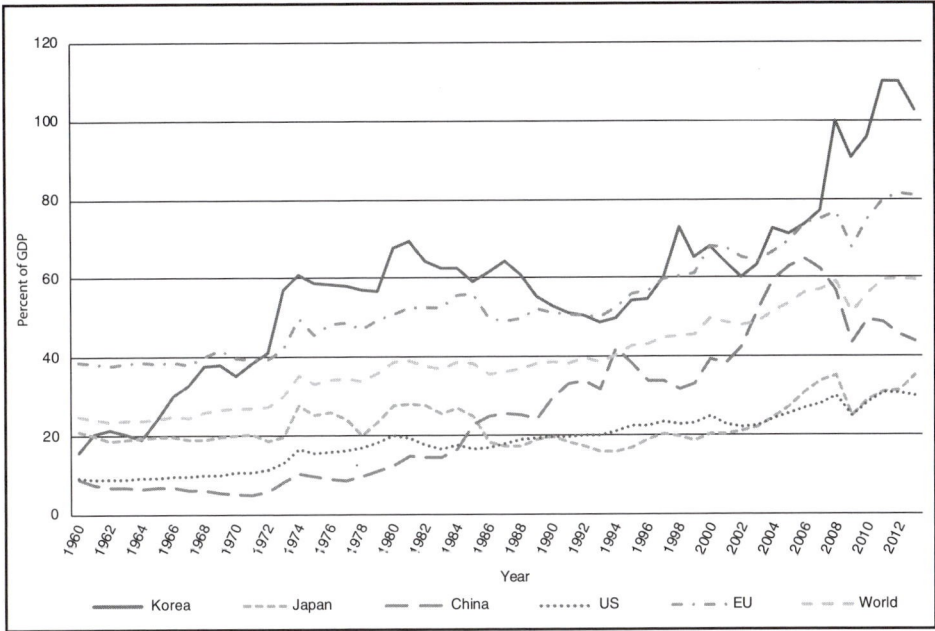

Figure 2.5. Trade dependency ratio trends 1960–2008. (*Source:* Created by the author from the World Bank database, http://databank.worldbank.org/data/home.aspx.)

namely South Korea's economic development, as the third factor. South Korea's trajectory to rapid economic growth has boosted the country's international influence and it now has trading partners around the globe. As a result, there has been nowhere for Japan's share to go but down.

However, while globalization might be proceeding worldwide, it is not having a similar impact directly on all countries. An extreme example is North Korea, which maintains a closed economic system that scoffs at a globalizing world. North Korea demonstrates that countries can, through their policies, shape to a certain extent the impact that phenomena like globalization have upon them.

So how has South Korea responded to these circumstances? Some valuable insights can be gleaned from figure 2.5, which traces trends in the trade dependency ratios of South Korea, Japan, the United States, China, the EU and the world as a whole. The trade dependency ratio (TDR) is the ratio of trade to gross domestic product (GDP), so a rising TDR means that trade is growing faster than GDP.

The graph clearly reveals completely different trends in Japan and South Korea. Despite the world economy increasing its TDR, Japan's has remained flat, with the figure even declining at some points. The TDR for South Korea, by contrast, not only evinces a steep rise but has held extremely high even compared to China, which has enjoyed the same rapid economic growth as South Korea.

Why has South Korea's TDR taken this trajectory? A closer look at the graph reveals the answer. The steepest increases occur over three periods: 1973–80, 1997–98, and 2008. It hardly needs to be said that these periods correlate respectively to the first and second oil crises, the Asian currency crisis of 1997, and the financial crisis that followed the collapse of Lehman Brothers, which is still fresh in our minds. Each of these episodes was a major blow to the South Korean economy, with the Asian currency crisis in particular taking it to the verge of state bankruptcy.[41]

The spike in South Korea's TDR accompanying each of these crises is the result of the government steering the economy sharply in the direction of trade dependence each time in order to overcome the crisis. Moreover, having spiked, the TDR does not return to its former level postcrisis but instead remains high. In other words, South Korea has met each crisis by instituting structural reform in the direction of greater dependence on the world economy to successfully survive fierce international competition. This stands in marked contrast to Japan, which failed to actively pursue structural reform after the collapse of the economic bubble and, as a result, has experienced a consistently low TDR.[42]

There are of course various reasons for the different paths the two countries have pursued. The most important has probably been circumstances around exchange rates. During global economic crises, people tend to sell won and buy yen because they worry about the won plummeting, whereas the yen is considered to be more stable. As a consequence, economic crises have created currency uncertainty for South Korea, but they have also provided an excellent opportunity to expand exports on the back of the weaker won. In the case of Japan, economic crisis always pushes up the value of the yen, keeping financial crises relatively confined but impacting heavily on the export industry. Due to their different circumstances, therefore, the South Korean government has been incentivized by crisis to steer the economy in the direction of globalization-oriented reforms grounded in export promotion, whereas the same crisis has simply brought about greater introversion in Japan's economic policy.[43]

I'll leave my analysis of economic policy and the underlying factors at that. What is important in the context of this book is that, since the 1970s,

South Korea has actively embraced the phenomenon that would come to be called globalization, continuing to reform the economy so as to absorb the brunt of globalization head on. As a result, the dwindling influence of the developed countries, the impact of globalization, and the expansion in trading partners prompted by economic growth have all manifested more strongly in South Korea than in other countries. And in terms of the Japan–South Korea relationship, they have manifested as a pronounced decline in Japan's importance to South Korea.

The Cold War and Korean War as Starting Points

However, these factors are insufficient to explain the rapid decline in Japan's presence in South Korea, because the starting point for Japan–South Korea relations was already unique. For example, as noted earlier in figure 2.3, in the early 1970s close to 40 percent of South Korea's trade was with Japan, which, added to the share of the United States as South Korea's second biggest trading partner, brought the total for these two countries alone to close to 75 percent. Seen from today's perspective, that in itself was extremely unusual and obviously presents the need to explain why South Korea found itself in that situation.

The answer is the Cold War, as is immediately apparent when we look, for example, at South Korea's trade figures immediately after the Korean War. South Korea's exports for 1954, the year after the Korean War ended, amounted to around US$24.25 million, while imports were US$243.32 million, almost ten times as much. Obviously, this unusual situation was supported primarily by the prodigious amount of assistance being provided by the United States. In other words, back then South Korea was able to make ends meet by using massive aid from the United States to import foreign goods. The same could be said of government finances. In the 1950s, the South Korean government depended on the United States for 30 to 40 percent of its revenue. Both the South Korean economy and government finances were literally reliant on US aid.[44]

Naturally enough, this heavy dependence on the United States made it impossible for South Korea to achieve any rapprochement with the Soviet Union, China, or any other member of the socialist bloc while the Cold War continued. Poverty-stricken South Korea had to import commodities from somewhere, and Japan filled that spot. South Korea found itself in the unique economic circumstances of receiving aid from the United States and exports from Japan.

As is widely known, this situation changed when the United States shifted its strategic attention from the Korean peninsula to Vietnam, slashing its aid to South Korea as a result. Park Chung-hee was already in power by that stage, and a serious shortfall in foreign reserves forced South Korea to pursue an export-led economic development strategy to obtain the necessary foreign funds. However, lacking primary products that it could export in large quantities, as well as the strength to pursue industrialization on its own, South Korea had little choice but to use foreign capital to build factories and export products made with cheap labor in labor-intensive industries to earn foreign currency. The trouble was that few countries were interested at the time in investing in a poor, politically unstable, divided country in the Far East, with the result that South Korea had to depend on Japan for much of that investment. Factories built in South Korea by Japanese companies moving into the country, usually in the form of joint ventures, used intermediate goods and production goods imported from Japan to make products that were exported around the world. As a result, South Korea's dependence on Japan continued to climb from the 1960s to the mid-1970s.[45]

However, this was also an abnormal situation created by the Cold War. In the 1970s, when the Vietnam War ended and the world entered an era of détente, South Korea's circumstances changed. In terms of statistics, a figure for trade with the Soviet Union emerged for the first time in 1974, and in 1980 a figure was officially released for direct trade with China. Exchange started to take place in areas other than the economy. One such example was sports exchange. When the Asian Games were held in 1986 as a de facto rehearsal for the 1988 Seoul Olympics, China sent along a huge mission, despite strong opposition from North Korea and the fact that it had no formal relationship with South Korea. The Soviet Union also participated in the Seoul Olympics, gracing the sporting event along with the mission from East Germany, which was a major Olympic competitor at the time.

As the Cold War wound down, it removed a major incentive for cooperation between Japan and South Korea on both the economic and security fronts. The change was particularly significant in South Korea. Confronting the huge threat of North Korea, backed by China and the Soviet Union, the South Korean government had developed an alliance with America as a counterbalance, and had also been forced to maintain friendly relations with Japan, where massive US military bases were located. The end of the Cold War changed the situation dramatically. North Korea lost its alliance with Russia, and its relationship with China also became decidedly rocky. Economic development had given South Korea a major boost in terms of military confidence, which also dramatically reduced the need for security cooperation with Japan. Even North Korea's nuclear missile program has failed to rekindle the hitherto smooth relationship.

Conclusion

To summarize the above findings, two key factors clearly underpinned the low degree of tension generated by the historical perception issue during this phase. One was generational change—from the prewar generation to the postwar generation—as epitomized by the positioning of the comfort women issue, along with many other issues of historical perception, as the rediscovery of history. The other was the relative decline in the importance of the bilateral relationship to the two countries. Japan became less important to South Korea both in economic and security terms. The loss of economic importance was due to globalization as well as South Korea's own economic growth, while the end of the Cold War played a major role in Japan's reduced security importance to South Korea.

The launch of South Korea's voyage of historical rediscovery and the diminished importance of the bilateral relationship together created a climate in which issues of historical perception were more likely to arise. However, a trigger issue was still needed that would turn a potential dispute into an actual one.

But these observations on the historical perception dispute have thus far been only hypothetical; now they need to be examined in light of actual events. The second part of my argument will therefore turn to the way in which the factors I have identified were reflected in the development of the dispute, looking specifically at two case studies: the textbook issue and the comfort women issue.

PART II

Case Study 1

Historical Disputes in the 1980s

THREE

The History Textbook Issue

1. The Root of the Issue

Why the Issue Is Important

In Part II, I examine how the factors identified in my theoretical observations manifest in actual cases, beginning with the history textbook issue.[1]

There are a number of reasons for addressing this particular issue. First, it is regarded as one of the most critical issues of historical perception between Japan and South Korea, epitomizing the distance between the two countries' views. That status is clearly demonstrated by the fact that the Japan-South Korea Joint History Research Project[2] conducted in the early 2000s—joint research not at the private-sector level but rather by committee members selected by both governments on the basis of the agreement reached at the 2001 Japan-ROK Summit Meeting—was set up specifically to address the history textbook issue. These days the publication of a new textbook in Japan inevitably signals another round of bickering between Japan and South Korea, to the extent that these rows almost seem to have become an annual event.

There are solid grounds for looking at the history textbook issue. For a start, government involvement in the process of textbook creation in both countries (albeit in different forms) means that revision of history textbooks can to some extent be regarded as mirroring changes in the historical perceptions of the respective governments and societies. Thus we can trace historical perceptions in both countries through changes in history textbooks and their references—which is my primary reason for electing to examine them.

My second reason is that the history textbook issue typifies those issues of historical perception foregrounded only as of the 1980s. In other words, a number of issues that today are regarded as central to the historical perception debate—history textbooks and the comfort women included— actually attracted scant attention prior to the 1980s. However, a major change in circumstances in the 1980s brought the history textbook issue in particular to the forefront of this debate.

The third reason is that the history textbook issue is a case in which the escalation of the situation cannot be directly explained by the actual status of the matters under debate. As I explained from the data in table 1.2, the textbook issue came to the forefront from the 1980s to around 2005, a period marked by a sharp rise in the number of textbook references to the era of Japan's colonial rule in the Korean peninsula and the years before and after. In other words, Japanese history textbooks during that period changed in a way that brought them more in line with South Korean demands—yet these same textbooks were lambasted by the South Koreans. By analyzing this apparent contradiction, we may gain a more concrete understanding of how the history textbook dispute developed and what factors shaped its course.

Finally, my fourth reason is that the juncture at which this particular issue came to the fore is so clearly defined. The immutable fact is that 1982 marks the first time a full-fledged dispute emerged between Japan and South Korea over Japanese history textbooks. This provides a very precise timeframe for exploring exactly what happened.

Naturally, the question then becomes: why 1982? And what was the trigger issue? Let's start there.

The Textbook Dispute and the Ienaga Lawsuits

The 1982 textbook dispute began with reports in the Japanese media on June 26 of that year. Due to the misunderstanding described earlier, the media reported that in the course of textbook screening that year, the Ministry of Education had ordered the publisher Jikkyō Shuppan to alter references to the "invasion of North China" to read the "advance into North China."[3] The textbook debate took off from there.

The June 26 reports were described above and do not require a detailed recounting here. However, there is one point that needs to be raised, which is why the Japanese media were watching the screening process so closely.

Photo 2. Press conference after the verdict in the first textbook lawsuit on July 16, 1974 (Jiji Press). Professor Ienaga presents his feelings in the form of a waka-style poem that reads "Win or lose, it matters not / I will continue the fight / For freedom of the spirit."

Given that textbook screening had been a regular event in the past, there must have been a specific reason that it drew media attention that year.

Clearly, the misreporting occurred as an extension of the Ienaga textbook trials that had been in the spotlight in Japan for some time.[4] It was 1965 when Tokyo University of Education professor Ienaga Saburō launched the first of three lawsuits against the Ministry of Education, arguing that its textbook screening was unconstitutional.

In his second suit, Ienaga demanded that the Ministry of Education reverse its rejection of his *Shin Nihonshi* [New Japanese History] in the

1966 screening. This suit was particularly important because Ienaga won victories in the courts of first and second instance, and because the second lawsuit moved ahead more rapidly than the first.[5] The judge's decision in the court of third instance—the Supreme Court—would therefore be critical in determining the direction of all the Ienaga suits—not only as the first to be decided in the Supreme Court but also because the direction of the verdicts handed down in the courts of first and second instance presented the strong possibility that Ienaga might actually win after the second instance.

Significantly in terms of the history textbook dispute, the Supreme Court's decision in the second Ienaga lawsuit was delivered in April 1982—barely two months before the misreporting incident—amid an unprecedented level of Japanese public and media interest in the textbook screening process.[6] However, the mood in relation to the lawsuit had already started to change as a result of the Japanese media starting to predict in early 1982 that Ienaga would lose his Supreme Court battle. In fact, the Supreme Court did reject the decisions of the courts of first and second instance and returned the suit to the High Court for retrial on the grounds that, as at 1982, the curriculum guidelines that set the standards for writing textbooks had been substantially revised, and as a result there was no merit to Ienaga's suit. This was effectively a loss for Ienaga, with the verdict significantly altering the direction of his lawsuits and the textbook screening debate.

So these were the unusual circumstances surrounding the history textbook issue in Japan when the 1982 textbook screening results were announced. The court case was expected to encourage the Ministry of Education to take an even tougher stance,[7] while Ienaga attracted such a degree of public sympathy that when his book *Kentei fugōkaku Nihonshi* [Japanese history: The version that failed the screening] was marketed as a general publication, it became a bestseller. Some felt that if the Ministry of Education responded with an even harder line with its screening, this might spur a new movement against textbook screening itself.[8]

Thus an erroneous report resulting from a basic misunderstanding by a single journalist spread instantaneously across Japan's media outlets. In short, because the mistake unintentionally met the expectations of the media and the public, it was widely received as fact.

2. South Korean and Chinese Responses

South Korea's Immediate Response

Of course this was not the first time that textbook screening made the front pages in Japan. By 1982, the Ienaga lawsuits had been underway for close to seventeen years, and the Japanese media had closely covered each new development. Some of the media had actually repeatedly problematized Japan's textbook screening system since the 1950s, even prior to the Ienaga case. Forced labor (later to become a focal point in the history textbook dispute between Japan and South Korea) and the history of Koreans permanently resident in Japan were being discussed in in terms of textbook content at least as far back as the early 1970s. So by 1982, the Japanese public was already quite familiar with the issues surrounding textbooks and their presentation of historical facts.

In contrast, South Korea had paid little attention to Japan's history textbook issues prior to 1982—and in fact, this lack of interest continued even after the 1982 issue initially arose. For example, on June 26–27, when the purported screening results were making headlines in the Japanese media, South Korea's two main papers at the time, *Chosun ilbo* and *Dong-a ilbo*, devoted only a few columns to the matter. As seen in figure 3.1, *Chosun ilbo* ran no more than a brief mention at the bottom left of the tenth page[9]—so small that only the most diligent reader would have even noticed it.

South Korea's limited interest in the Japanese textbook issue continued for some time. *Chosun ilbo* had nothing to say about it the next day or thereafter. It did include a small boxed article on the Chinese response in the issue of June 29,[10] but then fell silent again until July 8 when both *Chosun ilbo* and *Dong-a ilbo* suddenly ran editorials criticizing Japan's textbook screening.[11] In 1982, only two years after the de facto military coup d'état and the Gwangju Incident, the South Korean media was still tightly controlled by the Chun Doo-hwan administration,[12] so we can probably interpret the appearance of similar editorials in the two main newspapers on the same day as a government-driven response. However, following those editorials, South Korea's newspapers fell silent for a third time. Ultimately, contemporary reportage by the South Korean media on Japan's history textbook issue remained scattered and small-scale. In short, the media in South Korea initially revealed little interest in Japan's 1982 history textbook dispute.

Figure 3.1. Page in a South Korean newspaper (page 10 of the *Chosun ilbo* morning edition, June 27, 1982). The boxed area is the article referring to Japan's textbook controversy.

As noted in my theoretical framework in Part I, for an issue of historical perception to become a dispute it first needs to be discovered and invested with some degree of value. But the textbook issue had yet to be discovered as a major issue in South Korea and was not invested with significant value.

In late July, however, roughly a month after the issue had been foregrounded in Japan, the situation changed suddenly and dramatically. The South Korean media began to report on the Japanese textbook issue far more often and on a far greater scale, coverage that in turn incited a popular movement in South Korea. Newspapers covered details of "historical distortions" in Japan's history textbooks, and the anger and concern of the South Korean public grew quickly.

Below we consider why the South Korean people suddenly discovered the textbook issue and perceived value in it.

The Importance of China's Response

Why was the South Korean reaction to Japan's history textbooks so muted when the Japanese media misreported the issue in late June, only to erupt in late July, close to a month later? Obviously, something happened in late July.

The turning point was July 20, when China's *Renmin ribao* (People's Daily) issued a short commentary entitled "We must imprint this lesson on our memories," which formally criticized Japan's textbook screening.[13] The Chinese reaction was to a certain extent only natural, given that the main focus of attention in the textbook issue at the time was the suggestion that language referring to the Sino-Japanese War had been changed from "invasion" to "advance." Accordingly, it should have been far more an issue between Japan and China than between Japan and South Korea. It is not entirely clear why the Chinese government took nearly a month to produce an official response. China may have been expecting the Japanese government to work behind the scenes during that time to have the offending content changed.

When the Japanese textbook controversy, which until then had been reported and critiqued only in minor news articles, came under clear and ferocious attack by the *People's Daily*, the official organ of the Chinese Communist Party, it was received as an official protest from the Chinese government to its Japanese counterpart. As became immediately apparent from China's subsequent actions, this interpretation was not mistaken. On July 23, the state-operated Xinhua News Agency ran a discussion between the president of the Chinese Society of Education, the vice president of the Japan-China Friendship Association, and the leader of the Chinese

National Student Association as a vehicle for criticizing the screening results as "contrary to the spirit of the Japan-China Joint Communiqué and the Treaty of Peace and Friendship between Japan and the People's Republic of China," and observing that "Japan's history textbook screening is a challenge to the people of China."[14] On July 24, the *People's Daily* delivered another short commentary entitled "Falsifying the history of Japan's invasion of China is unforgiveable."[15] These broadsides marked the beginning of a full-scale Chinese government campaign against the Japanese government's textbook screening.

The Japanese government was deeply shaken by this vehement reaction from the Chinese,[16] which came barely four years after the 1978 signing of the bilateral Treaty of Peace and Friendship.[17] Japan was harboring high hopes for friendship between the two countries and believed that the bilateral relationship was making steady progress. In 1980, Premier Hua Guofeng became the first Chinese premier to visit Japan, and in May 1982, immediately before the incident, Japan received Zhao Ziyang as the new premier following Hua's downfall.

In 1982, Japan-China relations were at a turning point. The People's Republic of China had renounced all rights to wartime reparations in the lead-up to the Japan-China Joint Communiqué of 1972 as a counter to the Republic of China (Taiwan), which had taken the same step. Moreover, the Chinese government was working toward the conclusion of the Treaty of Peace and Friendship in 1978 and improving its relationship with Japan as East Asia's sole economic power at the time. Thus, as seen in Premier Zhou Enlai's careful avoidance of the Senkaku Islands issue, it shelved or offered concessions on many issues that would subsequently become involved in the historical perception dispute. This strategy was of course prompted by the continuing Cold War and the even more serious level of tension that had developed between China and the Soviet Union. Japanese government officials consequently never imagined that the Chinese government might choose to protest so stridently against an issue like the content of Japan's history textbooks.

In other words, both the Japanese government and public had regarded the history textbook issue as a purely domestic issue of how to approach textbook screening in light of the postwar constitution. The Chinese government's protest, however, elevated the issue to an international incident.[18] In that sense, China's fierce objection to the textbook screening process provided a crucial catalyst in transforming the nature of the Japanese history textbook debate.

Misperceptions of Reality

China's response to the textbook issue had a major impact not only on the Japanese government and society but also on the South Korean government and people.[19] Relations between South Korea and China at the time were completely different from today. When the textbook dispute first emerged in 1982, the world was still embroiled in the Cold War, and Deng Xiopeng was busy reforming China and instituting his open-door policies, while in South Korea, Chun Doo-hwan had been in power for only two years following his de facto coup d'état and the Gwangju Incident. Obviously, there could be no diplomatic relationship between a China run by the Chinese Communist Party and a South Korea led by Chun Doo-hwan's quintessentially anticommunist authoritarian regime, and there was virtually no direct trade between the two countries.[20] In other words, today's commonly perceived scenario of the anti-Japanese governments of China and South Korea working together to criticize Japan over issues of historical perception[21] was completely unimaginable back in 1982.

However, China's protest against Japan's textbook screening was still widely reported in South Korea and resulted in the government and people turning their attention again to an issue that at one point seemed as though it would be simply forgotten. Even so, South Korea was slow to react, for the very good reason that the focus was still on the Sino-Japanese War, with references to Korea yet to come under scrutiny. Consequently, on July 24, the South Korean government's only response was to order its embassy in Tokyo to look into the details of Japan's textbook screening system and textbook content and report back.[22] This suggests that the South Korean government had insufficient knowledge of Japan's textbook screening system and had little idea of how to proceed.

Subsequently, however, the situation would catch fire in South Korea as well. As exemplified by the government directive just mentioned, China's protest raised South Korean concern over references in Japanese history textbooks to a far higher level. The first thing that would emerge as a result was the discovery—scarcely surprising, really—that the content of Japanese history textbooks was quite different from that of South Korean textbooks. What should be noted here is the way in which the nature of the textbook issue changed along the way. When originally reported by the Japanese media, it was regarded as purely a Japanese domestic issue, focused on the rights and wrongs of textbook screening under the postwar constitution. China's protest turned it from a domestic problem into an international issue, but initially the focus remained on textbook screening and the changes this wrought in textbook language. However, in the course of debate in China and then South Korea, the spotlight shifted away from the screening process and onto the content of Japanese history textbooks.[23]

This was a natural development, in that the original legal debate in Japan on how textbook screening related to the ban on censorship under its postwar constitution was of no interest to China and South Korea. Rather than Japanese legal provisions concerning freedom of speech and the freedom of the press, what mattered to China and South Korea was where Japan was heading now that it had become an economic power. They were concerned above all about the reemergence of nationalism in Japan, a frequent accusation both in and beyond Japan. Both China and South Korea viewed the offending language in Japanese history textbooks as proof that nationalism was indeed gradually rearing its head in Japan, which is why they directed such searing criticism at the textbook issue.

However, there was a major flaw in this perception, namely that the wide divergence between the content of Japanese textbooks and Chinese and South Korean textbooks did not necessarily signify that the disparity was increasing. As I have already demonstrated with specific data, Japan's history textbooks were in fact including more references than before to colonial rule and Japan's invasion of the mainland, gradually closing the gap between treatment in Japanese textbooks and South Korean and Chinese textbooks. It should therefore have been impossible to say on the basis of textbook content alone that any change had occurred in terms of the emergence of Japanese nationalism. Rather than examining this rationally, however, people chose to shoehorn reality into a stereotypical notion that the difference between Japanese history textbook narratives and those in China and South Korea was evidence that Japan was shifting increasingly to the right. Put more figuratively, what was being distorted was not the historic reality of the past but rather the living present. Moreover, it was not only the Chinese and South Koreans who had this misshapen understanding of reality but the Japanese as well. As a result, the Japanese too failed to recognize the anomalous nature of the situation and could do nothing to stop it. Fueled by a subjective understanding divorced from the contemporary reality, the situation took on a life of its own.

Changing Perceptions in South Korea

Once South Korea began viewing the history textbook issue as evidence of the reemergence of Japanese nationalism, accompanied by a quickening militarist revival, this interpretation took almost no time to evolve into accepted wisdom. In August, the South Korean media started expounding on differences between history textbook content in Japan and South Korea, and South Korean "experts" explained plausibly how this signaled the rise of militarism in Japan.[24] Clearly, rather than seeking to engage in serious analysis of the visibly occurring changes in Japan's history textbooks, a one-dimensional discourse was allowed to hold sway.

I should point out that this discourse did not necessarily begin in South Korea, because the arguments of South Korean intellectuals at this point in time echoed that of the sector of Japanese opinion that had prompted and then supported the Ienaga lawsuits. In other words, the argument in South Korea was underpinned by a logic directly imported from Japan, based on which the South Korean public became increasingly dissatisfied with Japan's history textbooks.

With the protests of the Chinese government over the textbook issue therefore serving as the trigger event, the South Korean public discovered the issue and quickly absorbed the discourse then prevalent in Japan to imbue the issue with a degree of value.

However, we must also paint in the broader background issue to the discovery of the textbook issue in South Korea, namely the rapid change in the international situation surrounding South Korea in the 1980s. As noted in Part I, that change had heavily impacted on the situation surrounding the historical perception dispute in Japan-South Korea relations at the time, as I explore in the next section.

3. New Political Fluidity in Japan and South Korea

The South Korean Media and Japan's Shift to the Right

Let's start with the materials. Please read the following passage:

> In addition, the Japanese government's position is that, given the country's lack of resources, nuclear power plants are an important alternative energy source to oil energy, and even taking the dangers of nuclear power into consideration, technological management is possible.
>
> Despite this, Japanese public sentiment remains staunchly opposed. The public increasingly views Yasukuni Shrine visits and assertions of the constitutionality of the Self-Defense Forces as

marking a revival of militarism, and nuclear power plant construction as a path to destruction for the Japanese people.

Seen through outside eyes, Yasukuni Shrine is no different from the national cemeteries that exist in many other countries, and given that more than 80 percent of the public already approve of the existence of Self-Defense Forces, amending the Constitution to make it more realistic would be entirely natural.

When and in what country was this passage written? Many would mistake it for an excerpt from a recent nationalistic Japanese newspaper or magazine, but it was actually featured on the front page of a major South Korean newspaper—*Chosun ilbo*, in fact—more than thirty years ago on May 9, 1981, just over a year before the outbreak of the first history textbook dispute (fig. 3.2). Run under the headline of "Japanese society seized by 'opposition hysteria': New allergy towards a rightward shift," the excerpt was part of the eighth episode in a series entitled "A panorama of four billion people: The world today," which examined the current situation in countries around the globe. Above the article, the paper ran a large picture of a memorial service for the war dead held in Japan the previous year, with this caption below:

Memorial services for the war dead are held every year on the anniversary of the end of World War II. However, Japan's opposition parties and media have recently been reacting somewhat hysterically, arguing that ministers and Diet members paying their respects at Yasukuni Shrine where the souls of the war dead are enshrined represents a shift to the right.

The writer was Lee Do-hyung, Tokyo correspondent for *Chosun ilbo*.[25]

Chosun ilbo, which together with *Dong-a ilbo* has a history tracing back to the colonial period, is regarded as one of South Korea's most nationalistic papers. It would certainly surprise many people today to find such a paper running an article that seems to defend a Japanese shift to the right—and, moreover, on the front page. What is even more surprising, however, is that the article was written just over a year before the first textbook dispute emerged in June and July of 1982. In 1982, of course, the South Korean public would adopt the view expressed in Japan that the textbook screening results from that year were a manifestation of Japan's shift to the right, and it would criticize the Japanese government accordingly. The distance from the tenor of an article appearing only fourteen months earlier seems vast.

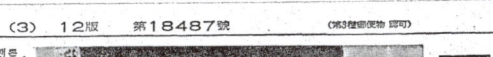

Figure 3.2. An article on the front page of the *Chosun ilbo* morning edition of May 9, 1981, highlighting the reaction of the Japanese public against a shift to the right.

For example, on July 25, 1982, right in the midst of the first textbook dispute, *Chosun ilbo* ran a dialogue between Seoul University professor Shin Yong-ha and Kookmin University professor Han Sang-il entitled "Is Japan Going to Repeat its Historical Crimes?"[26] In the course of the dialogue, Professor Shin, who would subsequently become one of South Korea's leading scholars of Korean nationalist historiography, observed as follows:

> Those individuals in their 60s who are making key policy decisions in Japanese politics in and behind the Liberal Democratic Party were young commissioned officers or paramilitary personnel during World War II. In recent years, they have been taking concrete steps to rearm Japan by changing the Constitution, and we have seen moves in Japan to develop publications and films that glorify its former militarist invasions: externally by securing the powerful foothold created by Japan's economic advance into Korea, China, and South East Asian countries, and internally by legitimizing those invasions. As a result, the ambitions that have been restrained to date are finally emerging into the daylight.

This is of course a typical South Korean condemnation of Japan's purported shift to the right that is still frequently voiced today. The important point is that this argument became accepted as self-evident in South Korea around 1982, as demonstrated by the huge difference in the tone of the South Korean media only a year before.

What was behind this change? I should first point out that prior to 1982 two lines of thought about Japan's supposed shift to the right existed side by side in South Korea. The first was the fear that Japanese militarism was reviving, as emerges from Professor Shin's observation above. It was perhaps inevitable that South Korea, as a country that had experienced Japanese colonial rule, would see Japan's transformation into one of the world's major economic powers and worry that it might again become a threat.

The Early 1980s

However, until around 1982, there was also support in South Korea for a Japanese shift to the right, as exemplified by the May 1981 *Chosun ilbo* editorial. The problem of course is why two completely different discourses should have existed at this point in time.

The domestic and international circumstances of both Japan and South Korea at the time hold the key to understanding this apparently anomalous situation—particularly the international circumstances in which South Korea had found itself until the early 1980s. As I have repeatedly observed, the Cold War was still very much a feature of the early 1980s, with the United States and the Soviet Union spearheading intense competition and hostility between the East and West. US president Ronald Reagan delivered his famous "evil empire" address in 1983, stressing the precarious position of the United States and the free world in the struggle between the East and West. South Korea, as a divided state on the frontlines of the Cold War, was still exposed to a major international threat.

Another aspect of South Korea in the early 1980s is that the Chun Doo-hwan regime had come to power following the assassination of Park Chung-hee and a series of coups d'état, followed immediately by the bloody Gwangju Incident. Because of this, Chun's administration suffered from a severe crisis of legitimacy. The support of South Korea's key Cold War allies, Japan and the United States, was seen as essential to maintaining the administration's grip on power, and Chun Doo-hwan visited the United States in 1981, the year after he took power, to strengthen relations with the newly elected Reagan.[27] He also took a proactive diplomatic line with Japan, in 1984 becoming the first South Korean president to officially visit Japan.

But South Korea's bilateral relations with Japan and with the United States were not proceeding smoothly, despite their importance. Developments in the United States were particularly critical. The shift toward détente in Asia that began in the late 1960s gathered momentum with the visits to China by US National Security Advisor Henry Kissinger in 1971 and then by President Richard Nixon the next year, and became even more evident after the Vietnam War ended in 1975. The biggest impact on South Korea was the reduction in US forces stationed there. The United States began troop cutbacks in the early 1970s, and when the Carter administration came to power in 1977, there was even talk of a complete withdrawal. The South Korean government reacted strongly to the US government's stance, placing the bilateral relationship under considerable strain.[28]

Parallel with the above developments, it came to light in 1975 that the South Korean government was involved in bribing members of Congress in relation to purchases of US agricultural surplus. Subsequent investigations saw this incident—dubbed "Koreagate"—evolve into a full-blown scandal when it was revealed that for many years the South Korean government had lobbied influential members of Congress and operated a bribery scheme to try to influence US Far Eastern policy to South Korea's advantage.[29] In 1979, former Korean Central Intelligence Agency (KCIA) director Kim Hyung-wook,[30] who had sought asylum in the United States and testified in Congress, disappeared in Paris. In January of that year, Taiwan, which, like South Korea, was anticommunist, lost its diplomatic relationship with the United States, and PRC de facto leader Deng Xiaoping made a visit to the United States immediately after. South Korea was deeply disturbed at this rapprochement between the United States and China, and South Korea-US relations reached their lowest ebb since the Republic of Korea was established in 1948.[31]

South Korea's relations with Japan were also deteriorating. The Kim Dae-jung incident in 1973—which involved the kidnapping and attempted murder of a political dissident by a foreign intelligence agency operating openly in the Japanese capital—was a barefaced violation of Japanese sovereignty. The Japanese government's confidence in the South Korean government was greatly undermined by this incident.[32] Conversely, the friction that arose between the two countries' investigative personnel over the 1974 Mun Se-gwang incident, in which Mun, a second-generation Korean resident in Japan, attempted to assassinate South Korean President Park Chung-hee, resulting in the fatal shooting of Park's wife, Yuk Young-soo, heightened South Korea's distrust of Japan. The main reasons were the fact that the weapon used in the attack had been stolen from an Osaka police box, as well as Japan's apparent failure to extend sufficient cooperation to investigations by South Korean authorities, who were convinced that persons connected to the General Association of Korean Residents in Japan (North Korea's de facto embassy in Japan) were involved. Needless to say, South Korea's misgivings also stemmed from the 1972 normalization of diplomatic relations between Japan and the People's Republic of China and the cessation of the diplomatic relationship between Japan and the Republic of China (Taiwan).

By the late 1970s, the South Korean government was growing increasingly concerned that it was being forsaken by its allies.[33] With both Japan and the United States cutting off diplomatic relations with Taiwan, as well as the fall of South Vietnam at the end of the Vietnam War, the international situation in the era of détente appeared to be operating greatly to South Korea's disadvantage as a member of Asia's anticommunist camp.

This was not just a South Korean perception. The situation in both Asia and the world at the end of the 1970s bore little resemblance to what it would be ten years later as the Cold War was drawing to a close. The countries of the so-called free world were recognizing in the late 1970s that they were far from victory. This was epitomized by the "evil empire" address by President Reagan mentioned earlier, in which Reagan stressed that the United States and the other countries of the "free world" needed to completely rebuild their strategy to overcome the perceived strength of the Communist bloc. The Carter administration's plan to withdraw all US troops from South Korea, the Moscow Olympics boycott in response to the Soviet invasion of Afghanistan, and the Reagan Doctrine were all different expressions of US frustration at finding itself in what it felt to be a vastly inferior position.[34] In Japan, too, John Hackett's novel *The Third World War: The Untold Story* was translated into Japanese in 1978 and became a bestseller.[35] From the end of the 1970s to the early 1980s, people were still speaking seriously about the communist threat and measuring their prospects in that light.

Japanese Political Fluidity

In the early 1980s, the South Korean people were afraid that they would be abandoned by both Japan and America, and the domestic situation in Japan also influenced the bilateral relationship. At the beginning of the 1980s, the "one and a half party system" in Japan—in which the Liberal Democratic Party (LDP) and a permanent opposition party, the Japan Socialist Party (JSP), consistently captured most of the vote—was still in place. However, the advance of the multiparty system had seen the number of LDP seats in the Diet continue to decline since the 1950s, and in 1976, the party lost its majority for the first time in its history. The same thing happened in the House of Representatives elections in 1979, destabilizing the government's political base.

Meanwhile, tensions were growing within the LDP, surfacing in a forty-day power struggle between rivals Ōhira Masayoshi and Fukuda Takeo. The result was an unusual situation in which both Ōhira and Fukuda stood for prime minister from the same party in the National Diet following the 1979 House of Representatives elections, with Ōhira as head of the main LDP faction narrowly winning the run-off to retain the prime minister's seat. The rivalry between Ōhira and Fukuda continued, however, and in 1980, Fukuda and other members of the opposing factions abstained from voting when a no-confidence motion was brought by the opposition parties against the Ōhira cabinet, causing the motion to pass by a majority vote. The Japanese political world was thrown into turmoil. Ōhira dissolved the House of Representatives in response to the motion's success, with elections in both houses scheduled to take place on the same day for the first time—and then Ōhira's sudden death during the election campaign eventuated in a resounding victory for the LDP.[36]

Clearly, Japanese politics was rapidly becoming far more fluid, making the future extremely difficult to predict. Moreover, at this time the JSP, the LDP's main opponent, still appeared to be a robust presence. The party had not abandoned hope of seizing power and swung between a coalition with the Japan Communist Party (JCP) and one with Kōmeitō and the Democratic Socialist Party as it sought a chance to achieve a JSP-led administration. In the 1970s, the JSP's strategy achieved great success at the regional level in the form of reformist local governments across Japan. Reformist politicians came to dominate key local governments in the Tōkaidō belt, including Tokyo, Kanagawa Prefecture, Kyoto, Osaka, Yokohama, Nagoya, and Kobe. This boom came to a rapid end with the string of defeats suffered by JSP- and JCP-backed candidates in the nationwide local elections of 1979. However, in the early 1980s, it was still impossible to tell whether this was really the beginning of the end or no more than just a temporary setback.[37]

The JSP-North Korea Honeymoon

Most troubling of all for South Korea was the Japan Socialist Party—Japan's largest opposition party—formally rejecting the legitimacy of the Republic of Korea and instead declaring its support for the Democratic People's Republic of Korea.[38] The JSP had not always been a supporter of the DPRK. Up to the mid-1950s, the party did not necessarily side with North Korea but maintained a neutral relationship with both halves of the Korean peninsula, as manifested in the JSP's position that North Korea rather than South Korea was responsible for starting the Korean War.[39] However, by the late 1950s when tensions heightened over the Syngman Rhee Line unilaterally demarcated by the South Korean government, the JSP started to become strongly critical of the South Korean administration.[40] In the early 1960s, when negotiations on the normalization of Japan-ROK relations began taking shape toward conclusion of the Treaty on Basic Relations between Japan and the Republic of Korea, in which South Korea would be recognized as the only legitimate government on the Korean peninsula, the JSP formally rejected the treaty.[41] In 1965, the party launched a large-scale protest against the Treaty on Basic Relations and decided the next year to foster exchange with North Korea.[42] North Korea subsequently utilized this, with the JSP and the North Korean government—or, more precisely, the Workers' Party of Korea (WPK), the ruling political party—drawing quickly closer. We could therefore say that the JSP was pushed toward the North Korean side by its opposition to the LDP-led Japanese government's normalization of relations with South Korea during the Cold War.

In the 1970s, relations between the JSP and North Korea made significant progress. Where exchange between the JSP and the WPK was originally conducted only at the level of ordinary Diet members, it began to extend to increasingly high-level representatives, with the 1970 visit to North Korea by JSP chairman Narita Tomomi marking the beginning of a tradition of JSP leaders making direct visits to Pyongyang.[43] Just two months prior to the May 1981 article in *Chosun ilbo* criticizing Japan's left wing, JSP leader Asukata Ichio and the sixth JSP mission to North Korea met with President Kim Il-sung. It was Asukata's second visit to North Korea, and the fourth JSP mission to be dispatched there since Asukata became JSP leader.[44]

At the meeting, Asukata observed that the JSP was currently opposed to bolstering Japan's Self-Defense Forces and would redouble its efforts toward achieving annulment of the US-Japan Security Treaty, nonalignment, and an active and unarmed neutrality. At the same time, the JSP's involvement in the movement for the elimination of nuclear weapons had led to engagement in the movement to abolish nuclear power plants. At the March 1981 Asukata-Kim meeting, the two leaders issued a joint declaration on the establishment of a nuclear-free zone of peace in East Asia. Media reports suggested that in response to the JSP's proposal of a nuclear-free peace zone that embraced Japan, the Korean peninsula, and environs, the WPK expressed concern about including the Soviet Union and China as nuclear powers, revealing that the JSP was spearheading that part of the declaration.[45]

Concerns of the Chun Doo-hwan Administration

Recognizing this special relationship between the JSP and North Korea is critical to understanding why the South Korean media might have welcomed a Japanese shift to the right around 1981. The elements included in the *Chosun ilbo* article cited earlier—opposition to nuclear power plant construction, opposition to making the Self-Defense Forces constitutional, and opposition to official visits to the Yasukuni Shrine—were plainly all consistent with JSP policies. In other words, the newspaper's criticism of Japan's supposed "allergy" was aimed directly at the JSP.

Given the JSP's close relationship with North Korea, South Korea would obviously have found a Japanese shift to the left unacceptable. In fact, at the March 1981 meeting, Kim Il-sung and Asukata concurred that

昭和56年)3月18日　水曜日　13版　総合　(2)

飛鳥田訪朝団長が寄稿

「非核・平和地帯」の宣言

反動動向への異議

【北京十七日＝佐野特派員】朝鮮民主主義人民共和国（北朝鮮）を十三日から訪問していた社会党訪朝団の飛鳥田委員長は十七日、北京で朝日新聞社に次のような一文を寄せた。

今回の訪朝の目的は社会党と朝鮮労働党の間で、まず第一に東北アジア非核・平和地帯の設置に関する共同宣言を行うこと、第二にアジアと世界のさし迫った情勢、運動の課題について意見の一致を遂げることであった。われわれはこの二つの目的で十分な満足すべき成果を得たと考えている。

東北アジアにおける非核・平和地帯の設置宣言は社会党がまだ政権についておらず、朝鮮側も統一国家を実現していない段階で、その効果が政府間協定と異なるのは当然である。それにもかかわらず、これは少なくとも日朝両国民とアジア諸国の大多数の民衆の切実な願望に合致しており、今日の平和のための諸運動に明確な目標と方向性を与え、強く激励するものといえる。

わが党はこの観点からすでに社会主義インタ加盟のオーストラリア、ニュージーランド両労働党との間で同じ趣旨の共同宣言を行っており、アジア太平洋地域の全域にわたる諸国民の平和維持の総結集に努めてきた。今回初めて社会主義国の党と積極的な合意を遂げたわけで、この意義は世界の非核・平和運動の歴史の中でも画期的なものと思う。

この宣言を実現していくための当面最大の障害は、東北アジア地域に核武装した外国軍隊が駐留していることであるのは言うまでもない。南朝鮮には現に七百発以上の核弾頭が配備され、日本でも沖縄や岩国をはじめ核部隊の存在が国民に不安を呼んでいる。レーガン大統領の軍拡路線の下で南朝鮮と日本を中心に軍備の急速な拡大が意図されているが、それは韓国の全斗煥体制へのテコ入れと相まって朝鮮の自主的平和統一の道を妨げ、日本国憲法の示す非武装平和への展望に逆らう動きといわざるを得ない。

今回の共同宣言は、こうした反動的なきな臭い動向に対して、日朝両国民のきっぱりとした異議申し立てを行い、東北アジア地域における真の安全と平和の革新的構想を提起したものである。これは日朝両国民のみならずアジアと世界の諸国民にとっても、平和のための共有財産となるべきものである。この観点から宣言文の取りまとめに際して、両党それぞれ注意深い配慮を注ぎ、広範な国と民衆の平和意思を最大限結集できるような表現を選んでいる。

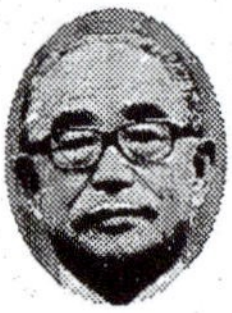

両党がこうした深い合意と一致を遂げるに当たって、私たち代表団と金日成主席との話し合いが決定的な意義を持ったことはいうまでもない。

主席が到着のその日から私たちと会見され、正式会談を含めて前後三回も話し合われたのは全く異例のことと聞いた。それほどわが党や日本国民との連帯が重視されているわけだが、いずれにせよ、一方ではアメリカの重圧を受け、他方では中ソの谷間にありながら、立派に自主性を貫き、非同盟・中立への志向を明確にされている主席の高い見識に私たちは心からの共感を覚えた。

私の訪朝は三年ぶりだったが、この短い間にも平壌の町並みは一段と美しく整備され、二十階、三十階建ての共同住宅が続々と建設されている。あと三年でこの百五十万都市の住宅問題は完全に解決されるという。私は西欧やアメリカの数多くの都市を訪れているが、こんなに美しい整った近代都市は他にないとさえ思う。

こうして静かに落ち着いた暮らしを営んでいる国が、どうして「脅威」などであり得ようか。全く根拠のない誤解や曲解に基づくレーガン政権の極東戦略と、それに追随する鈴木内閣の対韓、対朝鮮政策は一日も早く転換すべきである。そのために奮闘する決意を、私は今回の訪朝で一段と固めてきた。

Figure 3.3. Article by JSP Chairman Asukata Ichio after his visit to North Korea (*Asahi shimbun* morning edition, March 18, 1981, p. 2) military arrangements between Japan, South Korea, and the United States were moving ahead, and identified South Korean president Chun Doo-hwan as the "most dangerous element."

The JSP was a thorn in the side of the Chun Doo-hwan government not just because of its relationship with North Korea but also because of the vociferous criticism that the JSP had targeted at successive South Korean regimes' suppression of human rights since the 1960s, which also implied criticism of the military government. In particular, the JSP had maintained ties with Kim Dae-Jung and the South Korean democracy movement since Kim's kidnapping in 1973. On May 17, 1980, when Chun Doo-hwan and other members of the new military establishment staged their de facto coup d'état, placing the whole country under martial law and arresting and sentencing Kim Dae-Jung to death, the JSP responded by ramping up its criticism of the situation in South Korea and demanding that the Japanese government take a strong line with the South Korean government.

The JSP Shadow

In addition, the JSP was opposed to Japanese economic assistance to South Korea. Chun Doo-hwan sent his foreign minister, Lho Shin-yong, to Tokyo in August 1981 to demand a massive government loan of six billion dollars from Japan. While it has been completely forgotten today, the JSP was among the political forces most stridently opposed to this demand in Japan. In the Diet, the party declared that the six billion would end up being used for military spending and that such a huge loan would upset the balance of Japan's economic cooperation. The JSP went so far as to call on the Japanese government to place a total freeze on negotiations with its South Korean counterpart.[46]

The party's fierce opposition to providing government aid to South Korea was rooted in part in the 1976 Koreagate scandal in the United States, after which the JSP warned loudly against the political and economic collusion in relations between Japan and South Korea.[47] The party's negative view of government aid for South Korea remained unchanged in the early 1980s, and it regularly claimed that if Japan provided economic cooperation to South Korea, some of that capital would flow back to Japan and become a source of funding for ruling party politicians.

In the early 1980s, the JSP seemed to be thwarting the Chun Doo-hwan administration from all sides—including the party's cooperation with North Korea, support for the South Korean democracy movement, opposition to the Japanese government loan to South Korea, and its probes into corruption—even as the JSP's influence dwindled at home. The South Korean administration and its supporters could therefore definitely not allow Japan to shift to the left, with the increase in JSP power that this would imply.

The South Korean administration was prevented from piggybacking on the history textbook issue as pursued by Ienaga Saburō and his supporters within a purely Japanese domestic framework because one of the organizations supporting the Ienaga lawsuits was the Japan Teachers' Union, the political wing of which was the Political Federation of Japanese Democratic Education, which had close ties to the JSP. This was a different dimension of the Japan-South Korea relationship shaped by the international climate of the Cold War.

The key point is that the Cold War had an impact not just on international relations but also on Japan's domestic politics, which in turn forced the South Korean public to reconsider the Japan-South Korea relationship in that light. The situation in Japan until the early 1980s had created a situation whereby South Korea, and particularly those conservatives clustered around the South Korean administration, had good cause to regard Japan's "shift to the left" as a real threat. They were left with little choice but to seek the cooperation of Japan's conservatives to counter that threat, even if that required ignoring major differences in historical perception over Japan's colonial rule.

As noted in Part I, at this time the Cold War still played a major role in preventing the emergence of a historical perception dispute between Japan and South Korea.

However, the 1982 history textbook controversy would fundamentally transform that architecture. What happened between Japan and South Korea during the dying days of the Cold War? The next chapter considers the 1980s a critical turning point in the history textbook issue.

FOUR

The Turning Point of the 1980s

I. The Closing Days of the Cold War

South Korea during Détente

In the last chapter, I used the example of the history textbook issue to trace the transformation that occurred at a specific point in the 1980s in the context of the historical perception dispute, reflecting major changes in the circumstances of Japan and South Korea and their respective societies.

The shift toward détente in the 1970s had gradually changed the shape of the Cold War, which had been such a dominant influence in the region since World War II, and thus had a significant impact on the Japan–South Korea relationship, as evinced in the rivalry between Chinese and South Korean journalists in Tokyo over the textbook issue. In 1972, Japan resumed diplomatic relations with China, and many Chinese journalists were stationed in Tokyo as a result. Japan-China relations were excellent at the time, and Chinese journalists were awarded a considerable amount of respect. This did not go down well with South Korean journalists in Tokyo. China and South Korea had no formal diplomatic relations at the time, simply maintaining the truce that had existed between them since the Korean War. Coming from the Korean peninsula in its position as a front line in the Cold War, the South Korean journalists felt that Japan should treat South Korea better as a fellow member of the Western bloc. Instead the Japanese were busy enthusiastically embracing China while showing scant interest in South Korea.

Watching Chinese journalists launch into action in response to *People's Daily* reportage of the textbook issue and the way the Japanese government kowtowed to these newcomers, South Korean journalists were aggrieved that their country was not receiving the priority over China that they felt was merited given the thirty-five years of colonial rule to which South Korea had been subjected. Their response was to devote themselves to examining the Japanese government's historical perceptions just as closely as their Chinese counterparts, with the resulting denunciations of the Japanese government sent back to Seoul. This set the unusual tone of the international situation that pertained in the 1980s as the Cold War drew to a close.[1]

It should be noted, however, that the 1970s détente did not lead directly to the subsequent East-West reconciliation and the collapse of the Communist bloc. As symbolized by President Nixon's trip to China in 1972, framed in terms of an American president crossing the Pacific to visit Beijing, the major feature of the détente was that it manifested as a result of the Free World's subjective perception of the disadvantage at which it stood in relation to the Communist bloc—a perception that of course arose primarily from the United States' defeat in the Vietnam War. The political situation in the 1970s was consequently one in which the East Asian members of the Free World felt particularly exposed.

Most apprehensive of all was South Korea, positioned on the front line of the Cold War. Both the government and the intelligentsia feared that the changing international situation would marginalize the country and were consequently extremely wary of moves by the still-powerful Japan Socialist Party and other "revolutionary forces" in Japan. When Japan normalized relations with the People's Republic of China in 1972 with the conclusion of the Japan-China Joint Communiqué, it cut loose Taiwan's Kuomintang government without a qualm. The following year, the United States concluded the Paris Peace Accords with North Vietnam and withdrew its troops, effectively abandoning South Vietnam. It was therefore hardly unreasonable for the South Koreans to worry that Japan and the United States might next abandon another divided Free World nation— namely South Korea.[2]

I'll sketch a quick timeline to assist with a more accurate understanding of the situation. When Park Chung-hee was assassinated in October 1979, President Carter, who had at one time pledged to withdraw US forces from South Korea, maintained a firm grip on power in the United States and was also indicating strong interest in another term.[3] With the end of the Vietnam War and the Watergate scandal still fresh in the minds of the

American public, liberal Democrats continued to enjoy an edge over conservative Republicans, and in fact had swept the 1978 interim elections.[4] In addition to the incumbent Carter, Senator Edward Kennedy—known as even more liberal than Carter—had also revealed presidential ambitions, and the bulk of the media were predicting either Carter or Kennedy as the next president.[5] As noted earlier, in Japan, the lower house elections just before Park's assassination had left the Liberal Democratic Party in turmoil after losing the majority for a second time, and Ōhira Masayoshi and Fukuda Takeo had embarked on their fierce forty-day power struggle within the party.

Further afield, developments were also looking less than promising for South Korea. The Islamic Revolution rolled through Iran from 1978 to early 1979, producing an anti-American government in what had been an important US partner in the Cold War. This revolution led directly to the second oil crisis, heavily influencing the world economy. In December 1979, the Soviet Union invaded Afghanistan in its biggest military exercise since World War II. The sheer scale of the invasion prompted serious concern in certain quarters. The Soviet Union was not alone in increasing its military activity. In February 1979, China undertook a large-scale invasion of Vietnam, apparently mobilizing more than five hundred thousand troops for what became the Sino-Vietnamese War.

It is important to remember that the string of events which rocked South Korea—from the Park assassination to the December 12 coup d'état[6] (often referred to as the 12/12 Incident in South Korea) by Chun Doo-hwan and other members of the new military establishment in 1979 to the de facto coup staged on May 17, 1980, in order for Chun to take power, and the ensuing Gwangju Incident—took place against this dramatically changing international backdrop. Recognizing the great concern with which the military and other anticommunist forces in South Korea viewed contemporary international developments is essential to understanding their actions.[7]

However, immediately after Chun seized power, the world moved off in an entirely different direction. For South Korea, the most important developments were political changes in Japan and the United States. The turning point for Japan occurred in June 1980 when the upper and lower house elections were held simultaneously. The elections arose out of extraordinary circumstances—unrest within the LDP allowing the passage of the opposition's vote of no confidence—whereupon Ōhira's sudden death during the election run-up provided the LDP with an unexpected tailwind that propelled it to an historic victory.

The prime minister's seat was subsequently taken by Suzuki Zenkō as Ōhira's replacement, and this had a major impact on the distribution of power among the LDP's various factions. With two consecutive prime ministers coming from the Ōhira faction, Miyazawa Kiichi, a leading dove within that faction, now had little hope of taking power, while Nakasone Yasuhiro, a hard-liner sitting at number two in the Suzuki administration, enjoyed a meteoric rise in status.[8] Nakasone went on to become prime minister in 1982 and remained in power until 1987, the year of South Korea's democratization.

But what was of course far more critical was Ronald Reagan's election as US president in November 1980. Having come within a breath of beating the incumbent President Ford in the 1976 Republican primaries, Reagan was known in American politics for his heretical right-wing discourse, and at the start of the election campaign there was considerable skepticism about his prospects, even among party members.[9] However, having wrested victory from George H. W. Bush (whose turn would come later) in a tough primary battle, the boost he received during the presidential race from the domestic economic slump and the Iran hostage crisis (involving US embassy staff) that occurred just a few days before the election enabled Reagan to maintain his advantage over the incumbent Carter throughout the campaign. Reagan ultimately crushed Carter by more than 10 percent.[10] The emergence of hawkish, right-wing governments in both Japan and the United States was good news for South Korea as a divided nation, rescuing the country and its anticommunist camp from momentary crisis.

At the beginning of the 1980s, then, South Korea's international environment underwent rapid change. The fear of being abandoned that haunted the country at the end of the 1970s gave way to a much stronger international position, which obviously enabled the South Korean government to take a much firmer stance in relation to the Japanese government than it had previously.

This situation was accelerated by another factor raised in Part I, namely the shift in society from a prewar generation to a postwar generation. Below I look specifically at the effects of the generational change, whose importance was equivalent to that of the changing international situation during this period.

Emergence of a New Generation Unfamiliar with Japan

While the Park and Chun administrations each came to power in a coup d'état, they differed in a number of ways. One was the difference in the generation to which the members of the two administrations belonged. For example, there were fourteen years between South Korean presidents Park and Chun—born in 1917 and 1931, respectively—so when Chun came to power in 1980, he was still only forty-nine years old. While it is not often noted, Chun in fact belonged to a younger generation than subsequent presidents Kim Young-sam (born 1927) and Kim Dae-jung (born 1924).[11]

The emergence of a young president wrought major change throughout South Korean society. Serving military personnel and veterans exercised great political and social influence in South Korea, and the particular class at the Korean Military Academy (KMA)—the training ground for the military elite—to which they had belonged held particular significance for them. The successful coup d'état staged by Chun and his cohorts, most of whom were members of the Academy's eleventh class (which entered the Academy in 1951), had the effect of hastening the departure from center stage of South Korean society Academy graduates from the tenth class and before, as well as other members of the older generation who had ties to them—in other words, an entire generation actively involved not only in military affairs but also in the political arena and beyond.

One impact was the dramatic generational change in the Presidential Secretariat, which held huge sway in South Korean politics. For example, the "Three Fours"[12] (Heo Hwa-pyeong, Heo Sam-soo, and Heo Mun-do), who emerged as key members of the Presidential Secretariat early in the Chun administration, were all born around 1937 and still in their early forties when Chun took power. Given that key players in the Park Chung-hee administration such as Lee Hu-rak and Kim Jae-gyu were born in the mid-1920s, the change in administration pulled the age of core members of the president's office down by almost fifteen years—vividly illustrating the abruptness of the generational change brought about by Chun's new regime.[13]

What matters is that the members of the generation that sprang to the fore under Chun Doo-hwan were all born after 1930, and as such bore no responsibility for colonial rule. They had gained no social standing under colonial rule, nor had they served as officers or soldiers in World War II. Furthermore, Chun and many of his peers had not even received higher education under Japanese rule. Chun, for example, was only in his fifth year of elementary school when the war ended (because of a delay in his schooling resulting from his family moving to Manchuria then back home).[14]

Chun's generation accordingly had a completely different experience of Japan than the previous generation. Born in South Korea under Japanese rule and receiving their primary school education during the colonial period, they could understand a certain level of Japanese, but lacked the strong personal connections with Japan cultivated through life experience that was typical of those supporting the Park Chung-hee regime. In addition to their extremely limited knowledge of and connections with Japan, they had no particular interest in Japan.

As a result, South Korea's relationship with Japan underwent major change in this period. During the détente of the 1970s, South Korea felt deeply frustrated at its international isolation. Despite this, the generation that had received higher education under Japanese rule still held the political and social reins. Their approach was to exploit their personal networks to the full to maintain relations with Japan as the foreign country most familiar to them, and as the neighbor easiest to enlist in support of their activities—even while nursing considerable dissatisfaction toward Japan.

However, the rapid generational change that occurred in South Korean politics and society after Park Chung-hee's death combined with an upturn in the international situation to greatly reduce Japan's importance to South Korea. The country's improved relationship with the United States under the new Reagan administration had a special meaning for the new generation. It should not be overlooked that many of the military personnel in charge during the Chun years felt much closer to their American ally than to Japan even on a personal level.[15] Park Chung-hee and those occupying key positions under his administration had received only the most rudimentary and abbreviated education at military academies (including the former Imperial Japanese Army Academy) because of the disruptions of World War II and the extreme personnel shortages of the era when South Korea was founded and during the Korean War. By contrast, KMA graduates from Chun's eleventh class onward received a full four years of education at the Academy. In line with the wishes of South Korea's first president, Rhee Syngman, who had lived in self-imposed exile in the United States, the KMA curriculum adopted a West Point style that led graduates to idolize America. Many were also given the chance to study in the United States while at the KMA or after they were commissioned. It was hardly surprising that their hopes would rest more with the deeply familiar United States than with Japan, where they had never actually lived. Chun himself was a typical pro-American graduate who studied for two years from 1959 to 1961 at the US Army Center for Special Warfare.[16]

The key point here is that the members of the South Korean upper class during the Chun years were distinguished by their ability to speak Japanese while having no direct experience of Japan. Inevitably, once Chun and his contemporaries came to power, the administration adopted a very different policy toward Japan than during the Park Chung-hee years. Feeling little affinity with Japan and with limited personal connections to it, their Japan policy could sometimes be abrupt and haphazard. This was perhaps most clearly evident in South Korea's request of a six billion dollar loan from the Japanese government early in Chun's administration.[17] The improved US-South Korea relationship and South Korea's rapidly growing confidence in its own position have also been identified as factors.

2. Changing Japan-South Korea Relations

The New "Japan Cognoscenti"

Change was also afoot among the new "Japan cognoscenti," a loose group of South Korean academics, professionals, and leaders with a deep knowledge of Japan. What is significant here is that Japan and South Korea had no official diplomatic relations from 1945 to 1965. There was of course a certain amount of exchange of both goods and people even before relations were normalized, as evinced by the fact that many of the South Koreans who remained as long-term residents in Japan afterwards had come to Japan one way or another over that twenty-year period. However, the absence of official relations acted as a major obstacle to greater bilateral exchange, particularly at the elite level. This, together with the anti-Japanese stance of Rhee Syngman during his 1950s rule, prevented a new "Japan cognoscenti" from forming, so the relationship between the two countries had to rely on connections with the old group of cognoscenti formed during the colonial period.

Looking at concrete data in this regard, according to the 1967 *Korean Statistical Yearbook*, there were only twenty-two South Korean students in Japan (excluding long-term Korean residents) in 1966, the year after the normalization of diplomatic relations between the two countries. That figure, along with the fewer than 17,065 South Koreans officially entering Japan in 1966, attests to the limited nature of the bilateral relationship at that stage.[18] As a reference, in 2013, there were around 15,000 South Korean students in Japan and approximately 2,460,000 South Koreans visited the country, putting the scale of exchange between Japan and South Korea back in 1965 well below 1 percent of today's level.[19]

This situation changed dramatically with the normalization of relations, which prompted a boom in bilateral exchange exemplified by the eight-fold increase in the number of South Korean students in Japan in

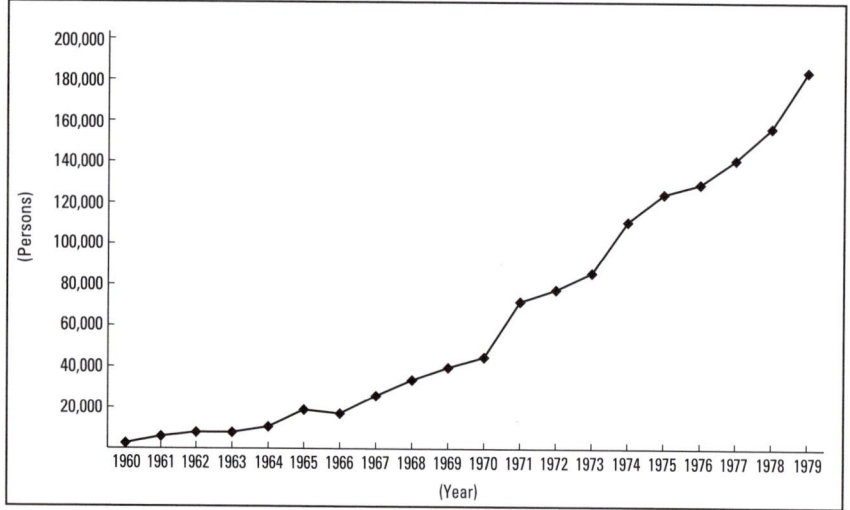

Figure 4.1. Visitors from South Korea. (*Source*: Created from Ministry of Internal Affairs and Communications Statistics Bureau, *Statistical Data*, http://www.stats.go.jp/data/index.html.)

1967 to 1971. The number of South Korean visitors to Japan also reached 25,791 in 1967, and went on to top the 100,000 mark in 1971.

Naturally enough, this new growth in bilateral exchange created a new group of Japan cognoscenti within South Korea. This group's experience of Japan was entirely different from that of the old cognoscenti of the colonial period. The old cognoscenti's knowledge of Japan was based on their experience under colonial rule and related to the old Japan that had brought about that colonial rule, whereas the new cognoscenti's knowledge was of the new Japan that had almost completed its postwar recovery and was in the process of becoming a major economic power.

More figuratively speaking, the old cognoscenti's bitter experience of colonial rule left them feeling a complex mix of hatred and reverence in relation to Japan. Having lived through the experience of total war, they simultaneously abhorred Japan as an oppressor while admiring a formidable strength far in excess of their own.

The Shock of Postwar Japan

The experience of the new Japan cognoscenti was different. To those born during the total-war period and experiencing their adolescence after liberation from colonial rule, Japan was a foolish country that had caused a reckless war—an irrational state that had ruled unjustly over the Korean peninsula. Under the anti-Japan Rhee Syngman administration, information on postwar Japan was limited and many South Koreans gave little thought to the changes occurring in their neighbor. In short, they regarded Japan as a contemptible country that should be shunned.

Postwar Japan therefore had a huge impact on South Koreans visiting for the first time following the normalization of relations.[20] Entering as students, businesspeople, or journalists, they were entirely unprepared for the country that greeted them. Much to their surprise, the Japan of the 1960s had staged a rapid recovery from its economic difficulties immediately after World War II and was now enjoying growth and prosperity. They also found that democracy had taken a far stronger hold than expected. While South Korea remained mired in poverty, Japanese society was affluent, peaceful, free, and orderly. They could understand why the United States as a victor in the war was so powerful and affluent, but why did Japan—a country that had essentially been driven out of the Korean peninsula—reemerge as such a potent force? They were shocked to the core by Japan's power and dynamism.

This might well have translated into a sense of awe toward Japan were it not for the intense discrimination against people from the Korean peninsula that remained embedded in Japanese society and which South Koreans living in Japan inevitably confronted on a daily basis. They experienced the same contradiction as many South Koreans coming to Japan subsequently—namely that many of the Japanese individuals with whom they developed a direct acquaintance were kind and admirable, but as a group the Japanese continued to discriminate against both visitors from South Korea and their compatriots who were long-term residents in Japan, refusing to accept them into Japanese society. These South Koreans were accordingly haunted by a deep sense of distrust toward Japan, feeling that while the Japanese might put on a good show, they in fact looked down on Koreans.

The complicated feelings toward Japan harbored by the new Japan cognoscenti were further aggravated in the 1970s by the kidnapping of Kim Dae-Jung and the attempted assassination of Park Chung-hee. These incidents damaged the general Japanese image of South Korea. As bilateral relations deteriorated, the new Japan cognoscenti started to think that while Japan might present itself as a friend of South Korea and a fellow member of the Free World, Japan and the Japanese were ultimately only interested in exploiting South Korea and its people, so South Korea should—indeed, must—develop a strategy for dealing with Japan accordingly. This position was only strengthened by the fact that Japan had just normalized relations with China, South Korea's enemy, accompanied by an upsurge in favorable Japanese popular sentiment toward China. South Koreans felt that Japan could not be trusted—nor could it be underestimated.

The Case of Heo Mun-Do[21]

Interaction between Japan and South Korea following the normalization of relations in 1965 spawned a new, albeit small-scale group of Japan cognoscenti of a different nature than those who came to maturity under colonial rule. Their outlook on Japan, which balanced amazement at Japan's achievement in becoming a developed democracy against dislike for the Japanese and their continued discriminatory attitude toward South Korea and the Korean people, progressively changed South Korea's Japan policy as well as its sentiment toward Japan.

As noted earlier, for the new Japan cognoscenti, the emergence of the Chun Doo-hwan administration and the attendant generational change represented a golden opportunity to have their view of Japan reflected in practical politics. A prominent member of this loose group was Heo Mun-do, one of the "Three Fours" identified above, who occupied the key post of chief political secretary in the Presidential Secretariat, which was itself extremely influential during the Chun years. After graduating from Seoul University in 1964, Heo went to work for the newspaper *Chosun ilbo*, which gave him the chance to study at the University of Tokyo immediately after the normalization of relations. In July 1974, he was officially appointed as the newspaper's Tokyo correspondent.[22] Heo spent close to five years working in the dark, cramped *Chosun ilbo* office in the basement of Japanese partner paper *Mainichi shimbun*.[23]

When Heo took up his Tokyo post, the kidnapping of Kim Dae-jung in Tokyo the previous year had tainted both bilateral relations and Japanese public opinion toward South Korea. Incidentally, Heo's predecessor and also *Chosun ilbo* acting editor-in-chief was Kim Yoon-hwan, who subsequently went into politics and climbed high enough as a conservative politician in the 1990s to be nicknamed "Kingmaker."[24]

The fact that the first article that Heo Mun-do wrote in Tokyo concerned the hijacking of Japan Airlines Flight 124 at Haneda Airport captures perfectly the nature of the times.[25] A more important incident, however, occurred immediately after—namely the attempted assassination of Park Chung-hee on August 15, 1974, otherwise known as the Mun Se-gwang incident. As noted earlier, this event brought Japan-South Korea relations to a new low, and huge anti-Japan protests raged throughout South Korea. In Japan, too, criticism of the Park Chung-hee administration became even more strident, and Heo Mun-do later recollected how that experience made him deeply distrustful of Japanese society. Heo would eventually become one of the new cognoscenti critical of Japan.[26]

Heo Mun-do entered the South Korean government in 1979 in the closing days of the Park Chung-hee administration, motivated by a deep respect for Park and a desire to work under him. However, Park was assassinated while Heo was still posted to the South Korean embassy in Japan as public relations (PR) officer, so he never had the chance to meet directly with the object of his admiration. Heo was concerned with the turmoil in South Korea, and when he came back to Seoul for a joint meeting among the PR officers from South Korea's embassies, Heo had the opportunity through the intermediary of a high school friend to meet with Chun Doo-hwan, who was rushing to seize power after the December 12 coup d'état. Heo returned briefly to Tokyo, but when Chun took control of the country, he was called back to Seoul to serve as an advisor to the new government, which led to Heo's appointment as chief political secretary. Kookmin University associate professor (at the time) Kim Young-jak, who had studied at the University of Tokyo at the same time as Heo, also came on board the administration, where he served primarily as mastermind for the ruling Democratic Justice Party. In this manner, the new Japan cognoscenti who had studied in Japan postnormalization would emerge onto the center stage of South Korean politics in the 1980s.

The Kuk-Il (Overcome Japan) Movement

What impact did the new Japan cognoscenti's Japan experience have on the South Korean political economy? Let's take the example of Heo.

First, one well-known policy was the pop culture event "Kukp'ung 81" (National Wind 81), which took place in May 1981.[27] Drawing more than ten million participants over just five days to Seoul's Yeouido Square, some parties claimed that the event was designed to contain students planning to protest over the Gwangju Incident of May 1980 and distract the public from politics—a set-up, in other words. It was apparently modeled on Japan's festival culture and intended to establish a similar culture in South Korea, and was of course the brainchild of Heo Mun-do and his fellow Japan cognoscenti.

But the experience of the Japan cognoscenti was most clearly reflected in more direct relations with Japan. The first history textbook controversy of 1982 was important in this context. As I have repeatedly observed, the essence of the dispute between Japan and South Korea was not that Japanese textbooks shifted to the right that year but rather that the difference between the content of Japanese history textbooks and those in South Korea and China was discovered as an important issue. In fact, when the first history textbook controversy emerged, neither the South Korean government nor the media had much concrete information about Japan's history textbooks, so when textbook content became an issue, some rapid information-gathering was required. The article about Japan's history textbook issue written in response to a request from head office by Lee Do-hyung, then the Tokyo correspondent for *Chosun ilbo*, was picked up to a far greater extent than Lee had expected, and he would later recall being taken aback by the exponential expansion of the reaction.

The way the postwar era unfolded meant that South Korean society of the 1980s did not in fact have much information about contemporary Japan. By that stage, more than half of South Korea's population had been born after colonial rule, and the group that had occupied the upper echelons of society during the Park Chung-hee years—who received their higher education under colonial rule and went on to achieve a certain level of social status—was rapidly disappearing.

Many South Koreans therefore had little concrete knowledge of Japan and lacked personal networks for acquiring that knowledge. The emergence of the history textbook issue forced them to turn their attention to contemporary Japan, which by the 1980s had become the world's second-largest economy and was enjoying a new prosperity. The history textbook issue led the South Korean people to rediscover contemporary Japan, going through essentially the same experience as the new Japan cognoscenti within the Chun administration who had visited Japan post-normalization.

Starting from the realization that they knew little about Japan, the new cognoscenti had worked hard to improve their knowledge. In other words, they "rediscovered" Japan, which also meant rediscovering the Japan of the past. To put it yet another way, regarding Japan as "other," they understood that coming to know that "other" would require conscious effort. As they reached the upper levels of South Korean society in the 1980s, these cognoscenti would turn their experience into a large-scale movement across South Korean society as a whole—namely the Kuk-il (Overcome Japan) movement led by *Chosun ilbo*, which spread throughout South

Korea immediately after the first history textbook controversy. On January 1, 1983, *Chosun ilbo* wrote as follows:

> The majority of Koreans are placed in the position of knowing absolutely nothing about Japan while having no choice but to engage in diplomacy, business and technical cooperation with a formidable people who once ruled over us. This is why Korea has pursued a good neighbor policy rather than hostile relations with the people of Japan—neighbors with whom both geography and history have forced us to engage.[28]

The slogan of the Kuk-il movement was "the road to overcoming Japan is to know Japan." This was a deliberate ploy on the part of the new Japan cognoscenti. Lee Do-hyung, *Chosun ilbo* Tokyo correspondent at the time, thought that it was driven by the personal relationship between Presidential Secretariat Chief Political Secretary Heo Mun-do and *Chosun ilbo* chief editor Choi Byeong-ryeo.[29] As noted earlier, Heo Mun-do worked for *Chosun ilbo* before he joined the government, while Choi was an earlier graduate of the same high school in Busan as Heo. Subsequently, Choi entered politics himself, becoming a heavyweight in various conservative parties linked to today's Saenuri Party.[30] The 1980s were therefore marked by the emergence of a new trend in Japan-South Korea relations in which the new Japan cognoscenti were deeply implicated.

What Was the First History Textbook Issue?

To summarize my argument above, the 1982 history textbook controversy clearly entailed the South Korean public discovering Japanese history textbooks as an issue and perceiving value for the first time in that regard. Two factors underpinned their discovery.

The first was the changing international situation. South Korea at the end of the 1970s was deeply isolated internationally as a result of the collapse of South Vietnam in the Vietnam War and the normalization of diplomatic relations between China and America and between Japan and China. The South Koreans, and particularly conservatives close to the administration, were working to rebuild relations with both Japan and America in order to reconstruct the foundations for South Korea's very survival.

In this endeavor, Japan's conservatives were invaluable partners for them. The JSP and other leftist elements in Japan remained strong and the

South Koreans were still extremely wary of them. It was therefore nearly impossible for the South Koreans to mount an outright challenge to the historical perceptions of Japan's conservatives as their partners in rebuilding the bilateral relationship.

However, political change in Japan and America in the early 1980s would bring about a major change in this situation. The emergence of the Reagan administration and the LDP's landslide victory in Japan's general elections, along with improved relations with the Japanese and American governments, gave Chun far greater confidence in his ability to run the administration.

Consequently, when the textbook issue suddenly broke out, rather than trying to suppress it, the Chun administration sought to use it. Another major driver in this regard was the generational change that was occurring. Unlike the Park administration, Chun's government was constituted by a generation that had no relationship with the Japanese colonial authorities, and therefore no reason to fear public criticism in that regard, so they were able to foreground issues of historical perception.

In addition, having had no involvement with colonial rule, the new generation were able to look frankly at their own ignorance of the truth in relation to the past and to the role that Japan played in that past, initiating a process of rediscovery of the past and of Japan.

Thus the lid was lifted on the Pandora's box of the historical perception dispute. Japan would also be affected by this new direction taken by South Korea, as I explore below.

3. The Second Textbook Dispute in 1987

Change in Japan

In any case, moves by the new Japan cognoscenti brought about major change in Japan-South Korea relations. Unlike the old cognoscenti who were thoroughly inculcated with a colonial education and could not help but see the bilateral relationship as an issue intrinsically relating to their own identity, the new cognoscenti were able to take a much more detached view. What this meant was that Japan-South Korea relations finally moved out of the shade of colonial rule in the 1980s and began evolving into a normal bilateral relationship.

This change in South Korea also necessitated a change in the other party to the bilateral relationship, Japan. For example, in the 1970s, as epitomized by President Park Chung-hee himself, it was not particularly unusual for a South Korean leader to use Japanese, even in bilateral diplomatic negotiations. For members of Park's generation, who younger compatriots mocked for "thinking in Japanese and speaking in Korean," engaging in complex and sometimes abstract conversation in Japanese presented no difficulty.

However, the situation changed dramatically with the Chun Doo-hwan regime. The departure of the old Japan cognoscenti from the upper echelons of government removed from South Korean politics the last of the generation who could speak Japanese with that level of proficiency, and this naturally had a significant impact on various working-level aspects of Japan-South Korea relations. A typical example was journalism. While it is hard to imagine today, until the end of the 1970s many Japanese media correspondents and company employees stationed in South Korea spoke almost no Korean, because most of the Koreans they dealt with had grown up during the colonial era and spoke Japanese fluently. Japanese journalists consequently felt no need to directly use the Korean language for their news-gathering or their jobs. Obviously there were some occasions when they had no choice, such as gathering and analyzing information printed by the South Korean media, but in those cases it was considered sufficient to enlist the cooperation of bilingual Koreans.

The same was true of academics. For example, there are distinct differences between books and papers written in Japanese prior to the 1980s about South Korean politics, society, economy, and history and those written from the 1980s onward. The former publications quote almost no works written in Korean and cite no primary academic materials from Korea—regarded today as essential—due to the perception prevalent among Japanese academics at the time that there was no great need to study Korean in order to study Korea, and certainly no need to speak the language.

From Vertical to Horizontal Relations

Another element underlying this era in which journalists, businesspeople, and academics felt no need to use Korean was the hazy sense of superiority that Japanese people felt in relation to South Korea. Moreover, the same could be said even of what South Koreans call Japan's "conscientious" citizens' groups, which supported the democracy movement in South Korea through those years. For example, when Kim Dae Jung was effectively living in exile in Tokyo in the 1970s, people simply expected him to speak and write Japanese. When a Japanese person does something for a Korean person, they should respect the Korean's pride to the greatest possible extent—which would obviously make it inappropriate to require the Korean to speak in a language forced on him or her under colonial rule. However, for a long time, many Japanese were not sufficiently aware even of this obvious point. The situation was quite different by the time Kim Dae Jung started to use Korean even in Japan during the 1980s.

Changes occurring in South Korean society in the 1980s forced the Japanese to revise their unconscious arrogance. The disappearance from the social stage of South Koreans who had received their higher education during the colonial era naturally made it extremely difficult for Japanese journalists to gather news using only Japanese. The new situation was vividly demonstrated by the fact that a string of Japanese journalists speaking fluent Korean appeared on the scene during this period, including a new generation well-versed in Korean peninsula issues such as Kuroda Katsuhiro from *Kyodo News* (currently at the *Sankei shimbun*) and Shigemura Toshimitsu from *Mainichi shimbun* (currently at Waseda University). The same held for academia. In the 1980s, figures such as political scientist Okonogi Masao, social scientist Hattori Tamio, and historian Yoshida Mitsuo developed their research in collaboration with fellow academics in South Korea. These scholars taught at key Japanese universities such as the University of Tokyo and Keiō University, where they were also training the next generation of academics, significantly altering the nature and quality of subsequent Japanese research on South Korea.[31]

In the 1980s, then, the vertical relationship between Japan and South Korea shaped by the legacy of colonial rule rapidly transmuted into a horizontal relationship. However, this development also signaled the advent of an era of fierce competition between Japan and South Korea. For example, just as with the new Japan cognoscenti in South Korea, the new Korea cognoscenti in Japan did not simply take Korean arguments on faith or advance arguments sympathetic toward South Korea. In fact, the new cognoscenti in Japan took a position diametrically opposed to their South Korean counterparts. Both groups belonged to a generation that had no actual social experience of the colonial era and were consequently able to freely discuss complex issues between Japan and South Korea, the colonial past included, with no constraints from their own pasts. In addition, because they operated from within companies and universities based in their home countries, they were able to observe the other country dispassionately—coolly, even. To each group, the other country was unmistakably foreign, or "other," which meant that compared to the old Japan and Korea cognoscenti, they engaged in their activities from a far more objective and dispassionate perspective. Thus debate between the two countries gathered rapid momentum, and an entirely new situation emerged.

4. Emergence of the Nationalistic *New Version of Japanese History*

Background of Japanese Nationalism

The advent of the new horizontal relationship did not simply bring out these two new groups of cognoscenti. In the case of Japanese society, the critical factor was the influence of the history textbook controversy in 1982. The history textbook debate in Japan was exacerbated by demands from both China and South Korea for ex post facto revisions to already certified textbooks. Prior to the 1982 controversy, the textbook debate in Japan had taken the direction of intellectuals like Ienaga Saburō arguing that textbook screening by the Ministry of Education was unconstitutional and seeking to broaden the freedom of publication in order to create more "progressive" textbooks. However, the waters were soon muddied for the progressive argument because the Chinese and South Korean governments, while initially appearing to share the views of these progressive intellectuals, actually wanted the Japanese government itself to take responsibility for textbook revision—revision from above, as it were.[32] Caught between its own claims that screening was unconstitutional and the Chinese and South Korean governments' demand for revision from above, the progressive movement splintered, its former cohesive power rapidly diminishing.

The outbreak of the history textbook controversy also spurred to action an entirely different group: supporters of Japanese nationalism. Here we trace that trajectory based on reportage in the *Asahi shimbun*.

Key to the nationalist upsurge were members of Nihon o Mamoru Kokumin Kaigi (People's Conference to Protect Japan). Formed originally in 1978 as the People's Conference for Realization of an Era Name Law, the group changed its name in 1979 with the successful formulation of that law. In 1997, it amalgamated with Nihon o Mamoru Kai (Group for the Protection of Japan) to become today's Nippon Kaigi (Japan Conference).[33] People's Conference members comprised around one hundred private associations, including Jinja Honchō (Association of Shinto Shrines) and other religious organizations, the Teachers Association of Japan and other educational groups, and various chambers of commerce and industry, as well as individuals. The group's executives included many well-known figures in Japanese society. For example, in 1986, key members included

Ibuka Masaru, honorary chairman of Sony Corporation, and Uno Seiichi, professor emeritus at the University of Tokyo.[34] The principal aims of the People's Conference as one of Japan's leading nationalist groups were to achieve constitutional revision, raise awareness of national defense, and "normalize" education.

The history textbook controversy triggered great alarm among members of the People's Conference, who felt this represented unwarranted interference by China and South Korea in the content of Japan's textbooks, resulting in distortion of textbook content. They reacted particularly strongly to the Japanese government releasing a statement in the name of Chief Cabinet Secretary Miyazawa Kiichi to the effect that corrections would be made at the government's responsibility.[35] Following the Miyazawa Statement, the "Neighboring Countries Clause" was added to screening criteria, stipulating that "due considerations should be made from the point of view of international understanding and international cooperation when dealing with modern history issues that involve neighboring Asian countries."

The People's Conference responded to the situation by deciding to create its own textbook, *New Version of Japanese History*.[36] On October 30, 1982, the group held a roundtable meeting in Tokyo on the history textbook issue, publicly calling for the "production of a distinguished history textbook that could be described as truly for the people of Japan." In March 1984, they proceeded to ask Murao Jirō, formerly the Ministry of Education's chief textbook examiner and chair of the Japan-Korea Cultural Association, to take up the post of editorial supervisor for their textbook, launching the production process into full gear. In April, the People's Conference revealed in its official organ *Nihon no ibuki* that it had begun writing a Japanese history textbook for high schools that would be finished in a year.[37] The text was eventually submitted to the Ministry of Education for screening slightly behind schedule on August 29, 1985, via the publisher Hara Shobō. It was apparently a personal relationship between Murao and the company president that led Hara Shobō to take on the publication project. In October 1985, Diet members such as Moriyama Kinji, Kaifu Toshiki, and Hayashi Kentarō formed the Kyōkasho Mondai o Kangaeru Giin Renmei (Diet Members' Alliance for Considering the Textbook Issue), actively pushing for the textbook to be approved.[38] With Kaifu joining the cabinet as minister of education immediately after in December, certification seemed almost guaranteed.[39]

However, the results of the actual screening proved very different from expectations. The Textbook Screening Council, which came under the auspices of the Ministry of Education, indicated major dissatisfaction with textbook content. In the end, on January 31, 1986, the Council gave the textbook a conditional pass, but a pass that was actually very close to a rejection, as the condition was that it be rewritten and resubmitted. The details of revisions suggested by the Council were communicated to the writers and editors on March 20, identifying a staggering 420 points in the text requiring amendment or improvement. Though the People's Conference resubmitted the text with the required changes, it continued to haggle with the Ministry until the textbook was finally certified on May 27.[40]

Even so, the battle was not yet won, as the textbook provoked a storm of protest from the Chinese and South Korean governments as well as from the Japanese public. Responding to a May 30 article in *Chosun ilbo*, all the South Korean papers immediately began to attack the certification of this "right-wing" textbook, warning that it signaled the rebirth of Japanese imperialism. On June 4, the Chinese government also lodged a formal protest, and the Ministry of Education was forced to postpone the textbook exhibition at which certified textbooks were traditionally revealed to Japan and the rest of the world.[41]

Nationalism Quashed by Conservative Politicians

What this process reveals is the eagerness of the People's Conference to have their textbook published, counterbalanced by the Ministry of Education's sustained effort to stall publication. In other words, it was clearly the private sector rather than the government that was driving the publication of this textbook. The Ministry of Education's string of ex post facto demands for revisions—previously a screening taboo—certainly seem to have been issued with a view to containing the situation.

That the Japanese government, far from leading a shift to the right in Japanese textbooks, was in fact using the textbook screening process to forestall the publication of right-wing textbooks became even more apparent from subsequent events. Despite Prime Minister Nakasone Yasuhiro's reputation as the 1980s' leading conservative and political hawk, he took a consistently cool line on the People's Conference textbook.[42] For example, a few days after the Chinese government registered its opposition to the textbook, Nakasone advised Kaifu as minister of education to pay due consideration based on the Miyazawa Statement.[43] He issued another warning to Kaifu a week later on June 13, clearly intent on closing down the situation. As a result, the Ministry of Education lobbied the People's Conference again behind the scenes over June 8–10 to make additional changes to the textbook. The Ministry is also said to have requested a cover-up—namely that the People's Conference say that the revisions had been made before the official screening deadline of May 30—which indicates the Ministry's very high level of sensitivity to the situation. When these unusual backroom negotiations over revisions ran aground in late June, Fujita Kimio, director-general of the Asian Affairs Bureau of the Ministry of Foreign Affairs (MOFA), apparently became impatient and decided to negotiate personally with Naruse Masato, president of Hara Shobō, to persuade the company to abandon publication of the textbook. As MOFA had no official role in textbook screening, under normal circumstances it should not have involved itself in the matter. The fact that even the Ministry of Foreign Affairs was impelled to take direct action is indicative of what a serious international issue this had become and the struggle that the Japanese government was having in addressing it.

The Fate of the New Version of Japanese History Textbook

In the end, on June 27, the Ministry of Education presented the People's Conference with further revisions amounting to eighty points across thirty items, going so far as to demonstrate specific examples. As it was glaringly obvious that the certification deadline was already well past, this was a fairly bare-knuckled demand.

The People's Conference called an emergency meeting of its executives and the textbook writing team to consult on a response. Their decision was that even if it meant bowing to outside pressure, it was important that they "endure the unendurable"[44] and get the textbook out, so they chose to accept all the government's demands.[45] Having gained the upper hand, the Ministry of Education immediately pressed its advantage by firing off a demand on July 3 for still more revisions. Following another fierce debate at the People's Conference on July 4, it was decided to accept those revisions. At last on July 7, the Ministry of Education notified the People's Conference that the textbook had been certified. At a press conference, Nishizaki Kiyohisa, director-general of the Ministry's Elementary and Secondary Education Bureau, was forced to account for this unusual course of events by explaining that while revision demands post-June 11 were a special measure not covered in the screening regulations, they were within the power of the Minister of Education.[46] The whole case clearly reveals the strong desire of the Japanese government, and particularly Prime Minister Nakasone, to prevent the textbook issue from impacting Japan's relationship with its neighbors.[47]

The 1986 *New Version of Japanese History* textbook incident now began to draw to a close. Subject to a torrent of criticism from both government and public opinion even prior to certification, the textbook continued to struggle during the adoption process. In the end, the adoption ratio was reportedly less than 1 percent.[48]

Thus the first stirrings of Japanese nationalism arising in the late 1980s in reaction to the new awareness of the historical perception issue in China and South Korea were ultimately contained by conservative politicians who prioritized the maintenance of relations with neighboring countries above nationalism.

Conclusion: Dominance by the Ruling Elite as an Additional Factor

The unfolding of events just described reveals two distinct characteristics of the historical perception dispute, and particularly the history textbook issue, in the 1980s—namely the new form taken by issues of historical perception as a result of the rise of a younger generation that had no direct experience of colonial rule, even as ruling elites were still seeking to control and use these issues. In Japan, the *New Version of Japanese History* ruckus was a case of the ruling elite using somewhat highhanded methods to contain moves by nationalist forces, while in South Korea, the emergence of the Kuk-il movement in reaction to the textbook issue was to some extent the result of the emerging new Japan cognoscenti using the history textbook dispute as an opportunity to educate the public. Importantly, their efforts met with some success at this stage. In short, the 1980s was a time when ruling elites were still managing to control issues of historical perception.

What this means is that a key element was missing from the theoretical framework in Part I—namely that if generational change and the declining importance of the bilateral relationship were factors in the dramatic change in the historical perception dispute, there must conversely also have been elements that prevented the dispute from gaining traction.

One of those elements was clearly the ability of the ruling elite to control the narrative space, the loss of which led the historical perception dispute to intensify. What was the mechanism that caused the ruling elite to lose control? Below I use a case study of the comfort women issue to examine this question more closely.

PART III

Historical Perception Dispute

Case Study 2: The Comfort Women Issue

FIVE

Japan-South Korea Relations at the End of the Cold War

1. From the Textbook Controversy to the Comfort Women Dispute

Revisiting the Contemporary Significance of the Historical Perception Dispute

We should recall that the unfolding of the historical perception dispute has been determined less by the historical facts and more by the interpretations of these facts and the significance attached to them by each particular generation. For example, the history textbook controversy escalated in 1982 because the textbook references in question were regarded as proof of the reemergence of militarism in Japan. Consequently, rather than paying attention to changes in the actual content of Japanese textbooks over the years around 1982—which, to reiterate, brought history textbooks far closer to the South Korean view of history than in the 1970s—attention focused solely on differences at the time between contemporary Japanese and South Korean textbooks and the orientation of screening. This led to the somewhat oversimplified understanding in South Korea that the Japanese government was producing textbooks of this nature because of an ambition to revive militarism.

However, relatively amicable relations at the governmental level between Japan and South Korea eroded this simple formula, forcing people to develop a different perceptual framework. Two views underpinned the construction of a new framework. First, the rapid expansion of the Japanese economic bubble in the late 1980s thrust Japan to the center of the world stage, giving arguments about the Japanese threat an unprecedented level of persuasiveness in South Korea.

The second arose from the explosive receptiveness to Marxism that manifested in South Korea in the late 1980s. Unlike in Japan, where Marxism and Marxist-influenced thought were the mainstream among the intelligentsia throughout the postwar period, South Korea's position on the front lines of the Cold War for many years made Marxism and extensions thereof taboo in South Korean society. That changed in the 1980s with the advance of détente and the slightly greater freedom of thought allowed by the Chun Doo-hwan regime. Where Marxism was already losing its luster in Japan following the campus unrest of the 1970s, in South Korea the earlier taboo lent this ideology an extremely fresh attractiveness. As a result, student groups and other elements of the democracy movement were strongly influenced by Marxism.

Where would the 1990s take these developments of the 1980s? This chapter offers a detailed examination of the comfort women as another critical issue in the historical perception dispute from the 1980s onward.

South Korea's Understanding

In the 1990s, a new narrative began to emerge in South Korea, one that was influenced by Marxism as well as the dependency theory then in vogue.[1] At the risk of oversimplification, the story went something like this. The modern world was controlled by multinational capital, and particularly that of the economic superpowers, Japan and the United States. This capital was using the power of its agents—the Japanese and US governments—to control the Korean peninsula, ruthlessly exploiting the Korean people. As the military regime ruling South Korea was no more than a puppet of Japanese and US giant capital, there was no way that it could seriously serve the interests of the South Korean people. The democratization of South Korea was a battle with this foreign-controlled regime, so the South Korean people had to take on not only the military regime but also its US and Japanese backers.

The comfort women issue took on an important meaning in this context. Which group among the exploited South Korean people was in the weakest position? The answer was women, and particularly sex workers, who were placed in the most humiliating position of all. As exemplified by the fact that most of their customers were American soldiers and Japanese tourists (this was the peak of the *gisaeng* tourism era), prostitutes were the ultimate embodiment of the oppression and exploitation of the South Korean people. Comfort women represented the past of those Korean women exploited through their engagement in prostitution. In other words, in addressing the comfort women issue, one was also addressing the issue of women in capitalist society, and indeed contemporary South Korea in general.

The key point here is that South Korean women came to view the comfort women issue as part of their own issue. They saw the comfort women as early victims of a Korean society distorted by capitalism and imperialism (itself a form of capitalism); as such, ignoring the issue would be tantamount to turning their backs on the issue of women in contemporary society. Women taking part in the democracy movement therefore should and quite naturally would take an interest in the comfort women issue.

In this manner, the comfort women issue was imbued with symbolic status within the new framework of the historical perception dispute, which clearly identified South Korea's ruling elite as the enemy while positioning the "conscientious intelligentsia" and the women's movement in Japan as allies of the movement in South Korea.

Power over the discourse on comfort women therefore shifted out of the hands of South Korea's ruling elite and into those of the counter-elite challenging their authority, with the ability that the former possessed in the 1980s to limit the discourse to their purposes now slipping away.

The Situation in Japan

As the power to control discourse—which had functioned as a brake on intensification of the historical perception dispute—began to slip from the hands of South Korea's ruling elite, what was happening in Japan?

The thing to note was the continuity in circumstances from the mid-1980s onward. As typified by the dispute surrounding the *New Version of Japanese History*, with the Cold War still smoldering the basic policy of the Japanese government was to inhibit and control the escalation of the historical perception issue with South Korea as a fellow member of the Free World, and to partner with China in containing a common adversary, the Soviet Union. That was why, even under the essentially conservative Nakasone regime, Japan's history textbooks were revised to more closely reflect the historical views of China and South Korea.

Needless to say, behind Japan's choices lay the dangerous level of Cold War tension that continued even in the mid-1980s. In other words, LDP politicians were conciliatory toward South Korea not despite but because of their conservative perception of the county as a fellow member of the Free World. Clearly, there was a certain solidarity among the ruling elite in Japan and South Korea at that stage that prevented the rapid expansion of the gulf in historical perception between the two countries that was gradually being exposed.

However, this premise for Japan-South Korea relations dissolved rapidly at the end of the 1980s, when Mikhail Gorbachev's appointment as general secretary of the Communist Party led the Soviet Union to pursue a more conciliatory policy toward the West, and the collapse of the Berlin Wall in 1989 effectively signaled the end of the Cold War. This sea change in the international situation removed the greatest incentive for Japan's conservatives to actively cooperate with South Korea.

Japan also experienced a major change in the political situation at home. In June 1986, the Nakasone administration swept the simultaneous upper and lower house elections following the infamous "play dead" dissolution of the Diet (in which Nakasone insisted until the last minute that he would not dissolve the Diet to hold elections, and then went ahead and did just that). But the LDP administration did not stay on course for long. Key political events were the consumption tax that Nakasone proposed immediately after the election and the Recruit stock scandal[2] that came to light after his resignation. The idea of introducing a consumption tax, which would by nature be highly regressive, provoked a storm of public criticism and caused support for the Nakasone administration to plummet. Nakasone suffered a major defeat in the nationwide local elections in 1987 and was forced to withdraw his proposal, resigning in disappointment in November that year.[3]

The LDP government's fortunes only worsened from there. Takeshita Noboru, Nakasone's successor, struggled with low support ratings from virtually the moment he took power. In addition, the Recruit scandal blew up in June 1988, with suspicion also falling on Takeshita himself. Takeshita went ahead regardless to table six tax reform bills, the centerpiece of which was the introduction of a consumption tax, and used the ruling party's overwhelming majority in both houses to get them through in December. As a result, Takeshita's support rating plummeted to an unprecedented low of less than 4 percent in April 1989, and he was forced to bow out from government. The day after he announced his resignation, a shocking incident occurred—the suicide of Aoki Ihei, who as Takeshita's top aide and safekeeper had come under investigation for his involvement in the Recruit scandal.[4]

Uno Sōsuke, who took over from Takeshita, was unable to retrieve the situation, and support for the LDP conversely foundered still further over allegations of Uno's scandalous involvement with a former geisha. At the House of Councillors election in July 1989, the LDP consequently suffered a historic defeat. Where the ruling party captured only 36 of the 126 contested seats, the greatest number—45 seats—went to the Japan Socialist Party (JSP), which made great strides thanks to the popularity of its new chairperson, Doi Takako.[5] The LDP still failed to seize anywhere near a majority in the upper house, including uncontested seats, and the administration lost even more momentum.[6]

As a result, Japan's ruling elite lost not only their reason for cooperating with South Korea but also their ability to control the domestic discourse.

Transformation of the JSP

What is critical for us here is that the control from above that the Nakasone government exercised over historical perception issues in the mid-1980s was premised on the stability of LDP rule. The decline in the ruling party's power—which was in fact only beginning—inevitably reduced the administration's capacity to maintain that control.

The other key development in Japanese politics at the time was the transformation of the JSP. It was not as simple as Doi Takako's popularity propelling the party temporarily to the forefront (not that this new prominence was necessarily seen as temporary at the time), with the greater influence of a party that had long maintained a close relationship with South Korea leading Japan to adopt a more conciliatory stance toward its neighbor.[7] The JSP could not by any means be said to have enjoyed a smooth relationship with either China or South Korea. As noted earlier, until the 1980s the JSP was known for its close ties to North rather than South Korea, and for standing by North Korea in rejecting South Korea's legitimacy as a state. The party placed a virtual taboo for many years on the idea of developing a relationship with South Korea, exemplified by the fact that even in 1985, at the height of the fight for democracy in South Korea, JSP Secretary General Tanabe Makoto flew to Pyongyang to seek Kim Il-sung's approval for the JSP to make contact with South Korea's opposition parties.[8]

The distance between the Japan Socialist Party and South Korea over issues of historical perception is apparent in the following episode. During Chun Doo-hwan's 1984 visit to Japan, Emperor Hirohito took the unusual step of expressing deep regret over colonial rule, but the JSP joined the

Japanese Communist Party in criticizing the emperor's comment. The JSP's reasoning was interesting. Yagi Noboru, JSP director of international affairs, noted that an apology needed to be made for Japan's long colonial rule, but he said that it would have been better if the emperor had apologized not just to the South but to all Koreans, including the citizens of the Democratic People's Republic of Korea.[9] In other words, the JSP's problem was not with the apology itself but the fact that it was not directed at North Korea. The JSP's coolness stood in sharp contrast to the favorable response from all the other Japanese political parties, the LDP included.[10] Bound by its relationship with North Korea, the Japan Socialist Party was in no position to fight alongside the South Korean government on issues of historical perception.

Subsequently, however, this was all to change, thanks to increased contact between the JSP and South Korea's opposition parties through Kim Young-sam, along with Kim Dae-jung a key player in the democracy movement.[11] In 1987, based on its interaction with Kim Young-sam, the JSP lifted its former ban in principle on visits to South Korea by JSP Diet members,[12] and while there were a few hurdles to be negotiated first, former JSP chairperson Ishibashi Masashi successfully visited South Korea in 1988.[13] In 1989, during talks toward the formation of a coalition government among the opposition parties, the JSP agreed to the "continuation" of the 1965 Treaty on Basic Relations between Japan and the Republic of Korea, finally granting de facto recognition of the legitimacy of the South Korean government. In response to this change in stance, the South Korean government formally granted visas for a JSP mission headed by the party's secretary-general, Yamaguchi Tsuruo,[14] resulting in the first visit to South Korea by incumbent party executives. That was not until 1989, however, meaning that the JSP had remained unable to develop a satisfactory level of contact with South Korea even after the latter's democratic reforms of 1987.[15]

In any case, the rapprochement between the JSP and South Korea's opposition parties inevitably also began to change the party's relationship with the South Korean government. For example, when Chun Doo-hwan's 1984 visit to Japan was repeated by his successor Roh Tae-woo in May 1990,[16] Emperor Akihito (who had succeeded Hirohito in 1989) told him that, "Reflecting upon the suffering that your people underwent during this unfortunate period, which was brought about by our nation, I cannot but feel the deepest remorse."[17] This time the JSP was much more receptive, noting that the words represented a frank expression of Emperor Akihito's feelings in his role as a symbol of the state and the unity of the

Japanese people.[18] Given how little difference there was between the actual words of Hirohito and Akihito, the JSP's response reveals how much the party's position on South Korea had changed.

Roh Tae-woo also met with JSP chair Doi Takako during his visit,[19] marking a moment of historic reconciliation between the JSP and South Korea.

The JSP position on issues of historical perception also began to coincide with that of the South Korean government as of around this time. The JSP was moving actively on issues related to colonial rule and had submitted a Diet resolution immediately before President Roh Tae-woo's visit calling for clarification in relation to atonement for colonial rule and responsibility for Japan's "war of aggression."[20] Doi also brought up this issue at her meeting with Roh Tae-woo, with the South Korean government apparently expressing strong approval.[21] The conditions (which remain to this day) were finally in place for the JSP and its next incarnation, the Social Democratic Party (renamed in 1996), to advance a position close to the South Korean government on issues of historical perception between Japan and South Korea.

It should be noted that their similar position on these issues also played a major role in improving the JSP's relationship with South Korea. Thereafter, the JSP would be viewed favorably in South Korea as representing progressive forces that were cooperative on issues of historical perception, as opposed to the LDP, which was conservative and uncooperative. The JSP's foregrounding of atonement for colonial rule made such issues the subject of heated debate in Japan's Diet. In other words, the situation was finally such that historical perception issues between Japan and South Korea ran along the same lines as the political divide in Japan.

A Rehearsal Visit

The hegemony of the Japanese ruling elite over control of the historical perception dispute in conjunction with South Korea's ruling elite was eroding rapidly. On the LDP side, the task of dealing with this situation fell on the shoulders of the new prime minister, Kaifu Toshiki, whose cabinet came to power after the 1989 upper house elections but was plagued from the outset by resistance from the opposition parties, who had gained an upper house majority. However, thanks to relatively strong public support for the young prime minister, as well as the backing of the LDP's dominant Takeshita faction, Kaifu somehow managed to keep his government in place. Kaifu's time in power—from late 1989 to 1991—coincided with a period of dramatic change in the international situation, with the Cold War coming to an end and the Gulf War breaking out in the Middle East. The Japanese government, as well as both the ruling and opposition parties, launched vigorous diplomacy to establish a place for Japan in this new status quo.[22]

One such diplomatic initiative was the September 1990 visit to North Korea made by LDP deputy president Kanemaru Shin and JSP vice chair Tanabe Makoto. The establishment of relations with North Korea had been considered the greatest outstanding challenge in Japanese diplomacy ever since the conclusion of the Treaty of Peace and Friendship between Japan and the People's Republic of China in 1978. However, the Cold War climate had made it difficult to simultaneously recognize both South Korea and North Korea on the divided peninsula. With the Cold War drawing to a close, the government, the ruling party, and the opposition were all keen to lock in a formal relationship with North Korea.[23]

Discussing the pros and cons of the Kanemaru mission is well beyond the purview of this book, nor is it necessary here.[24] What is important for us is that the effort to normalize relations with North Korea placed the Japanese government in the position of having to explain itself to South Korea, whose relationship with North Korea, while greatly improved since the Cold War days, nevertheless remained antagonistic. Accordingly, Kanemaru himself visited South Korea in October 1990, barely a month after his North Korea visit,[25] followed by Prime Minister Kaifu, who made clear his wish to consult with South Korea before the scheduled negotiations on normalization of relations between Japan and North Korea got fully underway.[26] Kaifu's visit also served as a return call for the above-mentioned official visit to Japan made by Roh Tae-woo in May of that year.

Kaifu's trip marked the first official visit to South Korea in eight years by a Japanese prime minister (since Nakasone's visit in 1983). South Korea civic groups tackling issues of historical perception between the two countries took the opportunity of the first major bilateral diplomatic event to take place in South Korea for some time to pull a major stunt—a large-scale protest denouncing the inadequacy of Japanese apologies for historical perception issues.[27]

This move was the result of the swift growth of various types of civic groups in South Korea between the time of Nakasone's visit in 1983 and Kaifu's visit in 1991. In 1983, just three years after Chun Doo-hwan had taken over the country in a coup d'état, South Korean public opinion was still closely controlled by the government. However, the country's shift to democratic rule in 1987 meant that by 1991 a number of dynamic civic groups had emerged. For some of these groups, addressing differences with Japan over shared history was the easiest and most reliable way to garner broad public support and sympathy, while Kaifu's visit offered a golden opportunity to raise their own profile. While he was in South Korea, Kaifu would express regret at colonial rule, noting that the past must not be forgotten, with remorse now utilized to open the way for an unclouded future.[28]

At this point, it appeared that Japan's ruling elite had the situation under control, but that control would dissolve in the space of only a year.

2. The First Katō Statement

Foregrounding the Comfort Women Issue

The major issue between Japan and South Korea in relation to historical perception when Kaifu went to South Korea in 1991 was the forced recruitment of Korean laborers during World War II, and activism by South Korea's civic groups was almost entirely focused in that direction. While the comfort women issue became central later on, at that stage it was still regarded as incidental—just one part of the forced labor issue—and accordingly neither the South Korean or Japanese governments, nor indeed the public, paid much attention to it.[29]

By contrast, when Prime Minister Miyazawa Kiichi visited South Korea about a year later, in January 1992, the attention of both governments and the public had refocused on the comfort women, signaling that something important must have occurred between the Kaifu and Miyazawa trips.

What happened was this. The comfort women issue, which had gradually been attracting more public attention as of the late 1980s, entered fully into the South Korean media spotlight for the first time in January 1990 when Yun Jeong-ok, who had been investigating the matter closely for some years, published a four-part column[30] entitled "In the Footsteps of the *Chôngsindae*"[31] in the progressive newspaper *The Hankyoreh*. Having succeeded in capturing huge public attention with her series, Yun sent a public memorandum to the South Korean and Japanese governments in October that year. Signed by thirty-six women's groups, including the group that Yun herself headed, the memorandum called for the facts of the comfort women issue to be laid bare and for compensation to be paid to the victims.[32] In November, sixteen of these groups formed the Chôngsindae-munje Taech'aek Hyôpuihoe (Korean Council for the Women Drafted for

Military Sexual Slavery by Japan, known as Chôngdaehyop),[33] with Yun taking on the role of Chôngdaehyop's first leader. South Korea's biggest advocacy group for the former comfort women, Chôngdaehyop remains active today.[34]

However, in early 1991, Yun had yet to spur either government to action. Even when Kaifu was in South Korea, the media in both countries treated the comfort women as no more than a side issue, with Yun and her fellow activists yet to achieve much of an impact. At the beginning of 1991, the main point of contention over historical perception between Japan and South Korea was the forced transport of laborers from the Korean peninsula during the total-war period, with the comfort women treated as no more than part of that larger issue.

A number of factors subsequently pushed the comfort women concern to the forefront as the key issue between Japan and South Korea. One was former comfort woman Kim Hak-sun coming out under her own name on August 14, 1991, and beginning to give testimony.[35] Other comfort women had also given testimony in the past,[36] but Kim was the first South Korean resident to do so under her own name, enabling the Chôngdaehyop and other South Korean activist groups to launch legal action against the Japanese government. Kim was inundated with interview requests, and her testimony appeared repeatedly in major features in the Japanese, South Korean, and international media. On December 6, 1991, Kim and a number of other former comfort women lodged a formal suit in the Tokyo District Court,[37] to which the Japanese government had no choice but to make a formal response.

Faced with this new development, what the government did first was to reaffirm its established stance. On August 27, 1991, when Shimizu Sumiko from the JSP asked a question in the Diet in response to Kim Hak-sun's testimony, Tanino Sakutarō, director-general of the Asian Affairs Bureau at the Ministry of Foreign Affairs, stated that in terms of relations between the two governments, the Japanese government's position was that issues such as these had been resolved in the 1965 agreement between Japan and South Korea, and he confirmed that the government would provide no new compensation.[38] His view was based on the Japanese government's understanding that no matter what issues existed in the past, "all issues relating to assets, rights, interests, and rights of claim" between Japan and South Korea as the parties to the Agreement on the Settlement of Problems Concerning Property and Claims and on Economic Co-operation between Japan and the Republic of Korea ("Claims Settlement Agreement"), one of the supplementary agreements to the 1965 Treaty on Basic

Relations between Japan and the Republic of Korea, as well as between the Japanese and Korean peoples, had been "completely and finally resolved," so no new compensation issue could arise between Japan and South Korea.

However, action by the South Korean government itself, as one of the parties to the Claims Settlement Agreement, upset this status quo. It began with the suit lodged by Kim and other former comfort women. On December 6, 1991, the day the suit was heard, Chief Cabinet Secretary Katō Kōichi stated on behalf of the Japanese government that no documentary materials indicating government involvement (in the recruitment of comfort women, etc.) had been found. Four days after the suit was lodged, on December 10, the South Korean government met with the Japanese ambassador to South Korea and requested that the historical truth be investigated.[39] This was the first time that the South Korean government had requested a formal response on this issue from the Japanese government. With both governments now officially in motion, the comfort women became a formal diplomatic issue. This was the second key factor in bringing the comfort women issue to center stage.

What complicated matters, however, was that a visit to South Korea by the new prime minister, Miyazawa Kiichi, had already been scheduled. Miyazawa had taken office in November 1991 after Kaifu was brought down by contention within the LDP over political reform legislation. Following Miyazawa's declaration that South Korea would be his first foreign destination, the government made an official announcement on November 29 of a three-day visit on January 16–18, 1992.[40] In other words, Kim and other former comfort women lodged their suit immediately after Miyazawa's decision to visit South Korea. For Miyazawa, the trip would mark his prime ministerial debut in international society. However, the growing seriousness of the comfort women issue meant that, at worst, the visit might even have to be postponed. The South Korean government's call on the Japanese government to take appropriate steps was actually an effort to prevent the situation from escalating.

Another factor is that by the end of 1991, the stable political foundation previously enjoyed by Roh Tae-woo's administration at the time of Kaifu's visit was already becoming shaky. The South Korean constitution created following democratization in 1987 banned presidential reelection, and the South Korean political world had already begun working toward the next presidential elections in December 1992. In addition, National Assembly elections were due to take place ahead of those elections in March 1992. A ferocious power struggle was already underway within the ruling party between the incumbent president, Roh Tae-woo, and Kim Young-sam, the leading presidential candidate.[41] As a result, it was already becoming difficult for Roh Tae-woo to maintain the old cooperative relationship with the Japanese government in relation to the comfort women issue when it was beginning to garner so much public attention.

Miyazawa's South Korea Visit

The combined impact of the coming forward of a former comfort woman, the launching of a lawsuit against the Japanese government, and the accompanying demand from the South Korean government for the truth to be uncovered brought the comfort women situation into a critical phase.

Receiving a formal request for investigation from South Korea on December 10, 1991, barely a month before Miyazawa's visit to South Korea, the Japanese government reluctantly decided to act. On December 11, Chief Cabinet Secretary Katō stated that documents indicating government involvement had not been found, so a thorough investigation was now underway. As this was not simply an issue of laws and treaties but one that had also injured many people and left emotional scars, the Japanese government wished to engage in an accurate investigation, he noted, effectively amending the statement he had made just five days prior.[42] On the same day, Katō told the Diet that, given the many testimonies and the historical investigations of multiple research institutes, he believed that there were individuals who had been forced to serve as comfort women.[43] In other words, the government had originally taken the relatively simplistic line that because documents indicating government involvement had not been found, the involvement of the Japanese military had not been proved, which in turn meant that there was no need for compensation. However, from the point of Katō's December 11 statement onward, the Japanese government acknowledged the possibility that it may have been involved in the comfort women issue. This was why the government was so explicit about its intention of conducting an "accurate investigation."

On December 13, the South Korean government followed up the above announcement of the launch of a formal investigation by conducting its own first interviews with former comfort women.[44] The issue was now being pursued from the angles of both documents and testimony, with documentary evidence being sought in Japan and official interviews underway in South Korea. Both governments were therefore at least superficially engaged in elucidating the facts, cooperating rather than opposing each other as they prepared for Miyazawa's visit the following month. In Japan, the JSP took a proactive approach, with Deputy Chair Itohisa Yaeko leading a delegation to the prime minister's official residence on December 16 to demand compensation and an apology for the comfort women.[45]

However, it was still unclear at this point which way the situation would go. To the extent that materials indicating government involvement were not found, the Japanese government could contend that it was conscientiously pursuing its inquiries and was therefore doing its utmost to respond to South Korea's wishes. Those inquiries were in fact still extremely perfunctory. According to historian Hata Ikuhiko, because the request from the government to the National Institute for Defense Studies (NIDS) Library, which held documents that later came to be known as "materials indicating military involvement," only asked for documents directly pertaining to South Korean comfort women, the library responded that it had no such materials.[46] South Korean public interest, too, was still extremely limited. For example, on January 8, 1992, Chôngdaehyop staged a demonstration outside the Japanese embassy demanding resolution of the issue, but only a little more than thirty people participated, most of them Chôngdaehyop members.[47] With only eight days left before Miyazawa arrived, both governments looked like they might succeed in riding out the situation.

The First Katō Statement

Barely three days later, however, on January 11, 1992, *Asahi shimbun* upset the status quo by running a major feature under the headline "Documents Discovered Indicating Military Involvement in the Korean Comfort Women Issue."[48] *Asahi* asserted that NIDS had documents showing that the military had been involved in advertising for comfort women and establishing "comfort stations" (*ianjo*), and it backed its story with pictures of these documents. This bombshell, coming only five days before Miyazawa was due in South Korea, upended the Japanese government position that no documents indicating military involvement had been found and forced the government to entirely rethink its stance.

Hata later described this report as a "surprise attack" on the part of *Asahi*.[49] Today we have no way of knowing what *Asahi*'s intentions were. However, given that an article in the same edition reports that the Hokkaido Colliery and Steamship Company also had documents indicating military involvement with the comfort women,[50] it seems highly likely that the paper had obtained its information some time earlier. It would be naïve to see no political motivation in running such a story just five days before the Miyazawa visit. At the same time, it has become clear that the government was also already aware of the existence of the documents days before the *Asahi* report. In that case, the story must have broken when the government was still in the midst of deciding how to handle its findings, leaving it with no choice but to cobble together an urgent response with its preparations still incomplete.

Clearly, the *Asahi* report forced the government to rapidly revisit its policy on the comfort women issue and make a public declaration. In the evening of the same day that the *Asahi* story emerged, Foreign Minister Watanabe Michio and Chief Cabinet Secretary Katō both made public statements acknowledging military involvement in relation to the comfort women issue, with the Japanese government effectively revising its hitherto official view.[51] On January 12, Katō went on to state that, legalities aside, the comfort women issue clearly raised serious problems, involving "wounds to the heart" beyond the simple interpretation of laws and treaties, and that Japan must convey to South Korea that the issue was accordingly being addressed with utmost seriousness. Katō's statement made it apparent that Prime Minister Miyazawa himself would make an apology during his visit to South Korea.[52]

The hurried response from the Japanese government also saw Katō hold a press briefing on January 13, 1992, at which he issued a formal statement on the comfort women issue. In light of the importance of this statement for subsequent developments, it is quoted in its entirety below.[53]

1. When we consider the suffering experienced by the so-called comfort women from the Korean peninsula, it is heartbreaking.

2. We know that materials have been discovered in the Defense Agency that appear to suggest that military authorities were involved in the comfort women stations, and we take this fact seriously.

3. Looking at the materials that have been discovered, testimonies from those involved, and materials already reported from the US military, etc., involvement by the military in some form in advertising for comfort women and operating comfort stations cannot be denied.

4. The Japanese government has repeatedly expressed deep regret and apologies concerning the past acts of Japan that caused unbearable suffering for the people of the Korean peninsula, but in this case, we want to again express our sincere apology and regret to those who endured suffering beyond description. The Japanese government is resolved that this should never happen again, and will staunchly maintain its status as a peaceful nation

while working to build a new Japan-Korea relationship toward the future.

5. We have been conducting an investigation since the end of last year in the relevant ministries and agencies as to whether the Japanese government was involved in Korean comfort women issue and will continue to pursue the facts of the situation in the best faith.

Katō made a further statement in July 1992 ("Statement by Chief Cabinet Secretary Kōichi Katō on the Issue of the so-called 'Wartime Comfort Women' from the Korean Peninsula"),[54] so to distinguish between the two, here we shall refer to the January statement as the first Katō Statement and the July statement as the second Katō Statement. In short, the first Katō Statement determined the direction of the Kōno Statement that was issued in August 1993 and already contained many of the features of the string of statements subsequently made by the Japanese government. Those features were as follows.

The first Katō Statement focused on whether military authorities and the government were involved in the comfort women issue, and it took the form of admitting that the previous view of the Japanese government was mistaken. This was because the somewhat confusing question of whether or not there had been government involvement in the comfort women issue was initially raised by the Japanese government itself. According to Diet records, the first time that the government referred to "involvement" in the comfort women issue was on December 18, 1990, when Kaifu was still in power.[55] As noted above, the Miyazawa administration made a number of similar statements following that same logic. The ultimate consequence was the chief cabinet secretary's statement on December 6, 1991, that documents showing that the government had been involved in the "recruitment, etc." of comfort women had not been found.[56]

The problem was that the term "involvement" was excessively nuanced. Hata Ikuhiko later noted[57] that the government really should have foreseen that the military authorities administering occupied territories during the war would have had some involvement, at least in establishing the comfort stations located there, as had in fact already been suggested by certain parties.[58] For the Japanese government to have taken a line premised on complete noninvolvement was an enterprise doomed from the outset.

Put another way, to the extent that involvement did not necessarily imply that the Japanese government bore responsibility for the issue, the government would have done better to approach involvement and responsibility as entirely different questions. However, when the comfort women issue came to the fore, the government repeated so often that there was no government or military involvement that it misled public opinion in both Japan and South Korea, as well as itself, into believing that this was the key issue in the comfort women debate. In short, the Japanese government failed to grasp the real heart of the issue, and it was this confusion that turned an already complex issue into something far more problematic.

Moreover, the government also repeatedly stated that it would conduct inquiries in order to resolve the issue. As is clear from the use of the term "in the best faith," the tone of the January 1992 statement had become quite different from Katō's initial response back in December 1991. The key issue here was that with its previous contention now in tatters, the government itself had lost confidence in the truth in relation to the comfort women. The Japanese government should have addressed the issue from the perspective of government responsibility—in other words, its responsibility to pay compensation. Instead, figuratively speaking, with absolutely no groundwork, it moved beyond its defensive perimeter to occupy the rather meaningless line of denying government "involvement." When that position simply crumpled because of a story emerging five days before Miyazawa's visit to South Korea, rather than stopping to think about where it should have drawn its line, the government lost its cool and plunged into blind retreat.

Clearly, by this stage Japan's ruling elite had already lost control of the situation. A growing social movement and a strong liberal media voice spearheaded by *Asahi shimbun* would plunge the government and the LDP into confusion.

3. The Miyazawa Visit

Ambiguous Remorse

Another feature of the first Katō Statement was its strong air of apology in the absence of any explanation of exactly what aspect of the comfort women issue the apology was for. For example, while expressing "deep regret and apologies concerning the past acts of Japan" that caused "unbearable pain and suffering," there is no concrete indication as to what those "past acts" were. This is hardly surprising given that the Japanese government still had no detailed information on what documents existed in relation to the comfort women issue and what had in fact taken place.[59] Partial disclosure of materials in the *Asahi* story and other reports had revealed to the public a certain degree of military involvement, but no conclusion had as yet been reached about the actual extent of that involvement or of government responsibility. However, where investigation of the materials should have preceded an apology, the government instead made a political calculation and put its apology first. This could in fact be described as the major feature of the first Katō Statement.

As a result, the statement simply threw matters further into turmoil. South Korean activist groups were naturally heartened, reading the statement as full recognition by the Japanese side of its wrongdoing and looking forward to the Japanese government paying compensation directly to the former comfort women. South Korean public interest also shot up, with the group of protestors in front of the Japanese embassy swelling more than ten times to over four hundred people.[60] A concerned South Korean government decided to boost the security detail for Miyazawa's visit from the usual five thousand to thirteen thousand.[61]

Growing Friction over Trade

On January 16, 1992, Prime Minister Miyazawa Kiichi visited South Korea. Again looking to newspaper reports for insight into the situation in South Korea at the time, the first thing we notice is that on January 14–15, just before Miyazawa arrived, the South Korean papers all ran major pieces on the fact that volunteer corps recruitment during World War II even extended to children of elementary school age.[62] These stories arose out of confusion in South Korea in relation to comfort women terminology.[63] As is apparent from the fact that even the Korean name for the Korean Council for the Women Drafted for Military Sexual Slavery by Japan (then and now the leading comfort women advocacy organization in South Korea) translates more literally as the "Council on the Volunteer Corps Issue," there was a tendency in South Korea to view interchangeably the terms volunteer corps, which meant conscripted laborers, and comfort women, which referred to sex workers, despite the clear difference between the two. As a result, the media reports assumed that girls of elementary school age had been recruited as comfort women, which came as a great shock to South Korean society.

However, this did not mean that the comfort women issue was the top priority in the talks between Japan and South Korea. For example, on the day that Miyazawa arrived in South Korea, *Chosun ilbo*, one of South Korea's leading papers, splashed across its front page the headline "Japan

Rejects Three Key Trade Deficit Reduction Demands,"[64] which suggests that the priority issue for the South Koreans in terms of the bilateral relationship was at that point not the difference in historical perception in relation to the comfort women and forced labor. Rather it was the more pragmatic issue of trade, driven by South Korea's growing trade deficit. From the time that South Korea became independent in 1948, it ran a consistent trade deficit until the late 1980s, when the account moved briefly into the black. In the 1990s, however, it slipped once again heavily into deficit, reaching a record high of US $9.6 billion in 1991, the year before Miyazawa's visit, much to the alarm of the South Korean government.[65] Moreover, US $8.7 billion of the deficit—over 90 percent—was with Japan, making it almost impossible for South Korea to claw its trade account out of the red without correcting this imbalance.[66] South Korea had consequently presented the Japanese government with three demands designed to redress the trade deficit: lower tariffs for key South Korean exports; the establishment of a new foundation for scientific and technical cooperation between Japan and South Korea to promote the transfer of industrial technology; and participation by South Korean companies in Japanese public works projects.

The importance of the trade issue in the bilateral relationship manifests clearly in the deliberate reference made to it by Roh Tae-woo in his New Year's remarks on January 10, when he stressed that friendship between Japan and South Korea would not be possible as long as the trade deficit with Japan remained outstanding. Held only a day before the Japanese media would be full of stories about military involvement, Roh's press conference mentioned not a single disputed historical perception, the comfort women issue included. It was universally apparent that the key item on the agenda for the Japan-South Korea summit was trade.[67]

However, the Japanese government took a hard line on the trade issue, arguing that South Korea's trade deficit with Japan was the result of the country importing intermediate goods from Japan and exporting finished products to other countries. In other words, it was caused by the structure of the South Korean economy, so trying to resolve it through concessions by Japan was essentially putting the cart before the horse—in other words, impossible. Japan consequently flatly rejected South Korea's proposal. When bilateral working-level talks held just before Miyazawa's visit stalled as a result, the issue was passed on for direct negotiation between the two leaders, a very unusual situation for summit talks.[68]

The times allocated for the various items on the summit meeting agenda also confirm that the comfort women issue was not a central topic of the talks. The talks were divided across January 16 and 17. In the original schedule, the 110 minutes of the first day were primarily allocated to trade and other international issues, and on the second day, too, most of the 75 minutes was to be spent on technology transfer, cultural exchange, and the emperor's visit to South Korea. Only 22 of the 185 minutes of the summit talks were set aside for discussion of the comfort women and other issues of historical perception.[69]

Remorse and More Remorse

This did not mean, however, that the comfort women issue did not play a major role in the summit talks, as is apparent from Miyazawa's schedule before and after the talks. Just two days before his departure for South Korea on January 14, 1992, Miyazawa held a press briefing for the South Korean media in Tokyo at which he said, in relation to the comfort women, that "I would like to express my heartfelt regret and remorse for those who suffered indescribable hardships. It is truly painful to the heart."[70] On January 16, Miyazawa arrived at Seoul Air Base and went straight to the Seoul National Cemetery to lay flowers before attending the first round of summit talks at the Blue House in the afternoon. Arriving at the Blue House, Miyazawa was to receive his first shock when, at talks that were meant to focus on international relations, Roh suddenly made reference to the need for Japan to have a "correct interpretation" of the "unfortunate past." Miyazawa promptly responded by expressing "regret and remorse."[71]

Both leaders then engaged in a long discussion about trade issues before moving on to the evening banquet, where Roh again set the stage for a Japanese response by remarking that both sides needed to make sincere efforts to break down emotional walls based on the foundation of a correct interpretation of history and humble reflection. Miyazawa chose his words carefully in responding that "We Japanese should first and foremost recall the fact that Japanese actions inflicted suffering and sorrow upon your people in a certain period in the past. We should never forget our feelings of remorse over this."[72]

What is noteworthy is the way in which South Korea gradually took over the direction of the summit. One feature of this summit was that it was the first to take place after working-level coordination had failed, which made the gamesmanship of the two leaders extremely important. The South Korean government appears to have sought to make optimal use of the comfort women issue, where it enjoyed a clear advantage. Having been forced to express remorse twice on the very first day of his visit,

Miyazawa found himself in an even more uncomfortable situation on the second day. As noted above, 22 minutes of the 75-minute talks scheduled for the morning of the second day had been allocated to the comfort women issue. According to *Mainichi shimbun*, Miyazawa expressed remorse and regret as many as eight times in those 22 minutes. At a rough calculation, then, he must have apologized at least once every three minutes in a 22-minute litany of regret and remorse—a situation unheard of in summit talks between sovereign states.[73]

At the press conference afterwards, Miyazawa noted in relation to the comfort women issue that "just hearing from those involved in the *chôngsindae*—known in Japan as military comfort women[74]—one could imagine the pain and suffering that they must have experienced," which was "truly painful to the heart." "I apologize from the bottom of my heart for those people who suffered indescribable hardships," he said.[75] The last major event scheduled for his visit was a speech to the South Korean legislature—the first ever delivered to that body by a Japanese prime minister. In it, Miyazawa again apologized humbly in relation to the comfort women issue and also expressed regret and remorse for colonial rule itself.[76]

The Collapse of a Premise

In all, judging solely from media reports, Miyazawa must have expressed remorse and regret at least thirteen times in his brief three-day visit.[77] This obviously also took a major psychological toll on him. In the old capital of Kyongju, the final stop on his trip, he noted that the talks had been "emotionally draining," and he was happy to now be enjoying the serenity of Kyongju.[78] At the same time, given that the Japanese side did not end up compromising with South Korea on the trade issue that was expected to be the major point of contention in the talks, it may well be that Miyazawa's strategy was, to borrow the words of a Japanese government official, to "apologize profusely" concerning the comfort women as a means of avoiding an attack from the South Korean government on this point.

There was, however, a major premise underlying Miyazawa's ability to pursue this "apology diplomacy"—namely that no matter how much he apologized, the Claims Settlement Agreement provided that "claims between the High Contracting Parties and between their peoples . . . have been settled completely and finally," and the Japanese government would not be responsible for making additional compensation. Crucially, both the Japanese and South Korean governments shared this perspective when the bilateral summit talks began in January 1992.[79] At that stage, they both believed that even if materials emerged that directly implicated the Japanese government in the comfort women issue, the existence of the agreement exempted Japan from making additional compensation. This was why the government was able to express remorse so freely without fearing that it might become liable for a payout. Apologies were free, and if the issue could be resolved simply by expressing remorse, what easier way could there be? It was scarcely surprising that the Japanese government chose a strategy of profuse apology.[80]

4. Insincere Apologies?

Structural Change in the Historical Perceptions Dispute

However, the foundation for the Japanese government's apology diplomacy collapsed immediately afterward. On January 21, 1992, just three days after Miyazawa's return home, the South Korean government changed its stance entirely, demanding that Japan conduct a full investigation and "take steps including appropriate compensation."[81] With all previous South Korean administrations following Japan's line regarding complete and final settlement having been reached under the Claims Settlement Agreement on the issue of reparations for Japan's colonial rule, this turnaround had huge significance, effectively dissolving the entire premise on which the Japanese government had based its approach to the comfort women issue. In short, this was the moment when the cooperative relationship that had previously existed between the ruling elite of Japan and South Korea collapsed.

As noted, Miyazawa's January 1992 visit and his repeated expressions of remorse were premised on the idea that the Japanese government would not incur any additional responsibility as a result. The South Korean government's sudden shift to demanding appropriate compensation placed the Miyazawa administration in a very difficult situation, since from a logical perspective the change in policy opened the way for the South Korean side to demand additional compensation in relation to other historical issues besides the comfort women. Specifically, if the Japanese government recognized the comfort women as an exception to the "complete and final settlement" of claims between Japan and South Korea, the same logic might be applied to other issues, opening the way for a flood of exceptions.

And in fact, after some twists and turns, the South Korean government did eventually widen the scope of exceptions to the original agreement, transforming the shape of the historical perception dispute between Japan and South Korea. In that sense, the South Korean government's January 21, 1992 decision was an even more pivotal moment than the *Asahi*'s January 11 scoop.

The Roh Tae-Woo Administration and the Democratic Liberal Party

What prompted the South Korean government to make such a major volte-face? Let's take a somewhat hypothetical look at the state of South Korean politics behind that move.

Back in February 1988 when Roh took power, it was in triumph over the "three Kims"—Kim Young-sam, Kim Dae-jung, and Kim Jong-pil—powerful rivals with whom he had engaged in a brutal election battle the previous December. Roh's victory was far from decisive, however. He collected only 36.3 percent, just over one-third of the vote, the lowest percentage of any South Korean president to the present day.[82]

The reason that Roh was elected despite attracting only a fraction of the vote was that the main forces behind South Korea's 1987 democratization split between Kim Young-sam and Kim Dae-jung and the rivalry between the two camps enabled Roh to scrape into power. But this also meant that his regime was built on extremely shaky ground.

Just how shaky it was became apparent in the National Assembly elections of April 1988, right after Roh took power. Roh's Democratic Justice Party took only 125 of the 299 seats, while Kim Dae-jung's Party for Peace and Democracy won 70, Kim Young-sam's Reunification Democratic Party won 59, and Kim Jong-pil's New Democratic Republican Party won 35. As a single-party minority government, the new administration found itself struggling to control the legislature, a predicament Roh needed to resolve immediately.[83]

As with presidential systems in many countries, the South Korean president has no power to dissolve the legislature, so the only option available to Roh was to explore cooperative relationships with other parties. Roh began negotiations behind the scenes beginning around 1989, and his efforts bore fruit in early 1990 when the ruling Democratic Justice Party merged with Kim Young-sam's Reunification Democratic Party and Kim Jong-pil's New Democratic Republican Party to form the Democratic Liberal Party (DLP). Because his Democratic Justice Party had been the biggest party before the merger, Roh Tae-woo became the head of the new party. Kim Young-sam, formerly head of the second-largest party, became the senior member of the DLP's executive council, of which Kim Jong-pil also became a member. Park Tae-joon, president of Pohang

Iron and Steel (now POSCO) and a National Assembly member from Roh Tae-woo's old party, was also appointed to the council to assist Roh with his heavy workload.[84]

The emergence of this massive new ruling party, which held close to 75 percent of the seats in the National Assembly, briefly stabilized the political foundations of Roh Tae-woo's government, but maneuvering soon began within the party in the run-up to the December 1992 presidential elections. At the center of the storm was Kim Young-sam, number two man in the party. Kim placed second in the 1987 presidential elections and was universally recognized as the strongest candidate in the 1992 elections. His greatest weakness, however, was limited support within the party, a problem he sought to overcome by wresting control from the strongest DLP faction—the former Democratic Justice Party, headed by Roh and Park. Kim exploited to the full his two advantages: the public negative image of the old Democratic Justice Party with its ties to the coup d'état-driven Chun Doo-hwan regime and Kim's own democratic legitimacy, earned through his role in the fight for democracy.

The Comfort Women Issue in South Korean Domestic Politics

The key point is that the foregrounding of the comfort women issue as a result of the January 1992 *Asahi shimbun* article and Miyazawa's visit to South Korea took place within the country as a power struggle within the ruling Democratic Liberal Party was reaching its peak. On January 7, Kim Young-sam observed that failing to identify the ruling party's presidential candidate—the public's greatest concern—was a cause of political, economic, and social instability, and publicly demanded that the DLP lock him in as its candidate prior to the March legislative elections.[85] His move had a major impact on the DLP, in that party members in the legislature with an election just ahead saw obvious benefit in fighting that election behind Kim Young-sam, a hero of the democracy movement who was popular with the public, rather than Roh Tae-woo and his falling support ratings. The number of party members changing their position to support Kim swelled rapidly.

Given this situation, Miyazawa's visit obviously provided excellent material for internal political maneuvering by South Korea's various political forces. The first moves were made not by ruling party factions but rather the opposition. The remaining members of the Reunification Democratic Party who had opposed the formation of the Democratic Liberal Party combined with Kim Dae-jung's Party for Peace and Democracy to create the Democratic Party. At the summit talks, the Democratic Party first made its presence felt by refusing to attend the banquet held on the first day of Miyazawa's visit. The banquet was a grand affair, bringing together eminent figures from throughout South Korean society, and was attended by numerous National Assembly members, among them Kim Young-sam, Kim Jong-pil, and Park Tae-joon, the three executive councillors of the ruling party. The absence of Democratic Party members was clearly an expression of objection to the summit talks and their content, an intention that would emerge in even more blatant form the following day.

On January 17, the Democratic Party put out a statement in the name of its Special Committee on Women.[86] It demanded "legal reparations" from the Japanese government, calling for Miyazawa as Japanese prime minister to make a clear apology concerning the comfort women issue during his visit and to clear up the Japanese government's legal responsibilities and the compensation issue. This was also a challenge to the position of the South Korean government, which remained that all reparations for colonial rule had been settled under the Claims Settlement Agreement. The Democratic Party further decided that its members could choose whether or not to attend Miyazawa's address to the National Assembly on January 18, with only twenty-three of seventy-five choosing to do so. In short, the majority of opposition party members boycotted Miyazawa's address.[87]

Significantly, the hard line taken by the Democratic Party served to highlight the conciliatory stance of the ruling party and the South Korean government toward Japan on the comfort women issue. The ruling party had also made its own preparations, of course. On January16, the Democratic Liberal Party released a statement in the name of its spokesman Park Hee-tae to the effect that Japan must demonstrate sincerity not only in words but also in a tangible form in relation to the trade deficit, technology transfer, and the comfort women issue. Moreover, it argued that, now that the truth had become evident in relation to the comfort women issue, Japan should pay compensation in good faith (putting the DLP ahead of the government in using the term "compensation").[88] However, the ruling party had not yet explicitly framed that compensation as legal reparations, continuing to run far cooler than the opposition.

What made things difficult for the Democratic Liberal Party was that Kim Jong-pil—one of its most powerful members—was a party to the negotiations on the 1965 Treaty on Basic Relations and its supplements. The biggest hurdle for the South Korean government in demanding reparations for the comfort women and other matters was that, as I have frequently noted, the agreement stated that a complete and final settlement of all claims had been made between the two countries and their peoples. This meant that Kim Jon-pil could potentially be required to take responsibility for his part in negotiating such an agreement.

Kim Jong-pil consequently issued a statement on Miyazawa's very first day in South Korea calling on Japan to acknowledge its moral responsibility and pay compensation. However, this only made matters worse, with coverage of Kim's comments by all the South Korean papers on January 17 conversely boxing in the DLP. For example, the leading paper *Dong-a ilbo* reported as follows:[89]

> At the center of the uproar is Kim Jong-pil. It is unlikely that any Korean of his age would be unaware of the comfort women, and yet when claim rights were being negotiated, he argued that neither Japan nor Korea had documentary evidence on the comfort women issue and that the facts could therefore not be ascertained, so nothing could be done.
>
> Such logic is tantamount to injuring someone and blaming the injury on the weapon. There were more witnesses back then than there are now, and there must have also been more materials. Having successfully led a coup d'état while still in his thirties, whether Kim was unable to resolve this particular issue because of a lack of experience or because he was involved in an unprincipled coalition with Japan is something that we shall not explore here.
>
> What we do want to question is the morality and understanding of history of one of the leaders of Korea's ruling party. Kim's statement is sadly distant from the imposing pronouncement of a political leader who has personally shouldered the responsibility for resolving Korea-Japan relations.

Kim Jong-pil's statement is also significant in revealing that the South Korean negotiators of the Claims Settlement Agreement were aware at least to some extent of the existence of the comfort women issue, clearly contradicting the claim of certain South Korean parties that the comfort women issue had not been in the minds of the negotiators.

This is a point that I would like to pursue elsewhere if the opportunity should arise. In any case, the apology diplomacy pursued during Miyazawa's January 1992 visit clearly put pressure on the South Korean ruling party and government. This was one reason the government altered its previous interpretation of the Claims Settlement Agreement, thereby crossing the Rubicon of the Japan-South Korea historical perception dispute.

Kim Jong-Pil and the 1992 South Korean Presidential Elections

The essential aspect of South Korean politics at the time of Miyazawa's visit was that the ruling DLP was a three-party coalition. A power struggle had developed between members of the old Democratic Justice Party, which had roots in the Chun Doo-hwan regime, and former Reunification Party members led by Kim Young-sam, the strongest candidate in the upcoming presidential elections. In addition, that struggle was staged in the context of the presidential candidacy battle taking place within the party.

Members of the old Democratic Justice Party initially regarded Park Chul-un as the most promising presidential candidate. The cousin of Roh Tae-woo's wife, Park Chul-un was said to have played a key role as Roh's right-hand man during Roh's ascent to the presidency. Roh had rewarded Park's efforts by appointing him almost immediately to an executive post, and those around Roh believed that the president viewed Park as his successor.[90]

However, the situation changed entirely with Roh's transformation into a lame duck in the closing days of his presidency. The key element in this was a fact-finding investigation into various matters occurring during the Chun Doo-hwan regime and its formation. This was partially the result of Roh Tae-woo's own political agenda, since immediately after he took power the greatest constraint on his political leadership was not opposition leaders such as Kim Young-sam and Kim Dae-jung but rather members of the Chun Doo-hwan camp trading on the prestige of the former president. Roh accordingly tackled with alacrity the work of fact-finding in relation to historical incidents from the 1979 coup d'état to the de facto coup of May 17, 1980, and the Gwangju Incident, so as to place Chun Doo-hwan followers at a political disadvantage.

However, the fact-finding process inevitably also cast suspicion on Roh Tae-woo himself, as he had been number two in Chun's government. As a result, Roh lost support, and Park Chul-un, who at one point was known within the administration as the "Crown Prince," saw his own influence rapidly wane.

But this did not end the hostility between old Democratic Justice Party members and Kim Young-sam's supporters. After the fall of Park Chul-un, the next Kim Young-sam rival to emerge was Park Tae-joon, another of the executive councillors of the Democratic Liberal party. While a former military man, Park was closer to Park Chung-hee than Chun Doo-hwan in terms of both generation and personal connections. He was also known as the legendary entrepreneur who had transformed POSCO, a former state-owned steel company, into an international player.[91] In other words, if Kim Young-sam stood alongside Kim Dae-jung as a hero of democratization, Park was a hero of economic growth. In modern South Korean history, economic growth rivaled democratization as a priority issue, and Park's heroic status in this regard was more than adequate in challenging Kim Young-sam's position.

This conflict between the ruling party's two major factions ultimately handed the casting vote to Kim Jong-pil as the third most powerful member of the party.[92] It was therefore highly significant that the opposition party and the South Korean media directed their criticism in relation to the comfort women issue at Kim Jong-pil. The political aim of the opposition was plain. By calling for legal reparations for the comfort women, they were able to differentiate themselves from the government and the ruling party, which had hitherto been unable to take the step of demanding compensation. In addition, where the ruling party and the government cited the agreement as the reason that they had been unable to demand compensation, the opposition was able to put even more pressure on the ruling party by demanding that its kingpin Kim Jong-pil take responsibility for his role in the negotiations.

Kim Jong-pil was very well aware of this. As noted above, it was the reason that he issued a statement immediately before the Miyazawa visit calling for the Japanese government to pay compensation for the comfort women issue.[93] Clearly, he was anxious to find some way to avoid being targeted. However, when the Japanese government did not go as far as offering compensation, Kim Jong-pil instantly found himself in a pinch. In the South Korean political context of the time, the comfort women issue equated to the treaty issue, and the treaty issue equated to the Kim Jong-pil issue. Despite this, the two major factions within the ruling party were unable to cut Kim Jong-pil loose. Not only did Kim's faction hold more than thirty seats, he had a powerful local base in Chungcheong-do, lending him major influence over the presidential candidacy battle within the party as well as the direction of the elections themselves.

The change in policy on the comfort women issue by the South Korean government immediately after the Miyazawa visit therefore held special significance in South Korean politics at the time. For example, a top official from the Korean Foreign Ministry stated publicly that the "volunteer corps" issue "could no longer be discussed purely in the legal dimension"; a new institution needed to be built at the governmental level to explore and uncover the truth, on the basis of which multifaceted consideration would have to be given to the issue of "compensation and other matters."[94]

The point here is that, unlike the opposition and others, the South Korean government did not use the term "legal reparations" but rather the more ambiguous expression "compensation and other matters." In other words, the South Korean government was seeking to resolve the issue outside the legal dimension as a way of avoiding discussion of the agreement—not least because that would allow Kim Jong-pil, who was right in the midst of the whirlpool, to be exempted and the ruling party and the government to avoid their own responsibility.

5. The Response of the Japanese Government

Apologies, Abstract and Concrete

Next it was the turn of the Japanese government, which was caught short by the sudden call from the South Korean government to address "compensation and other matters." The South Korean government's policy turnaround was simply too abrupt for the Japanese government. The fact that this was all happening only ten days after the *Asahi shimbun* report is indicative of how rapidly the matter unfolded, leaving the Japanese government with no choice but to make a serious response.

That response was certainly swift. On January 21, the same day that the Japanese government received a formal request for compensation from South Korea, Chief Cabinet Secretary Katō issued a statement indicating that it was his impression that the matter of individual compensation in relation to the comfort women issue was already resolved and that he wished to wait on the results of the court case.[95] In other words, the Japanese government reiterated that it did not intend taking part in additional consultations with South Korea on "compensation and other matters" related to the comfort women issue, effectively slamming the door on diplomatic negotiations.

However, this response would subsequently have a heavy impact on the historical perceptions dispute between Japan and South Korea by giving rise to a new discourse in South Korea. The South Korean public had seen the Japanese prime minister personally express remorse numerous times in the space of a few days, but his government now appeared to contradict that by immediately turning around and refusing to pay compensation. This left South Koreans with the impression that the Japanese apologies were not sincere but only for show. To resolve the historical perceptions dispute, it was now felt that Japan needed to make a real apology demonstrating its remorse. In this we see the emergence of an aspect of the South Korean understanding of the historical perception dispute that remains typical to this day.[96]

The underlying cause was the way in which the new spotlight on the comfort women issue changed the basic conditions of the historical perception debate. Prior to Miyazawa's administration, the Japanese government had in fact made a number of expressions of remorse to South Korea. The words of Emperor Hirohito at the time of Chun's visit to Japan in 1984 and of Emperor Akihito during Roh's visit in 1990 were typical examples. Expressions of remorse and apology were of course made not only by the Japanese emperors. During Roh's visit, for example, Prime Minister Kaifu noted that Japan was "humbly remorseful" for the "unbearable grief and suffering because of the actions of our country" and spoke of Japan's "frank feelings of apology."[97]

These expressions of remorse and apology by the Japanese government prior to the Miyazawa visit had one major commonality: they were all abstract apologies that did not focus on specific incidents or victims. By contrast, Miyazawa's expressions of remorse during his visit to South Korea were clearly directed to the comfort women themselves. Because abstract apologies do not identify specific injury or specific victims, it is difficult to connect them with specific compensation or reparations. However, an apology with a clear recipient opens the door for discussion of concrete responsibility and compensation. Accordingly, Miyazawa's repeated expressions of remorse conversely had the effect of highlighting the significance of the Japanese government's rejection of compensation.

In the end, the only effect of the repeated expressions of remorse by the Japanese government around the time of the Miyazawa visit was to give South Korean society the impression of underhandedness on the part of the Japanese government, making the position of the latter even more difficult.[98]

Backed into a Corner

At his January 21 press briefing, Katō also noted that he wanted to express a heartfelt apology in relation to the comfort women issue and to consider related measures.[99] He wanted, he said, to take some action to express Japan's feeling of apology. This comment reveals that the Japanese government was well aware that formulaic apologies had only exacerbated matters, and recognized that something would need to be done to remedy a difficult situation.

However, a new problem emerged. Where the South Korean government might have worked with the Japanese government to frame concrete proposals for a diplomatic resolution to the problem, it instead pulled back from positive and official cooperation with the Japanese government. In other words, having called on the Japanese government to pay compensation for the comfort women issue, the South Korean government then sank into silence on the issue of what specifically should be done.

There were two reasons for this. First, as Roh Tae-woo became more and more of a lame duck, his administration dwindled into a caretaker government that simply did not have the capacity to deal with the comfort women issue and the complex nationalist sentiments with which it was entangled. Neither did the ruling party seek to actively engage with the issue, burdened as it was with Kim Jong-pil and a number of other party members involved in the original treaty negotiations.[100]

More importantly, the most logical step for the South Korean government was probably to put the responsibility for finding a solution firmly in Japan's lap. Confusion over the comfort women issue subsequently continued in South Korea. The Roh administration was pushed out of power before it was able to make a formal claim from the Japanese government beyond the scope of "suitable measures, including compensation," while the Kim Young-sam administration that replaced it in 1993 took a step back from the issue, making it apparent that "material compensation" would not be sought from the Japanese government in relation to the comfort women issue.[101] Given the participation of ruling party members in the treaty negotiations, it would have been politically tricky for the South Korean government to engage in discussion in relation to the agreement, so instead it chose to avoid that discussion.

However, this did not mean the South Korean government returned to the collaborative line with the Japanese government that it had followed before the Miyazawa visit. While South Korea held back from making demands for "compensation and other matters" from 1993 to 1994, it maintained a consistent call for a sincere response from the Japanese government.[102]

The difficulty for the Japanese government was that South Korea gave absolutely no indication as to the specific content of the "sincere response" that it was seeking, and instead simply dropped the most difficult aspect of the comfort women issue—formulating a solution that could be viewed as constituting a "sincere response"—squarely in the lap of the Japanese government. Regardless of whether it was intentional or not, it was a masterly stroke, enabling the South Korean government not only to avoid a complicated legal question in which the government itself was implicated but also to reserve the right to ultimately reject the Japanese government's solution, regardless of what might be negotiated behind closed doors.

A process of trial and error followed as Japan sought to devise a model solution, resulting in the second Katō Statement of July 1992, the Kōno Statement of 1993, and the Asian Women's Fund. Below we take a closer look at that process.

6. The Second Katō Statement

South Korean Government Strategy and the Basic Structure of the Comfort Women Issue

The Roh administration's policy shift blindsided the Japanese government. However, as noted above, the greater problem was (and has since remained) the opacity of the South Korean government's stance on the issue. Contrary to common perception, even after the "Coomaraswamy Report,"[103] which was submitted to the United Nations in 1996, the South Korean government has not in fact formally pressed the Japanese government for legal compensation.[104] When Kim Young-sam took over from Roh, his government stated clearly and repeatedly that it was not seeking material compensation. The subsequent Kim Dae-jung administration as well effectively adopted a policy of nonintervention, simply announcing that the government had no intention of obstructing action by private-sector organizations to seek compensation.[105] After Roh Moo-hyun came to power in 2003, the Yasukuni Shrine issue and the outbreak of a territorial dispute led the government to take a hard line on the comfort women issue as well. In January 2005, it disclosed diplomatic documents from the negotiation process for the Treaty on Basic Relations and the various supplementary agreements, and then formed the Joint Private-Government Committee on Measures Pursuant to the Publication of Documents on South Korea-Japan Talks to analyze the documents. The committee published a report that concluded that the comfort women issue was beyond the scope of the Treaty on Basic Relations and the supplementary agreements, along with the issues of South Korean nationals in Sakhalin and atomic bomb victims. However, the government made no official diplomatic claim to the Japanese government for legal compensation in relation to the report.

What constrained the South Korean government was the Treaty on Basic Relations and the supplementary agreements. As became apparent through the Roh Moo-hyun administration's disclosure of diplomatic documents,[106] it was in fact the Japanese government that had argued throughout the treaty negotiation process for de facto compensation to be paid directly to individual claimants. The South Korean government, however, had pushed strongly for a lump sum to be paid by Japan that the South Korean side would then divide among the individual claimants. This was a major factor holding the South Korean government back from calling directly on Japan for compensation to individual victims.[107]

Understanding the importance of this requires a grasp of the legal structure of the comfort women issue.[108] While I am no legal expert, my understanding is that for South Korea to make a direct claim to the Japanese government on compensation and other matters in relation to the comfort women issue, it would need to clear four hurdles. First, there must have been an unlawful act, in the absence of which there is also no claim. Second, there must be proof that the Japanese government was responsible for this act. Even if there was an unlawful act, if the Japanese government was not responsible for it, the victims might be able to claim compensation from comfort station operators but not from the Japanese government. The first hurdle is therefore the question of the legality of the process of coercive recruitment of comfort women and the disregard of their human rights at comfort stations, while the second focuses on evidence relating to military and government involvement.

Clearing these two hurdles, however, would not be sufficient to claim legal compensation. The third hurdle is that the claim must be shown to be still effective. There are two major reasons why the claim might be null. The first is well-known—namely the argument that the provisions of the Treaty on Basic Relations and its annexes render individual claims on the South Korean side in relation to the comfort women null and void. The second is the statute of limitations in civil law. The Korean Supreme Court has ruled that the defendant's argument that it has no responsibility to pay compensation because the statute of limitations has expired is counter to the principle of good faith and is therefore inadmissible.

The fourth hurdle is that there must be proof that the ultimate payment obligation lies with the Japanese government. Even if the first three hurdles were successfully cleared, if the interpretation is that compensation should be paid from the economic cooperation funds that the South Korean government received under the treaty's supplementary agreements, South Korea becomes responsible for paying the final cost. The South Korean government has in fact recognized this in relation to compensation for wartime labor conscription and has paid de facto compensation to the relevant parties.

From the Roh Moo-hyun regime onward, the South Korean government has therefore avoided these issues by arguing that the comfort women represent a new issue not yet envisaged when the Treaty on Basic Relations was concluded, and accordingly calling for it to be handled outside the framework of the treaty's supplementary agreements.[109] However, as demonstrated earlier, the existence of the comfort women was known before the conclusion of the Claims Settlement Agreement[110] and the parties to the negotiations were well aware of this.[111] Moreover, because a strict interpretation of the articles suggests that what was paid under the respective agreements was not compensation but rather economic cooperation funds, it may not be particularly meaningful to argue about what kind of compensation these funds were used for.

Clearly, the Claims Settlement Agreement presents substantial hurdles to the South Korean government in seeking legal compensation from Japan, which is why successive administrations have in fact tried to avoid the issue. The Chôngdaehyop and other South Korean civil rights groups, however, have continued to press strongly for compensation from the Japanese government since 1992, and their position has always received a high level of support in South Korea.[112] Postdemocratization, it has been difficult for the government to directly oppose these groups because of the strong public criticism it would face.

Confronted with the serious dilemma of either directly challenging the Claims Settlement Agreement and having its demands flatly rejected by Japan or compromising to some extent with Japan and facing strident public opposition, the solution that the South Korean government chose to adopt—whether deliberately or simply because that was the way it turned out—was to leave the problem to the Japanese government to solve. In other words, what the South Korean government sought from Japan was not compensation for the comfort women but a way to resolve the matter, with the most fundamental issue—what that solution might be—left entirely to the Japanese government.

The Miyazawa Administration at an Impasse

It was only later that the importance of this legal structure became apparent. Confronted with the Roh Tae-woo administration's policy shift, the Miyazawa government had no choice but to take up the difficult question of what a solution to the comfort women issue might entail. Of the two main tasks this presented, the first was to determine the historical facts. Miyazawa's 1992 visit to South Korea had taken place only five days after the *Asahi shimbun* story on military involvement, at which point almost no specific historical facts had come to light on the comfort women issue. The Japanese government therefore first had to determine the facts of the matter in order to ascertain its own responsibility.

Second, Japan had to formulate a solution. Significantly, the Miyazawa administration tackled the tasks of determining the facts and formulating a solution simultaneously. On January 14, two days before Miyazawa left for South Korea, Chief Cabinet Secretary Katō had already revealed that alternatives to compensation would be considered in relation to the comfort women issue, so the basic direction of the government's solution was already outlined at this stage.[113] The contradictory approach of seeking a solution before fact-finding was completed was the result of the assumption on the part of both governments as well as public opinion that, as it was almost certain that the Japanese government bore some degree of responsibility for the comfort women issue, pursuing the facts would immediately make that responsibility even more apparent.

The meaning of the solution sought by the Miyazawa government therefore needs to be understood in its contemporary context—namely that it appeared to be only a matter of time before proof emerged that the Japanese government bore some degree of responsibility for the comfort women issue, but that the Claims Settlement Agreement effectively annulled the possibility that the government would incur any obligation to pay direct legal compensation. Accordingly, by proactively presenting a solution inclusive of an alternative to compensation at this stage, the Japanese government could demonstrate good faith to its South Korean counterpart and the South Korean public. Achieving this quickly would resolve the biggest cause of concern between Japan and South Korea, stabilizing both the Miyazawa regime and bilateral relations. This logic makes it easy to understand the Japanese government's actions.

However, these assumptions failed to come to pass due to a problem with the fact-finding investigation—the failure to find the expected evidence indicating clear legal responsibility on the part of the Japanese government.

Of course, many documents were found indicating Japanese government involvement in the comfort women issue. The explanation[114] given by Chief Cabinet Secretary Katō —what we have called here the second Katō Statement—on July 6, 1992, was that a series of investigations had discovered 127 documents—seventy at the Defense Agency; fifty-two at the Ministry of Foreign Affairs; four at the Ministry of Health, Labour and Welfare; and one at the Ministry of Education—revealing that the Japanese government had been involved in the establishment of comfort stations, the creation of recruiting regulations, comfort station management and surveillance, maintenance of hygiene in comfort stations and among comfort women, and the issuing of identification papers and other documents to comfort station personnel.

However, none of these documents directly indicated that the Japanese government had any legal responsibility in relation to the comfort women. Under prewar Japanese law, the existence of sex workers per se was lawful, and the fact that the Japanese government and military had some degree of involvement with these workers did not necessarily mean that it had directly engaged in unlawful acts. Above all, the documents that both governments and the public had most wanted and expected to be discovered—namely evidence that the Japanese government had been directly involved in illegal acts in the process of recruiting the comfort women—did not emerge.

The historical backdrop against which the comfort women surfaced is critical in understanding this point. As noted earlier, the focus of the historical perception dispute between Japan and South Korea in 1990–91 was on coercive labor conscription, with the comfort women issue regarded simply as part of this broader issue. As a result, at that time the greatest point of concern regarding the comfort women was—and in Japan, perhaps even today, still is—the issue of whether or not coercion had been involved in the recruitment process. This was epitomized by the heated 1992 debate between Yoshimi Yoshiaki and Hata Ikuhiko concerning narrow and broad definitions of coercion.[115] Those positing Japanese government responsibility and those denying it shared a belief that the real heart of the issue was whether or not coercion had been used in the recruiting process, which was why this point was argued so fiercely.

However, contrary to the predictions of many people, no documents were found providing direct evidence of the Japanese government's legal responsibility in the recruiting process. What might look today like a happy turn of events for Japan was regarded by the government at the time as a major constraint, in that the prime minister himself had already extended an apology over the issue, and had also acknowledged that some alternative to compensation would be explored. This was why Katō was forced in his second statement to express the government's "sincere apology and remorse" and commit to "consider sincerely in what way we can express our feelings to those who suffered such hardship."[116] Bound by its own prior words and actions, the Japanese government was now struggling to find a way out.

7. The Kōno Statement

A Watershed Moment in the Historical Perception Dispute

The foregrounding of the comfort women issue that began with the January 1992 *Asahi shimbun* report led to Miyazawa's apologies in South Korea and the Roh Tae-woo administration's policy shift. At that point, it was widely anticipated that documents relating to the forced recruitment of comfort women would come immediately to light, and both governments took action on that premise.

However, the situation took a change for the worse when the all-important documents failed to emerge. The second Katō Statement acknowledged the involvement of the Japanese government in the comfort women issue on various levels, but it also revealed that it had been unable to uncover materials related to coercive recruitment. The South Korean government and public reacted angrily to this unwelcome result of the Japanese investigations.[117] In some quarters, the announcement was even regarded as proof that the Japanese government was trying to cover up the truth.

The South Korean government countered by announcing the results of its own investigations, concluding that it was obvious from the testimonies of former comfort women that de facto coercion had taken place.[118] One South Korean government official said at the time that "if the Japanese are going to argue that there was no coercion, then we must prove otherwise."[119] Clearly, while the discussion might be ongoing, the conclusion was regarded as foregone.

The crucial point here is the divergence that occurred in Japanese and South Korean historical perceptions of the comfort women issue. The issue attracted little interest until the 1980s, and neither society had a particularly fixed view on it as an important diplomatic issue between Japan and South Korea. Following the *Asahi shimbun* revelation of government involvement, both governments began operating on the assumption that coercive recruitment of comfort women had in fact occurred, with their historical perceptions in fact appearing to coincide. The situation changed again, however, in the process of fact-finding. In South Korea, the weight given to testimony from former comfort women led to the perception that coercion was involved. In Japan, by contrast, the lack of documentary evidence created the perception that it was not. In this sense, the comfort women issue might be described as a typical example of how both countries developed new but divergent historical perceptions some decades after the end of the war.

The Search for a Political Solution

This divergence in historical perception cast a long shadow over the concurrent efforts of the Japanese government to develop solutions for the comfort women issue. On August 1, 1992, about two weeks after the second Katō Statement, the Japanese government revealed that a foundation entirely funded by the Japanese government would be established in South Korea as an alternative to compensation.[120] Given that the organization that was subsequently established—the Asian Women's Fund—was funded partly by the government and partly by the private sector, and was headquartered in Japan,[121] the original proposal by the Miyazawa administration was obviously far more in line with South Korean demands than what was ultimately realized by the Murayama administration. But South Korean advocacy groups for the comfort women expressed their opposition to the proposal,[122] and the South Korean government then demurred as well.[123] The reason given was that the facts had not been sufficiently investigated, and their basic argument was that no initiative would be acceptable if the Japanese government would not admit to coercive recruitment. The calculation may well have been that if only they could force the Japanese government to admit to coercion, South Korea would stand at a huge advantage in any subsequent negotiations.

What made things even more difficult for the Japanese government was the international attention that the issue was now drawing. Developments between Japan and South Korea spurred to action other countries involved in the comfort women issue. Governments and private-sector groups in China, Taiwan, the Philippines, and other countries began demanding that the Japanese government investigate the facts of the comfort women issue in their countries and provide appropriate compensation.[124] The issue even affected the negotiations on the normalization of relations between Japan and North Korea that were underway at the time. The North Korean government announced that it supported the view of the South Korean government and also demanded compensation from the Japanese government.[125] As a result, the comfort women issue escalated from a bilateral one between Japan and South Korea into an international concern that would later be taken up by the United Nations Sub-Commission on the Promotion and Protection of Human Rights.[126]

It was then that the Japanese government had a stroke of luck. As noted above, in February 1993, Kim Young-sam, who had taken over the presidency from Roh, announced that he did not intend to seek material compensation from Japan, and that the key issue was for the Japanese side to uncover the truth, with assistance for the victims to be provided out of the South Korean government budget. This was on March 13, 1993.[127]

Significantly, Kim's announcement was consistent with the position of the Japanese government, namely that all claims had been settled under the Claims Settlement Agreement. The Japanese side took this as evidence that Kim wanted to resolve the issue quickly and build a new bilateral relationship, and thus expedited its efforts to find a solution.[128] The day after Kim's comment, the Japanese government made a complete turnaround on its former position that oral testimony did not constitute proof and announced its intention to conduct its own interviews with former comfort women living in South Korea.[129] In addition, it released a new definition of coercive recruitment that included not only physical coercion but also cases of coercion through threats and other such nonphysical means.[130] In other words, the government adjusted its definition of coercion in order to widen the target area for its upcoming investigation. One paper summed this up neatly as the Japanese government recognizing that documentation alone could not provide the proof of coercion required by the South Koreans and opting instead to change its policy.[131]

The South Korean government responded to these Japanese moves by stating that individual victims would still be free to make claims for compensation or press lawsuits, opening the way for Japan's proposed remedy of establishing a foundation. The government also made additional demands, such as the inclusion of references to the comfort women issue in Japanese history textbooks.[132] On May 18, the Korean National Assembly passed legislation on the provision of financial assistance to secure a steady livelihood for those who had served as comfort women during Japanese colonial rule, laying the groundwork for the South Korean government to pay de facto compensation to former comfort women.[133] The only remaining issue appeared to be the Japanese government's fact-finding investigations—and specifically its interviews with former comfort women.

Rushed Statement

However, the Japanese government immediately ran into trouble with its investigations when the Chôngdaehyop, South Korea's most influential comfort women advocacy group, reacted to these efforts by the Japanese and South Korean governments to reach a political solution by refusing to cooperate on the grounds that they were inadequate.[134] In the absence of documentation demonstrating coercion, the Japanese government needed the testimonies of former comfort women in order to be able to acknowledge that coercion had actually occurred. Caught at an impasse, the two governments could only watch time slip needlessly by.

Meanwhile, major political change was underway in Japan, bringing the Miyazawa administration to a rapid end. In May 1993, a schism surfaced in the LDP between the party's executives and young Diet members pushing for political reform, leaving the LDP seriously divided. As a result, some Diet members sided with a no-confidence motion tabled by the opposition on June 18, forcing the Miyazawa cabinet to dissolve the lower house. The internal dispute ended with the LDP splitting and two new parties forming: the Japan Renewal Party, led by Ozawa Ichirō and Hata Tsutomu, and New Party Sakigake, created by Takemura Masayoshi.[135]

With the cabinet under threat, the usual procedure would be for the government to suspend all action on important diplomatic issues (such as the comfort women issue) because there would be no guarantee that it could meet commitments made in diplomatic negotiations. The Miyazawa administration, however, rushed to resolve the comfort women issue. On June 29, eleven days after the no-confidence motion passed, the government sent its foreign minister to South Korea, apparently because of a de facto agreement between the two governments to resolve the comfort women issue while their current administrations were still in power.[136]

It should be remembered, however, that with the lower house dissolved but general elections yet to take place, at the time there was still a chance that the Miyazawa administration might remain in power.[137] In fact, the July 18 general elections saw the LDP seize more seats than it had remaining after the party split, holding on to its status as top party.[138] What toppled Miyazawa and the LDP was losing the coalition battle with the anti-LDP group led by the JSP and the Japan Renewal Party.[139] Both sides were vying to bring on board the Japan New Party and New Party Sakigake to form a coalition government, and Miyazawa, finding himself under attack from both within and outside the LDP as the major obstacle to that coalition, announced on July 22 that he would step down.[140]

Even then, the Miyazawa cabinet continued its efforts on the comfort women issue. Going back to July 16, two days before the general elections, the Association of Pacific War Victims and Bereaved Families, the second most influential comfort women advocacy group in South Korea after the Chôngdaehyop, had decided that it would allow Japan to conduct a study, and the Japanese government sent an investigation team to South Korea.[141] Interviews with sixteen former comfort women were initially scheduled to be conducted on July 26 and 27 (actually continuing until July 30)[142]—in other words, after Miyazawa had decided to resign his post. Meanwhile, back in Japan, the anti-LDP group continued to work on a coalition, agreeing on July 29 to create an administration with Hosokawa Morihiro at the helm.[143] Effectively left out in the cold, the LDP elected former Chief Cabinet Secretary Kōno Yōhei as party president the next day.[144] This was the long summer in which the LDP finally relinquished its decades-long hold on power and crossed the aisle into the opposition seats.

On August 4, Kōno himself announced the results of the comfort women investigations.[145] Specifically, the government released a document entitled "On the Issue of 'Comfort Women'" in the name of the Cabinet Councillors' Office on External Affairs, and this was supplemented by the "Statement by Chief Cabinet Secretary Kōno Yōhei on the Result of the Study on the Issue of 'Comfort Women,'" otherwise known as the Kōno Statement.[146] With an extraordinary Diet session already scheduled for August 5 to appoint a new prime minister, it was also Kōno's last press conference as chief cabinet secretary. The statement dealt with the key issue of coercion as follows:

> The recruitment of the comfort women was conducted mainly by private recruiters who acted in response to the request of the military. The government study has revealed that in many cases they were recruited against their own will, through coaxing, coercion, etc., and that, at times, administrative/military personnel directly took part in the recruitment.[147]

It should be noted that while the two Katō Statements focused primarily on the recruiting of comfort women from the Korean peninsula, the Kōno Statement covered comfort women in general, including those from other regions. It had already become clear from materials that the Imperial Japanese Army had coercively recruited comfort women from the Chinese mainland and parts of Southeast Asia. To that extent, the Kōno Statement's observation that "*at times*, administrative/military personnel directly took part in the recruitment" (emphasis inserted by the author) was certainly not a mistake. In other words, the statement skillfully manages to admit that the recruiting of comfort women was in fact coercive by adding the results of investigations in South Korea to already verified cases in China and Southeast Asia. In fact, at the press conference after his statement,

Photo 3. Chief Cabinet Secretary Kōno Yōhei gives a press conference on the comfort women issue (August 4, 1993). (Jiji Press.)

Kōno made specific reference to the Semarang incident, which involved coercive recruiting of comfort women in what is now Indonesia. According to reports at the time, government officials clearly acknowledged that the Kōno Statement had been created with incidents such as these in mind.

What is sometimes misunderstood is that the statement is not a concrete admission of direct and organized conscription of comfort women by the Japanese government, much less a declaration that all comfort women were coercively recruited. In fact, Deputy Chief Cabinet Secretary Ishihara Nobuo recalled in an interview conducted by the Asian Women's Fund that he had thought there was no question that most of the comfort women had been recruited by private recruiters.[148] It is also clear from the testimony of other government officials at the time that they did not believe that all comfort women had been coercively recruited. From this perspective, the Kōno Statement was a very cleverly crafted piece of language, typical of the deliberately ambiguous responses that Japan-South Korea relations were producing at the time.

If there was a clear problem with the statement, it lay more with the hasty nature of its announcement in the last days of the departing Miyazawa administration.[149] In any case, in the context of the times, the Kōno Statement was the product of political compromise between the Japanese and South Korean governments, which meant that both governments had to bear responsibility for it. However, the Miyazawa cabinet was dissolved before it could meet its obligations, and eventually the Kōno Statement would end up being abandoned even by the South Korean government.

8. From the Murayama Statement to the Asian Women's Fund

An Indian Summer under the Hosokawa Administration

The Kōno Statement drew varied assessments. For example, *The New York Times* felt that it marked "welcome progress" in the historical perception dispute.[150] China's Xinhua News Agency also regarded the statement as an official admission and apology from the Japanese government for coercively recruiting women from Asia, and particularly from the Korean peninsula, as comfort women.[151]

However, advocacy groups were far cooler in their response. The Association of Pacific War Victims and Bereaved Families in South Korea, which had earlier cooperated in the Japanese government's investigations, criticized the statement for going no further than a vague admission of Japanese government involvement, while the Chŏngdaehyŏp was even more dismissive, excoriating the statement as an attempt to bring investigations to a close while avoiding examination of the real heart of the issue. At the United Nations Sub-Commission on Prevention of Discrimination and Protection of Minorities, a representative from a South Korean private-sector association criticized the Japanese government report as "far from the truth," joining with the North Korean government's representative in attacking the statement.[152]

The South Korean government initially welcomed the Kōno Statement with open arms as closely reflecting its own viewpoint. The issue could now be removed from the diplomatic agenda between the two countries, the government said approvingly, adding that the greatest obstacle between South Korea and Japan had been removed.[153] The South Korean government had been seeking a way to wind up the comfort women issue and seized upon the Kōno Statement as the perfect opportunity. The Japanese government was also strongly hopeful that the statement would bring a final resolution to the problem, as evinced in Kōno's assertion that "the investigations have now been concluded."[154]

In addition, the advent of a new administration in Japan provided an opportunity to further improve relations between the two countries. The Hosokawa administration that came to power in 1993 was the first non-LDP government in thirty-eight years, and together with Kim Young-sam's emergence as South Korea's first nonmilitary leader in thirty-three years, seemed to set the stage for a new, "future-oriented" Japan-South Korea relationship.[155]

Both sides were well aware of the importance of this opportunity. Immediately after his appointment as prime minister, Hosokawa Morihiro remarked that the Pacific War had been a war of aggression and a mistake, going beyond any previous administration in expressing his historical perception of this issue.[156] Hosokawa's position was warmly welcomed in South Korea,[157] and the two countries agreed to hold summit talks at the earliest possible opportunity.[158] The summit was realized with Hosokawa's November 1993 visit to South Korea.[159] At the meeting, which opened with the two leaders offering each other encouragement in relation to the political reforms each was undertaking at home, Hosokawa said:

> I would like to express my regret and deep apologies to the victims for the unbearable suffering they have experienced through the Japanese colonial rule, for example as "comfort women" or conscripted laborers or through the fact that Koreans were deprived of the chance to learn their own language at school and that they had to change their surnames to Japanese names.

Kim lauded this apology, noting that the South Korean people were deeply moved. It was an Indian summer for Japan-South Korean relations.[160]

The Murayama Cabinet and the Historical Perception Dispute

However, this came to a sudden end on April 8, 1994, only five months after the highly successful summit talks, partly due to Hosokawa's resignation in the face of a political donation scandal.[161] Subsequently, the bilateral relationship deteriorated rapidly, as epitomized by Kim Young-sam's slangy comment at a November 1995 South Korea-China summit that South Korea would "give Japan a licking and cure it of its bad habits"—a manifestation of South Korea's irritation with Japan.[162] Given that this was only a year and a half after Hosokawa's resignation, the speed with which the situation was changing is apparent.

This seems strange, because the Hata and Murayama cabinets that followed the collapse of Hosokawa's government, and particularly the latter, are regarded in Japan as more proactive than any of their predecessors in efforts to resolve the historical perception dispute. Murayama Tomiichi, known for his August 1995 statement—"On the Fiftieth Anniversary of the End of World War II," or the Murayama Statement—was probably the most committed in this regard of all Japan's postwar prime ministers.[163] Moreover, he was supported in his efforts by foreign minister and LDP president Kōno Yōhei—the same Kōno who released the Kōno Statement.[164] Despite these apparent positives, however, the Murayama administration struggled with various aspects of the historical perception dispute from the time it took power in June 1994.

What was the problem? A comparison with the Hosokawa administration may be instructive. The first difference between the two administrations lay in the extent to which they were seeking a concrete resolution of the historical perception dispute. Hosokawa held power from August 1993 to April 1994, during which time he made positive comments on the issue but did not attempt to produce any concrete results (in part because of the brevity of his administration). Despite this, Japan-South Korea relations remained relatively tranquil during this period, for the obvious reason that, with both governments anxious to avoid the comfort women issue as a diplomatic concern in the wake of the Kōno Statement, doing nothing actually constituted a major diplomatic action.

This was an issue that reached to the heart of the historical perception dispute between Japan and South Korea. As I have already noted several times, issues of historical perception are not as concerned with the facts of history as they are with our perception of the historical facts. For dispute to arise over an issue, in addition to discovery of the issue, two other conditions must pertain: there must be differences in historical perception and importance must be ascribed to these differences.

There are accordingly two conditions for the escalation of disputes over historical perception. One is that differences in perception become apparent, and the other is that meaning is attributed to them. Conversely, therefore, to the extent that neither South Korea nor Japan clearly identify the differences in their perceptions nor grant importance to those differ-

Photo 4. Prime Minister Murayama Tomiichi making his statement on the fiftieth anniversary of the end of World War II (August 15, 1995). (Jiji Press.)

ences, disputes will not escalate. In this sense, Hosokawa made the right choice when he offered up various isolated comments on issues of historical perception but never drew them together into a coherent and substantive statement. This enabled the Japanese and South Korean governments and media to interpret his comments as they saw fit, with the differences in the two countries' perceptions never clearly emerging.

Murayama, however, set out from the start to resolve the dispute and sought to use the opportunity of the fiftieth anniversary of the end of World War II to announce a coherent position on historical perception as a key cabinet policy.[165] In short, his administration itself declared that historical perceptions were important and set out its own perceptions in a coherent form. However, as is the case today, there was an insurmountable barrier between Japanese and South Korean historical perceptions, and those expressed by the Murayama cabinet were inevitably far from what the South Korean government had hoped for. The South Korean government consequently rebuffed this overture and the chasm between the two governments ultimately deepened. In the end, what Murayama managed to do was satisfy the precise conditions required to escalate the historical perception issue into a dispute by clearly identifying the differences in the respective historical perceptions of Japan and South Korea and flagging them as important. As a result, the Murayama Statement and the actions of the Japanese government in the lead-up to it virtually threw down a gauntlet to the South Korean government over the historical perception issue—exactly the opposite of Murayama's own intentions.

Statements by Weak Governments

There was another major difference between the Hosokawa and Murayama administrations. During the former, ministers and key ruling party figures barely responded to Hosokawa's comments about issues of historical perception. In the case of the Murayama administration, however, a whole string of comments—characterized as "irresponsible statements" by the South Korean side—were made by both ministers and key ruling party figures that clearly contradicted the historical perspective expressed by Prime Minister Murayama himself.[166]

Table 5.1 compiles various "irresponsible statements" made on key issues of historical perception during the 1980s and 1990s. The exceptional situation during the Murayama administration is apparent at a glance—and not just in terms of the number of incidents. For example, the "irresponsible statements" during the Nakasone and Takeshita administrations were made by individual politicians with opinions of their own on issues of historical perception, none of whom enjoyed particularly high status within the cabinet or the ruling Liberal Democratic Party, and most were promptly dismissed following their comments.

In the case of the Murayama administration, however, most of the "irresponsible statements" were made by ministers and key figures from the LDP—one element of the coalition government—whose status within

Table 5.1. Key "irresponsible statements" of the 1980s and 1990s

	Prime Minister	Source of statement	Status	Subject
9/17/1984	Nakasone Yasuhiro	Fujio Masayuki	Chairman, LDP Policy Research Council	Imperial Rescript on Education
7/25/1986	Nakasone Yasuhiro	Fujio Masayuki	Minister of Education	War of aggression
9/6/1986	Nakasone Yasuhiro	Fujio Masayuki	Minister of Education	War of aggression, annexation of Korea, Nanking Incident
4/22/1988	Takeshita Noboru	Okuno Seisuke	Director-General, National Land Agency	War of aggression
5/10/1988	Takeshita Noboru	Okuno Seisuke	Director-General, National Land Agency	Aggression, Yasukuni Shrine
5/4/1994	Hata Tsutomu	Nagano Shigeto	Minister of Justice	Aggression, Nanking Incident
8/9/1994	Murayama Tomiichi	Shimamura Yoshinobu	Minister of Education	War of aggression
8/12/1994	Murayama Tomiichi	Sakurai Shin	Director-General, Environment Agency	War of aggression, "good" colonial rule
10/12/1995	Murayama Tomiichi	Murayama Tomiichi	Prime Minister	Annexation of Korea
10/24/1994	Murayama Tomiichi	Hashimoto Ryūtarō	Minister of International Trade and Industry	War of aggression
6/3/1995	Murayama Tomiichi	Watanabe Michio	LDP Vice President	Annexation of Korea
11/9/1995	Murayama Tomiichi	Etō Takami	Director-General, Management and Coordination Agency	Annexation of Korea, "good" colonial rule, enforced name changes

Source: Created by the author from *Maisaku* (*Mainichi shimbun*) and Kawano Noriyuki, "Kakuryo shitsugen no seijigaku" (The political science of ministerial gaffes), *Kokusai kyōryoku ronshū*, Vol. 7, No. 1, 2001, Hiroshima University Graduate School for International Development and Cooperation.

the administration was extremely high. Consequently, the reaction of the South Korean government to their comments was inevitably much stronger. In the face of repeated "irresponsible statements," the South Korean government became disillusioned with the Murayama administration's apparent lack of good faith and Japan-South Korea relations deteriorated still further, with a vicious cycle emerging.

Why did this situation develop? The cause was extremely simple. Despite working hard to develop a coherent ministerial position on historical perceptions, Murayama lacked the necessary political base to bring his ministers on board. Established in 1994, the Murayama cabinet was a three-party coalition comprising the LDP, the Japan Socialist Party, and the minor New Party Sakigake. Murayama was merely the leader of the second-largest coalition partner, the JSP. The LDP and the JSP had been on opposite sides of the ideological fence during the Cold War, and their perceptions of Japan's past were also extremely different.

Reconciling the historical perceptions of the two biggest parties within the coalition was therefore essential. An additional problem was that the JSP had opted to base the administration's official perspective on issues of historical perception on its own position, in exchange for bringing its stance on security closer to that of the LDP. This choice was shaped by the high priority that Murayama himself placed on resolving Japan's historical perception issues with other Asian countries. Murayama's commitment to this campaign was so great that he would later suggest that it constituted the entire meaning of his prime ministership.[167]

However, since he was only the leader of the second-largest coalition partner, Murayama lacked the political muscle to force LDP politicians to share his historical perception. The same could be said of LDP president Kōno Yōhei, who was number two in the administration. Kōno's political clout as party leader had declined significantly with his failure to seize the prime minister's seat across three administrations—Hosokawa, Hata, and Murayama—and by this point he could not even hold his own faction together.[168] When he allowed the opposition New Frontier Party to gain a significant edge in the July 1995 upper house elections, he was forced to give up his leadership of the party. Ironically, he was replaced by Hashimoto Ryūtarō, who had come out with one of the highest-profile "irresponsible statements" under the Murayama administration.[169]

The Annexation of Korea—Lawful or Unlawful?

Among the string of "irresponsible statements" by ministers during the Murayama administration, the first major stumble was Hashimoto's assertion that it was a matter of "subtle definition" as to whether Japan had intended to wage a war of aggression against its Asian neighbors.[170] Hashimoto was serving in the key post of minister of international trade and industry and was recognized as a leading LDP hardliner, so his words were headlined by the South Korean media. The South Korean government also condemned the comment as an attempt to gloss over Japan's invasion of Asia, and the Japanese government had to scramble to calm the situation.[171]

The situation was still not that serious, as the South Korean government subsequently chose to accept the Japanese government's claim that Hashimoto's comment was premised on his acknowledgment of Japan's invasion of China and its colonial rule over the Korean peninsula—reflecting the South Korean government's desire at that stage to prevent the issue from blowing up any further.[172]

The critical turning point came with remarks made by former deputy prime minister Watanabe Michio, a senior politician and a strong candidate for the LDP leadership after Hashimoto, on June 3, 1995. Watanabe observed that "the government's position is that the annexation of Korea was in accordance with international law. . . . The Treaty of Annexation was an amicably concluded international agreement."[173]

What is important here is that while the Hashimoto and Watanabe comments might appear to be similar, they actually contain clear differences. First, Hashimoto's comment was made in the context of remarks about Japan's past, whereas Watanabe's comment was made in isolation. This was why Watanabe's comment was greeted by the South Korean government and public as a provocation directly targeting South Korea. There was another, more important difference—the fact that Watanabe raised the issue of the legality or illegality of the annexation, which had major implications for the legitimacy of South Korea as a state. For example, the preamble to the South Korean Constitution of today begins, "We, the people of Korea, proud of a resplendent history and traditions dating from time immemorial, upholding the cause of the Provisional Government of the Republic of Korea born of the March First Independence Movement of 1919. . . ."[174] The implication is that the Republic of Korea is the legitimate successor the Korean Empire, proclaimed in 1897, with sovereignty passing from the absolute rule of the Korean emperor to the Korean people.

It should be noted that this ignores Japanese colonial rule, which occupied the period between the Korean Empire and the Republic of Korea. South Korea's reasoning was that Japan's colonial rule was unlawful, and therefore legally null and void. In other words, Japan's colonial rule was not based on a legally valid agreement between Imperial Japan and the Korean

Empire but rather unilaterally imposed through Japanese military force. Premised on this understanding, the period of Japanese colonial rule was referred to in modern Korean history textbooks as a period during which Korea was forcibly occupied by Japan. According to this interpretation, if the annexation of Korea was legally void, then the sovereignty of the Korean Empire continued to exist even subsequent to the annexation, to be inherited by the Republic of Korea. Between these two governments lay the Provisional Government of the Republic of Korea, established immediately after the March First Independence Movement of 1919. In other words, state legitimacy on the Korean peninsula passed from the Korean Empire to the Provisional Government to the Republic of Korea directly, untouched by Japanese colonial rule.[175]

This argument was originally used by South Korea to assert the superiority of its legitimacy over that of the Democratic People's Republic of Korea in the northern half of the peninsula. However, South Korea's grounding of its own legitimacy as a state in such an argument inevitably cast a long shadow over the debate between Japan and South Korea on colonial rule, in that it required Japanese colonial rule to be regarded as unlawful. Japan's consistent official view was that its annexation of Korea was legal under international law at the time, and this was regarded as a line that could not be crossed in the various discussions on compensation for colonial rule.[176]

Accordingly, South Korean and Japanese governments prior to the Murayama administration made various efforts to avoid this tricky issue of principle. One such effort was Article II in the 1965 Treaty on Basic Relations between Japan and the Republic of Korea, which states, "It is confirmed that all treaties or agreements concluded between the Empire of Japan and the Empire of Korea on or before August 22, 1910, are already null and void." The Japanese side interpreted this to mean that all past agreements including the Treaty of Annexation were rendered null and void by the Treaty on Basic Relations, while the South Korean side interpreted the same article as meaning that all past agreements including the Treaty of Annexation had been null and void from the outset.[177] While it might be unthinkable today, at the time, though government officials openly pointed out these different interpretations of the same article to their respective parliaments, these differences did not become a major issue for either government or their peoples. Efforts to avoid problems in relation to legal interpretations of the annexation continued even in the 1980s. For example, when Fujio Masayuki asserted in 1986 that the annexation was carried out through mutual agreement, Prime Minister Nakasone promptly fired him.[178]

Watanabe's comment about the legality of the annexation therefore opened up a Pandora's Box that both governments had worked very hard to keep shut. Faced with criticism of his comment, Watanabe immediately issued a statement retracting his reference to an amicable annexation, but he did not withdraw his claim that the annexation was lawful,[179] for the very good reason that his assertion that the annexation of Korea was in accordance with international law was in fact consistent with the Japanese government's official position.[180]

The Collapse of Historical Perception Efforts

Even more important was the timing of Watanabe's remarks, which came right as discussion was heating up over the content of a proposed Diet resolution on the fiftieth anniversary of the end of World War II, which would lead directly to the Murayama Statement. Watanabe's comments were made in the midst of debate on this subject at the convention of Tochigi Prefecture LDP branches. What they reveal is the strong opposition within the LDP to the Murayama cabinet's perception of history.

In fact, there was a serious division of opinion within the ruling coalition over the content of the proposed Diet resolution. A group of 210 lower house Diet members from the LDP formed the League of Parliamentarians on the Fiftieth Anniversary of the End of World War II to protest the Murayama administration's proposed resolution, saying that they could not accept a resolution that would create historical problems for the future.[181] After various twists and turns, consensus was reached within the ruling parties on this issue on the evening of June 6, only three days after Watanabe's remarks.[182]

Drafted amidst the peculiar political circumstances of the time, the resolution was inevitably flawed. Power relations within the coalition meant that the resolution had to be equivocal, and in fact it represented a retreat from the historical perceptions expressed during the Hosokawa administration.[183] As a result, despite Murayama's strong commitment, the announcement of the resolution and the concomitant turmoil were viewed overseas as evidence that Japan's historical perceptions were in fact shifting to the right. The resolution was savaged by some elements of the Japanese media and also failed to garner a positive reception from many Asian countries.[184] The state-run Korean Broadcasting System (KBS) criticized the removal of the terms "apology" and "renunciation of war,"[185] and the South Korean government also responded negatively, arguing that the resolution sought to avoid taking direct responsibility for Japan's colonial rule of Korea and other matters.[186]

The Failure of the Asian Women's Fund

The turmoil within the Murayama administration over historical perceptions also had an impact on measures related to the comfort women. As noted earlier, from the time of the Miyazawa administration, the Japanese government had been considering creating some sort of foundation to pay former comfort women a solatium as a way of resolving the issue. The Murayama administration introduced the concept of establishing a foundation that would be funded entirely by the private sector, but when this was criticized by the public and by South Korean advocacy groups, the organization was launched as a private foundation funded half by the government and half by the private sector, and named the Asian Women's Fund (AWF).[187]

The AWF concept emerged in June 1995, the same month that the final decision was made on the content of the Diet Resolution on the Fiftieth Anniversary of the End of World War II.[188] The South Korean government commented immediately after the announcement that it was a sincere gesture that reflected to some degree the demands of the parties involved, so it would appear to have not regarded the AWF negatively at the outset.[189]

Subsequently, the South Korean government's stance would change dramatically. In 1996, it formally made additional demands to the Japanese government concerning the AWF on the grounds that it wanted to see a resolution that would satisfy the victims.[190] Then, in 1997, the South Korean government asked that solatium payments from the AWF be terminated.[191]

This change in the South Korean government's attitude to the comfort women issue was not the result of internal political circumstances such as a change of government or reshuffling of key personnel, as Kim Young-sam remained president throughout, while his foreign minister was Gong Ro-myung, a diplomat known as one of South Korea's leading Japan hands.[192]

What, then, caused the change? A key factor, along with activism by South Korean comfort women advocacy groups, was the government's rapid loss of faith in the Japanese government. Ironically, this dwindling confidence was primarily brought about by the comment of none other than Prime Minister Murayama, who stated at an October 5, 1995 plenary session of the House of Councillors his belief that in the historical context of international relations at that time, Japan had signed and carried out the Treaty of Annexation legally.[193] As noted earlier, the South Korean government regarded the question of the legality or illegality of the annexation of Korea as directly involving the legitimacy of the South Korean state and

Photo 5. "Wednesday demonstration" in front of the Japanese Embassy in Seoul (March 13, 2002). (Jiji Press.) This was the 500th Wednesday demonstration.

could not afford to make any concession on the issue, which is why the South Korean government and public reacted so angrily to Murayama's remark.[194]

However, the Japanese government and public did not really understand the importance of the issue. Most of the Japanese media paid little attention to Murayama's remark, which first received coverage only days later when North Korea lodged a protest.[195] Even after that media coverage, Murayama's response was that his real intention was quite clear from the plenary session minutes, clearly revealing that the prime minister had no idea the uproar his comment would provoke in South Korea.[196]

However, the South Korean reaction was extreme. In Seoul, major anti-Japan demonstrations broke out and effigies of Murayama were burnt in the streets.[197] One person infuriated by Murayama's comment was none other than President Kim Young-sam. Immediately after the remark became public, Kim observed that Japan continued to make comments that distorted history, and he extended his dissatisfaction to the Murayama administration's policy toward North Korea (which really had nothing to do with the issue), saying that Japan was obstructing unification.[198] Given that Kim Young-sam had a cordial relationship with the Japan Socialist Party dating back to the 1980s, his comments are indicative of how deeply he was affected by Murayama's remarks. His confidence in Japan would never recover, and his offhand comment mentioned earlier about curing Japan of its bad habits was in fact made at the South Korea-China summit talks held immediately after the Murayama incident.[199]

In any case, the Murayama administration's efforts to address the historical perception issue ultimately caused significant injury to bilateral relations—exactly the opposite of what Murayama had intended. Kim Young-sam lost any desire to cooperate with Japan, which left the AWF high and dry and dealt a fatal blow to the strenuous efforts made by many individuals to get the AWF to that stage. In addition, with Japan wasting the valuable diplomatic card of providing what was effectively compensation paid through a Japanese-funded foundation, the comfort women issue would slip into an even deeper quagmire.

Conclusion

In this chapter I examined the evolution of the comfort women issue from the early 1990s to the middle of the decade, demonstrating this to be the time in which the influence of and solidarity between the ruling elites of Japan and South Korea that had prevailed until the late 1980s finally broke down.

In South Korea, control of the comfort women issue moved into the hands of a progressive anti-administration movement, with the influence of the ruling elite over the matter dwindling rapidly. In the end, court action by newly active civilian groups forced both the Japanese and South Korean governments to respond officially to the issue.

The power of the ruling elite was also declining in Japan. A January 1992 scoop by *Asahi shimbun* forced the Japanese government onto the defensive, and it initiated a series of confused responses. Talks between the Japanese and South Korean leaders during this period led to a loss of the solidarity that had previously existed between the ruling elites when the South Korean side opted to play the comfort women card against the Japanese side in response to Japan's failure to help South Korea out with the trade deficit between the two countries. This decision was influenced by the political situation in South Korea prior to a presidential election, which led the South Korean ruling elite to sacrifice Japan-South Korea relations momentarily for the sake of political benefit at home. The period in which the imbalance in economic power between the two countries forced an economically weak South Korea to rely on the economic giant of Japan and, consequently, to make perpetual concessions to it, was drawing to a close.

The two key factors were the end of the Cold War and South Korea's own economic growth. Without the Cold War, there was no further reason for close security cooperation, and this began to change the way in which the ruling elites of both countries dealt with each other. The end of the Cold War also influenced the domestic situation in both countries, manifesting in the form of greater activism in civil society. Both ruling elites consequently lost their ability to control the situation, as well as their political leeway. Repeated rash statements in relation to the historical perception dispute made by LDP politicians during the Murayama years and the South Korean reaction to these closed the door entirely on cooperative ties.

As the situation evolved, the ruling elites of both countries began to foreground issues of historical perception, damaging bilateral relations. In the next chapter, I look at how this new situation developed, with a particular focus on Japan.

SIX

Issues of Historical Perception during Japan's "Lost" Twenty Years

1. Changing Japanese Society

The Textbook Reform Society

Bilateral relations became deadlocked over the historical perception dispute in the mid-1990s, primarily as a result of the comfort women issue. However, this development had an impact on more than just international relations between the two countries. In the early 1990s, the historical perception dispute changed Japanese society in a way that had major consequences for the subsequent trajectory of historical perception issues—in other words, the emergence of nationalism. As we have seen, these issues typically followed a predictable course: the South Korean side would raise an issue, and the Japanese side would respond. This was partly due to lobbying by liberal—or, in the Korean terminology, "conscientious"[1]— Japanese in support of South Korean initiatives. There were only a few sporadic efforts on the Japanese side to oppose or counter South Korean moves (the case of the *New Version of Japanese History*, for example), and their impact was extremely limited.

However, the escalation of bilateral issues of historical perception inevitably heightened awareness in Japanese society, prompting new attempts in the late 1990s to respond proactively to actions by South Korea and other neighboring countries. A key example was the Society for History Textbook Reform (below, "Textbook Reform Society"), formally launched in 1997.[2]

The implications of the social climate in Japan in the late 1990s become apparent when we compare how matters stood in 1997, when the Textbook Reform Society was established, with the situation back in 1986, when the *New Version of Japanese History* was published. As observed earlier, it was the Nihon o Mamoru Kokumin Kaigi (People's Conference to Protect Japan), established in 1981, that spearheaded the development of the *New Version of Japanese History*. The group's prior incarnation was the 1978 People's Conference for Realization of an Era Name Law, the brainchild of former Supreme Court Chief Justice Ishida Kazuto.[3] As is evident from the political circumstances surrounding the Era Name Law, the agenda of the People's Conference to Protect Japan was closely linked to the ruling Liberal Democratic Party, and particularly its hardliners. The roster of People's Conference executives featured major corporate executives and leaders of pressure groups supporting the LDP. In short, the People's Conference was made up of members of the ruling elite—officials of the LDP administration, its right wing, and their close associates. Therefore, in the dispute over the *New Version of Japanese History*, the Japanese government found it relatively easy to control fellow members of the elite.

The origins of the Textbook Reform Society were entirely different from that of the People's Conference. Inspired by Fujioka Nobukatsu's "liberal" view of history (which advocated a revisionist, "positive view" of Japanese history), Nishio Kanji and fellow intellectuals held their first press conference in December 1996, announcing the group's formal establishment and inaugural general meeting in January 1997.[4] It is interesting that the first major effort by the Textbook Reform Society was to call on the Ministry of Education to remove references to the comfort women from textbooks.[5] This was in December 1996,[6] even before the Textbook Reform Society's inaugural general meeting, and epitomized the way in which the group's activities followed the trajectory of the comfort women issue in the early 1990s.

In addition to Nishio Kanji, who became the first chairman of the group, the Textbook Reform Society's original proponents were Agawa Sawako, Kobayashi Yoshinori, Sakamoto Takao, Takahashi Shirō, Hayashi Mariko, Fukuda Yūsuke, Fujioka Nobukatsu, and Yamamoto Natsuhiko.[7] One of the group's key characteristics was the absence of any of the major corporate leaders and executives from major pressure groups who had held key posts in the People's Conference. The group set itself clearly apart from traditional conservative groups even in its method of appealing to the public, as exemplified by the fact that when the Textbook Reform Society was first established, its de facto spokesman was the cartoonist Kobayashi Yoshinori. Kobayashi had built up his own following through his controversial manga series Gōmanism Sengen (literally the "Arrogance Manifesto," which offered right-wing political and social commentary with a nationalist slant) since publication began in 1992, and he was a pivotal figure in the Textbook Reform Society's early activities.[8]

Of course, like the People's Conference, the Textbook Reform Society also had many supporters who were corporate executives, leaders of major pressure groups, and so forth—but they had a minimal role in the group's activities. In fact, when the Textbook Reform Society was first established, its chair, deputy chair, and directors were all academics like Nishio or writers like Saikawa Eita.[9] The only representative from the world of finance among the directors—Koga Tadashi, a Toray Rayon counsellor—was so exceptional as to be striking.[10] As is apparent from the subsequent fierce battle over the chair and directorships, it was the individuals in these posts who exercised the real power, leaving the group's supporters with a very limited influence.

Why did this movement, so different from anything previous, gain traction in Japanese society in the late 1990s? And what impact did that movement have on the trajectory of the historical perception dispute between Japan and South Korea?

Changing Textbook Content

The emergence of the Textbook Reform Society was indicative of the major changes then occurring in the situation surrounding the historical perception dispute. The first of these concerned history textbooks. As noted earlier, contrary to popular understanding, Japan's history textbooks were rapidly becoming more liberal during this period. There was also a huge increase in the number of references to modern Japan-South Korea relations—incomparably more than in the 1960s and 1970s.

This was mainly due to the growing seriousness of the dispute over Japan's history textbooks. A key issue was the existence of the "neighboring country clause" added to the textbook authorization criteria in 1982, which called for textbooks to show understanding and seek international harmony in their treatment of modern and contemporary historical events involving neighboring Asian countries. Yet the clause was not actually invoked with any frequency in the textbook screening process. According to *Yomiuri shimbun*, it was first applied in 1991, and then again in 1992 and 1993, but there is no evidence it was used after 1994. In other words, it appears that the neighboring country clause was implemented in only a very limited number of cases.[11]

Yet this did not mean that the editorial process of textbook publishers was not influenced by the clause. For example, in 1998, after the Textbook Reform Society had formed, there was an incident in which the chief textbook examiner commented in a roundtable discussion organized by a monthly magazine that textbooks really should state that Japan was wrong to stage a war of aggression, and that Japan's overly rigid system was to blame—and found himself replaced as a result.[12] Regardless of the mechanism, the existence of the neighboring country clause undeniably exerted influence, albeit indirectly, on textbook editing.

However, around the period the Textbook Reform Society was launched the situation was changing, with the debate over the comfort women issue playing a major role in the steady increase in the number of references to comfort women in history textbooks. For example, in 1992, when the issue came to the fore, only one of the twenty Japanese history textbooks used in Japanese high schools contained a reference to comfort women,[13] but references to the comfort women appeared in all nine of the high school Japanese history textbooks that passed the June 1993 screening conducted just before the Kōno Statement.[14] This trend continued despite various complications, and all junior high school social studies textbooks in the 1996 screening included references to comfort women.[15]

It was at this time that the Liberal View of History Study Group emerged under the leadership of Fujioka Nobukatsu, who had founded the Textbook Reform Society alongside Nishio Kanji.[16] Fujioka was a professor of education, not a historian, and his criticism was directed from the outset not at the historical facts but at history education in Japan. He and his colleagues were dissatisfied with the way in which Japan's history education was dominated, on the one hand, by a Marxist perspective with a negative view of post-Meiji Restoration Japan, and on the other, by a view of history shaped by the Tokyo war crimes trials. Fujioka's group sought to redress what they regarded as a sorry state of affairs,[17] a perspective that would form the framework for their subsequent criticism of what they regarded as "masochistic" readings of history.[18] They pointed to the references to the comfort women issue in a growing number of textbooks as the epitome of that masochism and launched a national movement to have comfort women references removed.[19]

As noted above, the efforts of Fujioka and company subsequently crystallized in the Textbook Reform Society, supported by Fujioka's fellow founder Nishio Kanji. As a result, the comfort women issue had a central place in the Textbook Reform Society's initial program. The new organization provoked a major social response even before it was officially formed. In politics, for example, the Diet Members' Alliance for a Bright Japan, a group within the LDP, adopted a resolution in September 1996 calling for the removal of comfort women references,[20] which was followed in December by the Diet Members' League for the Transmission of a Correct History, a group within the New Frontier Party (Japan's other major party alongside the LDP in the mid-1990s), also adopting a resolution for action to amend the content of comfort women references.[21] These trends at the heart of the political world spread immediately to rural Japan. After the Okayama Prefectural Assembly adopted a resolution calling for the removal of comfort women references in December 1996,[22] many other prefectural assemblies around the country too were flooded with petitions for the adoption of similar resolutions, as well as counterpetitions calling for these to be rejected.[23] As the movement caught on, the media began to pay close attention to comments by Fujioka and Nishio, with the comfort women issue serving as a catalyst for the Textbook Reform Society's activities.

There was an immediate impact on textbook references to comfort women. Three of the seven junior high school history textbooks that passed the 2000 textbook screening already contained no references,[24] and by 2005 the term "comfort women" had disappeared from all the successful textbooks. Only one publisher's textbook contained references to comfort stations.[25] It should be noted, however, that references to comfort women continued to appear in high school Japanese history textbooks.

In any case, though references in Japanese history textbooks showed no sign of drifting to the right from the 1980s to the mid-1990s, some textbooks did in fact start shifting in that direction in the late 1990s. Then, in 2001, the Textbook Reform Society submitted its own junior high history textbook for screening. When the examiners came back with 137 suggested revisions, mainly in relation to modern and contemporary history—addressing, for example, the textbook's presentation of the legality of the annexation of Korea and the Nanking Incident—the Textbook Reform Society agreed to all 137 and their textbook was passed.[26] Probably the most noteworthy aspect of the suggested revisions was that none were based on the neighboring country clause. In that year's screening, the Japanese government announced publicly that it did not intend to engage in political interventions in response to external considerations, making it politically difficult to apply the clause.[27] Consequently, though the neighboring country clause was at one stage a major factor, its influence waned rapidly at this time.

The Cold War Finally Ends

However, this did not mean that the Textbook Reform Society's textbook found its way immediately into classrooms. After passing its screening in 2001, its adoption rate (private education included) was under 0.1 percent.[28] In 2004, the Society produced a revised version with softer claims in order to get the textbook into more schools, but the rate remained a very low 0.4 percent.[29]

Subsequently, frequent clashes occurred within the Textbook Reform Society over its course of action and differing personal views among its directors effectively split the group.[30] In 2014 the only original director remaining was Fujioka. Other former directors had either left the movement or were continuing their activities as members of the Nippon Kyōiku Saisei Kikō (Japan Educational Revival Organization), which broke away from the Textbook Reform Society to pursue its own path. This organization has a textbook publishing program of its own. While the adoption rate for the Textbook Reform Society's textbook stood at 0.08 percent in 2011, the Japan Educational Revival Organization textbook recorded 3.9 percent, with the breakaway organization outperforming its parent in the textbook market.[31]

Despite the turmoil within the Textbook Reform Society, its activities were no mere flash in the pan. Against the background of the major social changes occurring at the time, their claims exerted a major influence on the subsequent historical perceptions of the Japanese people.

A key aspect here was the effect on Japanese society of the end of the Cold War in the early 1990s, which destroyed the previously accepted left/right political polarization. It is easy to understand how those who had ascribed to a leftist ideology might have been severely shaken by the end of the Cold War, exemplified by former Japanese Communist Party member Fujioka's identification of the 1991 Gulf War as the turning point in his thinking.[32] The launch of the Textbook Reform Society coincided with the dwindling of the Japan Socialist Party from one of Japan's two major parties during the Cold War era into just another minor party (and in 1996 an official name change to Shakai Minshutō, or Social Democratic Party). This decline was matched by the waning of the former influence of progressive intellectuals.

Photo 6. Nishio Kanji and other members of the Textbook Reform Society giving a press conference on textbook screening results (August 16, 2001). (Jiji Press.) (From left, Kobayashi Yoshinori, Tanaka Hidemichi, Nishio, Fujioka Nobukatsu, Nakajima Shūji, Takamori Akinori.)

More importantly, however, the end of the Cold War also had a significant impact on the conservative camp, as evidenced by the strong affinity felt by the leaders of the Textbook Reform Society in its early days for anti-American conservatism—not the LDP's traditional pro-American conservatism.[33] In other words, the end of the Cold War enabled the conservative camp to cast a more skeptical eye on Japan's cooperative relationship with the United States, which had previously been absolutely essential from a security perspective. As a result, anti-American conservatives who had constituted no more than a minority faction under the hegemony of the pro-American conservatives suddenly found themselves with far more scope for action.

The Elite under Fire

The change in climate manifested clearly in the formation process of the Textbook Reform Society, which was the product of collaboration between Fujioka, who had shifted over from the left, and Nishio, who had been part of a minor right-wing faction. This did not mean that the movement was simply an unprincipled coalition of parties that had splintered off from their respective camps—there were clear points of agreement between the two sides.

What exactly were these points of agreement among the original members of the Textbook Reform Society, who joined forces only to break up almost immediately? They shared a negative view of Japan's postwar regime, regarding both the mainstream conservatives and progressives who had previously exerted such a major influence over public debate as accomplices in creating that regime—an old, corrupt elite who should be overthrown.[34] The formerly leftist Fujioka savaged the Japanese Communist Party of which he was once a member, while the anti-American conservative Nishio occasionally lambasted those taking a pro-American conservative line. Consequently, they were able to position themselves as critics of all the old elite, both left and right.

The Textbook Reform Society's clearly confrontational attitude toward the old elite was one of the reasons that their activities came under the spotlight, supported by another peculiar feature of the time—the protracted economic recession that began in the 1990s. The Textbook Reform Society was born in the midst of that recession, with its activities reaching a climax in 1997–98, when the Asian currency crisis plunged the national economy into its worst crisis in Japan's entire "lost" twenty years.[35] The long-running recession amplified public distrust of the ruling elite and particularly the bureaucrats regarded as its heart. As a result of that distrust, the early twenty-first century would see the "maverick populist" Koizumi Junichirō approach his structural reform program from the top down.

As members of the ruling elite such as Koizumi began themselves to play the role of reformists of the postwar regime, the claims of the Textbook Reform Society were pushed out of the limelight and gradually lost their appeal.

2. An Era of Populist Nationalism

The Domestic Impact of Globalization

The development of the historical perception dispute between Japan and South Korea has not been shaped solely by the facts of their shared past, and in fact belongs more to those inhabiting the present. Diverse aspects of each particular era have thus played a critical role in the development of the dispute.

One key factor shaping current Japan-South Korea relations has been globalization. Progressing swiftly since the 1990s, this phenomenon has affected both countries in various ways. One example discussed earlier is the diversification of economic relations that has made Japan and South Korea less important to each other.

However, the influence of globalization has not stopped there and has shaped the relationship directly and indirectly through changes it has wrought in the political, economic, and social situation of both countries. One factor in this was the loss of faith in the established elites previously believed to have led economic growth in both countries, and the concomitant change this brought about in both countries' political situations.

Economic Downturn and the Lost Prestige of the Ruling Elite[36]

An important aspect in that loss of faith was the memory of the strong economic growth that both countries enjoyed for much of the postwar period. In the 1980s, a spectrum of views began to emerge on the role of the state in both countries' economic growth, at one end highlighting the state's role as a control tower for economic expansion, and at the other rejecting the notion that the state played any significant role at all. What is critical here is that, regardless of the objective situation in both countries, it was believed that the ruling elites had played an important role in the economic growth process.

It should be recalled that despite the clash between Japan and South Korea over issues of historical perception and territory, they were actually quite similar in terms of their domestic political, economic, and social structures. In both countries for many years, academic elites produced by a hierarchical education system with top universities such as the University of Tokyo and Seoul National University at its apex had gone on to become the top-ranking bureaucrats, politicians, and business leaders who ran the government and society. In other words, it was an era in which certain universities and certain workplaces were universally recognized as superior, and within which, unlike today's universities and workplaces tailored to the individual, it was still taken for granted that everyone would ascend the same career ladder.

During that era of unconditional belief in the value of the elites, their superiority was accepted without question by the bulk of society. And in fact the societies of both countries appeared to be performing very well under the established elite leadership. Economic growth rates were high and the distribution of income was believed to be more equitable than in other countries. So the ruling elite could be confident of their own success, and there was considerable public faith in what they said.

Yet everything changed in the 1990s, with the failure of the buoyant economic conditions that had most significantly underpinned people's faith in the ruling elite. Japan's bubble burst, and the ensuing recession dragged on far longer than initially expected. The government's fiscal policies had little effect, and numerous banks watched their bad debts increase to alarming levels. By around 1995, the crisis had deepened to the point that small and medium-sized banks were starting to collapse. The failure of the various prescriptions presented by the ruling elite to free the economy from a seemingly endless recession ate steadily away at the credibility of this previously unchallenged segment of society.

South Korea experienced a similar phenomenon. While the South Korean economy had sustained strong growth despite considerable volatility, the steep downward trajectory that began in 1995 saw several small and medium-sized *chaebol* (family-owned business conglomerates) start to crumble in early 1997. A more serious problem for South Korea began when the domestic economic crisis was compounded by the emergence of the Asian currency crisis in July 1997. With South Korea locked in a trade deficit and heavily dependent on short-term finance from abroad, the opacity of the Kim Young-sam administration's handling of the *chaebol* shattered the international market's confidence in the country. By the end of 1997, the swift outflow of foreign capital brought South Korea to the edge of default. The beleaguered South Korean government asked the International Monetary Fund for a bailout, in return for which it was forced to accept a humiliating structural reform program.

The Asian currency crisis also impacted heavily on the Japanese economy, an effect amplified by the tight monetary policy instituted by the Hashimoto administration. Financial markets contracted, and in 1998, the Long-Term Credit Bank of Japan, the Nippon Credit Bank, and the Hokkaido Takushoku Bank failed in quick succession.[37]

In this period both countries were swamped by a wave of economic globalization. On the one hand, the advent of globalization meant the demise of the so-called convoy system on the basis of which Japan and South Korea had previously operated their economies. At the same time, it should be noted that not all the ruling elites of both countries suffered the same loss of credibility, which was rather concentrated among the political elite— more specifically, bureaucrats and politicians. According to a 2000 survey, the institutions that people felt were most in need of reform in Japan were not only the police force (which was reeling under a series of scandals) but also the government bureaucracy and the Diet.[38] The same trend was even more marked in South Korea. In 1998, a year after the Asian currency crisis, the newspaper *Dong-a ilbo* conducted a survey on institutions most in need of reform in which almost half of the respondents identified politics and government.[39] Interestingly, relatively little criticism was directed at the economic elites and financial institutions, which should logically have attracted similar blame. The Japanese and South Korean public evidently regarded the grim economic situation as the result of a policy failure on the part of political rather than economic elites.

The New Populists

It is not surprising, then, that a strong call emerged for political and administrative reform in both South Korea and Japan from the end of the 1990s to the early twenty-first century. However, this presented a major dilemma—the fact that the loss of prestige suffered by the political elite in both countries affected not only bureaucrats but also the politicians tasked with instituting these reforms.[40] Having lost the confidence of the people, how could the political elite engage in administrative and political reform that would inevitably attract stiff opposition from vested interests? At the beginning of the new century, political leaders in both countries faced a real problem.

The political elites of both countries—whether consciously or not—made the same choice. They selected as leaders politicians who had a different style from the established political elite and who had personal popularity unrelated to political affiliation. The two new leaders that emerged at the beginning of the twenty-first century were consequently Koizumi Junichirō and Roh Moo-hyun.

Unlike the United States and Europe, where the rise of populism began to be noted in the 2010s, populist leaders with quite different origins than established elites sprang up all over East Asia in the early years of the twenty-first century. The era in which Koizumi and Roh were operating on the political stage also saw former film star Joseph Estrada elected as president in the Philippines, while former businessman Thaksin Shinawatra wielded power in Thailand as the country's prime minister. Chen Shui-bian, with his strong nationalistic message, came to the fore in Taiwan, while in Malaysia, Mahathir Mohamad pursued populist politics well beyond the UMNO's traditional political base.[41]

Why did populism emerge in East Asia at an earlier point than in the United States or Europe? What happened was this. A loss of faith in the political elite as a whole emerged in the region, partially triggered by the Asian financial crisis. It manifested in falling popular support for the ruling and opposition parties alike, and a growing number of independent voters. As a result, it became difficult for any party to maintain a stable administration based solely on their own traditional base of support, so they had to devise other means of boosting their ratings. A number of parties selected a political leader whose personal popularity would enhance party popularity and nudge them toward electoral victory. In short, at a time when the parties' own support was flagging, selection of a leader on the basis of personal popularity was logical and to a certain extent necessary in terms of winning elections. As a result, this era saw the emergence in East Asia of leaders from different backgrounds and with different leadership styles than in the past.

Despite their apparent opposition to each other and the differences in their views, Koizumi and Roh in fact had much in common.[42] First, they were both strongly committed to political and administrative reform, which they justified by proclaiming it necessary as a response to globalization. Second, both adopted a political style of speaking directly to the public, using not only television and other traditional media but also new media such as email magazines and Internet bulletin boards. They spoke far more plainly than their predecessors and did not hesitate to use emotional language on occasion to convey their message more effectively.

Third, they positioned themselves as distinct from the existing political elite and ruthlessly discarded anyone regarded as part of that group. Just as Koizumi eliminated those within the party who opposed his reforms in the 2005 elections (the only big issue in which was his plans to privatize Japan's postal service), Roh called in the Millennium Democratic Party members who had supported him in the presidential elections to form the Uri Party. Fourth, while both presented themselves as political outsiders, they were in fact ruling-party politicians who had matured within the old political circles. Koizumi was the son of a politician and served as head of the Mori faction when Mori was LDP president, while Roh was a minister in Kim Dae-jung's administration and was also supported through part of his career by Kim Young-sam, who was a major force in Roh's home province of South Gyeongsang.[43]

Populists Become Nationalists

The historical perception dispute worsened significantly during the two leaders' time in power, beginning in 2001 when Koizumi marked his appointment as prime minister by pledging to make official visits to Yas-ukuni Shrine; this was also the year that the Textbook Reform Society's textbook was authorized. By 2005, when Shimane Prefecture passed its "Takeshima Day" ordinance, the dispute had reached its worst point since the normalization of relations. In April 2006, when two Japanese Maritime Self-Defense Force vessels were dispatched to the waters off Takeshima Island to conduct a hydrographic survey, Roh Moo-hyun instructed mari-time police that if South Korea's territorial waters were invaded, they were to attack and sink the Japanese vessels.[44]

This was not to say that Koizumi and Roh both took hard-headed nationalistic stances from the moment they arrived in power. Koizumi's pledge to visit Yasukuni Shrine was probably influenced by his awareness that his major rival in the LDP presidency elections, Hashimoto Ryūtarō, was former chairman of the Japan War-Bereaved Families Association, while the Textbook Reform Society's textbook only passed its screening because the group accepted all the revisions suggested by the Ministry of Education.[45] Similarly in South Korea, in June 2003, shortly after Roh came to power, Japanese foreign minister Asō Tarō suggested that Koreans had changed their names because they wanted to (rather than being forced to do so by the Japanese),[46] yet Roh insisted on going through with his visit to Japan despite domestic opposition, and he declared that issues of historical perception would not be raised as points of contention during his administration.[47] In fact, for the first few months after Roh became presi-dent in 2003, the bilateral relationship ran very smoothly. He reaffirmed his intentions at the 2004 summit talks, repeating that issues of historical perception would not be officially raised as points of contention during his term.[48]

However, in 2005 the situation deteriorated markedly as a result of Shimane Prefecture formulating its Takeshima Day ordinance. What prompted these developments?

3. The Historical Perception Dispute in an Era of Populist Nationalism

From Populism to Nationalism

As noted above, from the end of the 1990s to the early 2000s, old-school political leaders in Japan and South Korea were replaced by politicians with a new political style. The newcomers were unanimous in demanding a break from the old political establishment, reform of the old regime that had brought about economic recession, and the overturning of various taboos that had underpinned that regime. Similar phenomenon occurred throughout Northeast and Southeast Asia—all areas that had experienced the Asian currency crisis.

Importantly, many of the challenges the new leaders sought to mount against established taboos had a nationalistic aspect. For Koizumi, it was visiting Yasukuni Shrine; for Roh, it was challenging old historical perceptions both at home and abroad; and for Chen Shui-bian, it was claiming Taiwan's independence. The phenomenon of populist leaders inciting nationalist sentiment occurred across Northeast Asia.[49]

Premature Lame Ducks[50]

However, this era did not last long. A number of the populist leaders who attracted public attention in their early days in power through new political styles and radical criticism of the political status quo almost immediately came up against their own limitations. Criticizing the old regime was certainly a clear and persuasive message, but these politicians did not necessarily possess a clear vision of how to build a new regime to replace the one they had destroyed. Their proposed reforms tended to be vague or not as effective as claimed. So while they initially stirred great public expectations, their support slipped precipitously as it became clear that their reforms were not producing substantial results.

But the manner in which this phenomenon manifested differed between Japan and South Korea in certain respects. In Japan, it was in the lower house elections of 2005, when the LDP was internally divided, that Koizumi scored a triumphant victory with his promise of a reform program built around postal service privatization. Immediately after those elections, he announced that he would be leaving office the following year. In September 2006, Abe Shinzō stepped into Koizumi's shoes, again initially attracting strong support ratings. However, that support rapidly dissolved, and he slunk out of office barely a year later. The next prime ministers chosen by the LDP over the following two years—Fukuda Yasuo and Asō Tarō—came up against a similar problem. Fukuda's early slide in the support ratings damaged his credibility within the party, and he gave up his seat after a year. Asō's ratings fell even faster than those of Abe or Fukuda, causing the LDP to lose the August 2009 lower house elections and cede power to the Democratic Party of Japan.[51]

The DPJ administration, however, was to experience no better luck. Hatoyama Yukio, whose platform was reform without tax hikes, immediately found himself struggling with the holes in his reform program, while his rash promise to shift the US Futenma military base out of Okinawa ran into such stiff opposition at home and abroad that it became essentially impossible to implement. When Hatoyama left power just nine months later, the new prime minister, Kan Naoto, struggled to run the country with his own party in a state of turmoil, even before the eruption of the Senkaku Islands issue in September 2010 caused his support ratings to tumble. Noda Yoshihiko took over in September 2011, six months after the Great East Japan Earthquake, experiencing similar problems. The DPJ was ultimately defeated in the December 2012 lower house elections and the LDP returned to power.[52]

In the six years after the Koizumi administration, therefore, the next six Japanese prime ministers—Abe, Fukuda, Asō, Hatoyama, Kan, and Noda—all experienced a rapid drop in their support ratings immediately after entering office and gave up their posts after about a year (table 6.1). This curious situation was partly due to Japan's parliamentary cabinet system, which means that if a prime minister's support ratings drop below a certain level—or, more precisely, sink close to the level of the ruling party's overall support ratings—his credibility within the party rapidly dissolves as party members begin to worry about the impact on the next election. Once that level has been reached, the ruling party therefore tends to step in and change the leadership. Due to the widespread political distrust occurring in Japan at the end of 1990s, all parties' ratings were down, forcing them to field a popular party leader to boost their support and help them achieve election victory.

The situation was different in South Korea, which has a presidential system. As in Japan, support for political leaders who came to power on a reform platform tended to dissolve early on when their proposed reforms turned out to be vague and ineffective. However, in South Korea presidents are guaranteed their term in power to the extent that they do not commit a clear legal violation or other similar impeachable offense, so removing a leader prematurely is not easy even for the ruling party. Accordingly, even if a president loses public support early in their term and becomes a lame duck, they still remain in office until the end of their term.

Political Destabilization and Escalation of the Historical Perception Dispute

Naturally, these circumstances destabilized the political situation in both Japan and South Korea that influenced the historical perception dispute between the two countries.

Table 6.1. Trends in support ratings for Japanese, Korean and Taiwanese administrations from 2002 (within one year of inauguration) in percentage

Month	Abe (1st)	Fukuda	Asō	Hatoyama	Kan	Noda	Abe (2nd)	Roh Moo-hyun	Lee Myung-bak	Park Geun-hye	Ma Ying-jeou
1	51.3	44.1	38.6	60.6	41.2	50.1	54.0	72.1	57.4	50.4	37.8
2	51.4	41.3	38.8	54.4	31.8	42.2	61.4	59.6	45.0	45.3	27.0
3	41.9	40.1	16.7	46.8	36.0	35.5	61.4	40.2	19.7	53.5	36.1
4	40.7	34.5	17.8	47.1	45.6	32.4	62.1	—	21.5	61.5	24.9
5	34.9	32.5	16.4	35.7	39.2	28.4	60.2	—	26.9	59.6	23.6
6	34.7	30.9	17.6	30.9	27.8	24.9	57.4	33.4	32.8	58.8	29.8
7	40.6	27.6	25.2	23.7	21.0	27.4	53.6	28.6	25.4	67.0	30.3
8	39.4	19.9	26.3	19.1	21.3	21.7	54.2	25.5	33.2	59.0	28.7
9	28.8	19.1	24.1	—	17.8	23.3	61.3	—	34.7	58.1	34.5
10	25.7	21.1	16.3	—	18.9	24.3	55.8	23.9	34.0	53.2	28.6
11	22.6	23.6	16.7	—	20.5	21.3	56.6	—	34.8	54.5	32.8
12	25.5	—	13.4	—	21.9	19.8	47.1	25.1	38.5	56.6	38.9
Source:	Jiji Press	Jiji Press	Jiji Press	Jiji Press	Jiji Press	Jiji Press	Jiji Press	Gallup Korea	EAI	Realmeter	Global Views

Note: The figures for Japan indicate the cabinet support rating, while the figures for Korea and Taiwan are presidential support ratings. For Roh Moo-hyun, figures are only given for the months in which Gallup Korea ran a poll.

The South Korean situation is easy to understand. Whenever a president is appointed, the new leader announces to Japan that they will not make a political issue out of whichever issue over territory or historical perception is under the spotlight at the time, but as the end of their term nears and their support wanes, they change their stance entirely and bring that issue to the top of their agenda. In recent years, with the premature lame duck phenomenon occurring as a result of the dwindling political confidence explained above, presidents' political bases have begun to crumble even faster, leading the South Korean government to attack the Japanese government fiercely over issues of territory and historical perception much earlier than was previously the case. Typical examples include the hard line that Roh Moo-hyun took on territorial issues as of February 2005, and Lee Myung-bak's foregrounding of the comfort women issue and Takeshima Island beginning in December 2011.

The impact on Japanese society of these initiatives by South Korea was exacerbated by the domestic situation in Japan. It was just as difficult in Japan for an administration with diminishing support to cope with the pressure from nationalistic public opinion, and Japanese governments from Koizumi onward started to adopt a much tougher approach toward South Korea (whether actively or passively) as well as China, with whom issues of territory and historical perception had also begun to intensify.

As a result, territorial and historical issues between Japan and South Korea became increasingly serious and the situation deteriorated rapidly. For political leaders in both countries, foregrounding such issues, on which there was a high level of public consensus, offered a sure boost to their falling support ratings with very little possibility of damage, so both sides began using these cards more often as their administrations' terms neared their end and their support ratings fell. This in turn heavily influenced public opinion in both countries, as each became aware that nationalist feeling was rising in the other country, accompanied by growing criticism of their own country. Such awareness was enhanced by the rapid spread of the Internet and the emergence of multilingual Internet sites. Once upon a time, remarks made in one country were accessible only to experts who could understand the language of that country; now they were suddenly available even to ordinary people. Moreover, using machine translation, ordinary people could also engage in direct dialogue with people from that country.

As a result, ordinary people now came into direct contact with the perception gap between Japan and South Korea over matters of territory and history, something that was previously known only to a limited group. The differences in perception were old news to experts, but the general public was shocked and sometimes angered by this discovery. The historical perception dispute between Japan and South Korea consequently entered a new phase of direct confrontation between public opinion in the two countries.

4. Deteriorating Bilateral Relations

Ken-Kanryū and the Emergence of Japanese Oversensitivity to South Korea

Let's again go back a little in time to Japan under Koizumi, when several changes occurred that would be important in terms of subsequent perceptions of South Korea. One was the joint hosting by Japan and South Korea of the FIFA World Cup in 2002. When the Fédération Internationale de Football Association (FIFA) chose Japan and South Korea as hosts in 1996, both countries regarded the occasion as a golden opportunity to deepen their exchange and cement their bilateral relationship.[53] A variety of events were planned in both countries in conjunction with the World Cup, and regardless of the effectiveness of these, Japanese feeling toward South Korea certainly took a turn for the better during this period.

In 2003, just after the World Cup, Hallyu (the "Korean Wave," a term referring to the new popularity of Korean pop culture across Asia and other parts of the world) came to Japan. The South Korean television series *Winter Sonata*, picked up by NHK after a dogged South Korean marketing campaign and subsequently rerun several times, prompted a social phenomenon that became known as the "Yon-sama boom" in reference to Bae Yong-joon, the series' male lead. Bae's first visit to Japan in 2004 brought as many as four thousand fans to Narita Airport's arrival gate, with both countries declaring the official arrival of a Hallyu boom in Japan.[54] The boom was expected to have a positive impact on bilateral relations, and the optimistic expectation was expressed in various quarters that the unprecedented scale of the Korean pop culture success in the Japanese market might change perceptions in both South Korea and Japan, positively influencing the debate over issues of historical perception in both countries.

However, these expectations were roundly disappointed. As can be seen in figure 6.1, warm Japanese feeling toward South Korea reached its peak in 2002 when the two countries cohosted the World Cup, but it subsequently continued to cool. During this period, there was a sharp rise in the

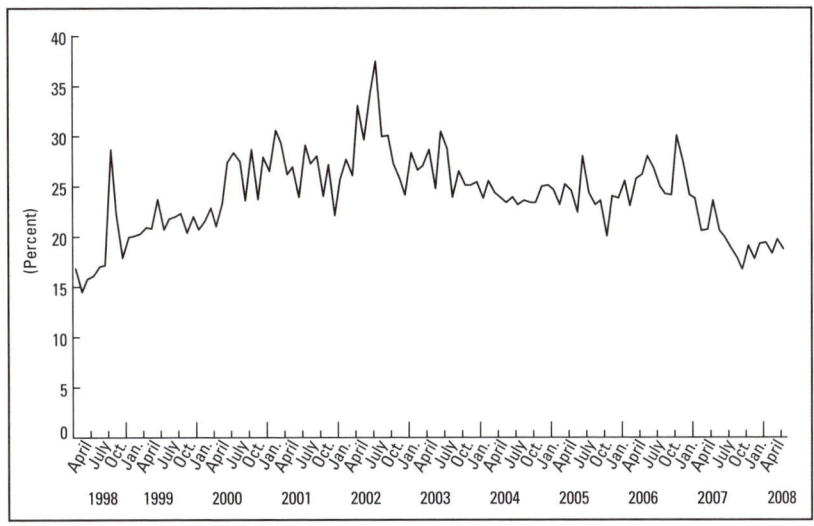

Figure 6.1. Ratio of Japanese identifying South Korea as "a country important to Japan." (*Source:* Created by author from a Jiji Press public opinion poll.)

number of emotional and rancorous comments about South Korea on the anonymous textboard 2channel and numerous other websites. That Internet discussion eventually gave rise to a bestseller—Yamano Sharin's manga *Ken-Kanryū* (Hating "The Korean Wave"), published in 2005. As Yamano later noted, the manga drew on the discussion posted on Internet bulletin boards like 2channel, which effectively gave it a readership even before it was published.[55]

However, *Ken-Kanryū*'s influence was not limited to an online audience who already shared the views that the manga expressed. Instead, it carried a discussion from the virtual world out to the real world, vastly expanding its reach. Moreover, the deterioration in bilateral relations caused by the outbreak of the Takeshima Island issue just at this time drew even more attention to the publication. As a consequence, emotional and rancorous discussion about South Korea that had been confined to the Internet gained much more widespread support.

Changing Japanese Nationalism and the New US-China Cold War

During this period, the Japanese public suddenly became almost oversensitive to government, media, and even Internet discussion on the South

Korean side. This was of course a complete departure from the previous pattern in Japan-South Korea relations. For example, where the 1980s disputes over Japan's history textbooks and other issues of historical perception provoked public uproar in South Korea, in Japan the general attitude could be generously described as cool and less generously as indifferent. In the 2000s, however, Japanese public opinion became in some cases even more thin-skinned than the South Korean side over the same issues.

A key factor in this new development was the change occurring in Japanese nationalism that emerges clearly in the remarks of Ishihara Shintarō, one of Japan's leading nationalist politicians. *The Japan That Can Say No*, one of Ishihara's most influential works from the 1980s (coauthored with Morita Akio, one of Sony's founders), targeted the United States.[56] Today, however, Ishihara barely touches on the United States; instead, he makes constant reference to China and South Korea.[57] A similar change in focus is evident among many other Japanese nationalists.

Seen from a broader perspective, what happened was this: during the Cold War, Japanese nationalists' hypothetical enemy was naturally the leader of the socialist bloc, the Soviet Union. As Japan emerged as an economic power and the Cold War drew to a close, the situation gradually changed, with some nationalists instead shifting to an anti-American stance. However, the economic slump that began in the late 1990s combined with the economic and military rise of Japan's Asian neighbors to bring about yet another change. Faced with the growing military threat posed by China and North Korea, Japan once again began to need the United States, prompting the nationalists to redirect their criticism away from the United States and toward China and North Korea as hypothetical enemies. The new mood manifested clearly in the growing sense of danger that emerged after Koizumi's visit to North Korea in 2002.[58]

The focus on China and North Korea initially seemed as though it would improve relations between Japan and South Korea as fellow American allies, on the grounds that if emerging China and North Korea were the hypothetical enemies of both countries, they would need to cooperate with each other. However, that scenario failed. Instead a number of factors—among them South Korea appearing to side with China on issues of historical perception and territory; the unstable relationship between South Korea and the United States under the Roh Moo-hyung administration, which came to power on the back of the South Korean public's anti-American sentiment; and the appeasement policy that both the Kim Dae-jung and Roh Moo-hyung administrations observed toward North Korea—left the Japanese public with the vague sense that South Korea was siding not with Japan and the United States but rather with China and North Korea.[59] The advance of the so-called new Cold War between China and the United States consequently exacerbated Japanese ill-feeling toward South Korea—the opposite result of what had been expected.

The Bitter Legacy of the New Administrations

That said, some optimism did remain concerning Japan-South Korea relations in the 2000s. A particularly important factor was the change in administration that occurred in both countries between 2008 and 2009. The Lee Myung-bak administration, which came to power in February 2008, was South Korea's first conservative government in ten years (since Kim Young-sam). This, together with the fact that the president himself was born in Japan just before the end of World War II, created a strong expectation in Japan that Lee would address the deterioration in bilateral relations that had occurred under the progressive Roh administration.[60] Hatoyama Yukio, the head of the new DPJ government inaugurated in September 2009, was already known as being proactive on resolving issues of historical perception such as the comfort women issue, and also proposed the East Asian Community concept, leading to the expectation in South Korea that Japan might make some compromises on historical perception issues.[61]

Initially, it appeared that these expectations might become reality. From the outset, Lee emphasized the importance of the bilateral relationship[62] and also steered his country skillfully through the 2010 centenary of Japan's annexation of Korea, which had been a cause of concern in some quarters. Despite the fizzling of Hatoyama's East Asian Community concept due to the indifference of the Chinese and South Korean governments, bilateral relations entered a period of comparative stability.[63]

But it was all too brief a springtime. In August 2011, the Korean Constitutional Court ruled that the failure of the South Korean government to resolve the comfort women dispute under Article 3 of the Claims Settlement Agreement was unconstitutional.[64] The South Korean government was thus obliged to take some action to resolve the issue, and Lee used the December 2011 summit talks in Kyoto to announce a policy turnaround[65] and press the Japanese government to produce a solution.[66] Already soured by this incident, the bilateral relationship was dealt an even heavier blow in August 2012 by Lee's visit to Takeshima Island[67] and his demand that the Japanese emperor make an apology to South Korea[68]—events that still remain fresh in Japanese minds.

Photo 7. Comfort woman statue outside the Japanese Embassy in Seoul (December 14, 2011). (Jiji Press.)

Japan-South Korea relations continue to be deeply scarred by these developments even today. The fact that relations did not improve but instead disintegrated under apparently promising new administrations devastated remaining public hope in both countries that a solution might be found. In other words, from 2005 to 2006, both countries still regarded the historical perception dispute as a temporary phenomenon created by two atypical political leaders: Koizumi and Roh Moo-hyung. People still expected that if these two leaders were replaced, the two countries would be able to restore their former cordial relationship. However, despite the appointment of new leaders who the people were confident would repair the relationship, relations instead significantly worsened. As a result, the public began to think that rather than the historical perception dispute arising simply out of the personal qualities of certain political leaders, it might be caused by larger factors such as public opinion and national character.[69]

Dwindling Expectations

The period up to 2012, therefore, decisively closed two avenues of hope in both countries for a better bilateral relationship: more active exchange and a shift to potentially friendlier administrations. With the prospect of improved bilateral relations lost, a serious deadlock emerged from 2012 onward. Neither the second Abe administration that came to power at the end of 2012 nor the Park Geun-hye administration inaugurated in February 2013 turned the situation around. Conversely, Park made it clear from the outset that she intended to take a hard line toward Japan on the comfort women issue and other issues of historical perception, with the relationship deteriorating to the point that the two countries could not even manage summit talks in 2013.

Conclusion

So what should we make of the situation from the late 1990s to the present?

Examined chronologically, we first see outsider activists spurred by the worsening of the historical perception dispute embarking on nationalistic campaigns. With sentiment hardening on both sides, their campaigns bore some fruit and eventually came to the attention of the ruling elites. Struggling with dwindling popularity amid ongoing economic recession, they adopted these outsider causes as a means of boosting their own support, launching an era in which the ruling elites themselves actively raised issues of historical perception.

With the embrace of historical perception issues by the ruling elite, previously marginal nationalistic discourses invaded the social mainstream. These hegemonic discourses eventually gained a stranglehold on reality, forcing Japan and South Korea into a deadlock over historical perception issues that continues today.

In the following chapter, I will summarize my findings on the development of the historical perception dispute between Japan and South Korea.

SEVEN

Revisiting the Japan-South Korea Historical Perception Dispute

1. Generational Change, Mutual Loss of Importance, Collapse of Cooperation between Ruling Elites

Let us return to the hypothesis that I put forward in Part I.

I made two key points. First, I noted that the situation between Japan and South Korea in relation to the historical perception dispute has continued to deteriorate for many years. Second, I identified the shift from the prewar generation to the postwar generation and the reduced importance of Japan-South Korea relations resulting from the end of the Cold War, globalization, and South Korea's economic development as factors in this ongoing deterioration.

How was the actual impact of each of these factors measured? The impact of the generational shift was clearly confirmed by the evolution of the textbook and comfort women controversies. In other words, the generational shift between the Park Chung-hee administration and the Chun Doo-hwan administration was an important one, playing a significant role in the South Korean ruling elite of the time discovering the textbook issue.

The generational shift was also important in relation to the comfort women issue, as exemplified by the initial framing of the issue as a search for actual comfort women, with the surprise accompanying the discovery of the issue becoming part of the foundation of this movement.

The change in the importance of the bilateral relationship brought about by the end of the Cold War and changing economic conditions also clearly cast a long shadow over this issue. The key factor in the development of the textbook issue in the 1980s was the change in the security environment surrounding South Korea. The international environment in the late 1970s placed South Korea at serious risk, but it improved rapidly in the early 1980s, providing part of the footing on which South Korea was able to raise the textbook issue during this era in rivalry with China. In the case of the comfort women issue, the reduced importance of the Japan–South Korea economic partnership was critical, as exemplified by the January 1992 summit talks. When the Japanese government showed no sign of concessions on the trade deficit issue that was South Korea's greatest concern, the South Korean government responded, not with concessions of its own, but rather by utilizing the comfort women issue to bolster its own domestic position.

My case studies of two key aspects of the historical perception dispute—the textbook issue and the comfort women issue—revealed that the generational shift and the reduced importance of the bilateral relationship noted above manifested in the collapse of the narrative space that had previously been controlled by the ruling elites in both countries regarding issues of historical perception. The historical perception dispute had been kept from escalating beyond a certain level prior to the 1980s because these ruling elites cooperated with each other to keep the bilateral relationship stable.

In the 1990s, however, the status quo dissolved on two levels. First, in parallel with growing public distrust of politics, the ruling elites lost their ability to control domestic discourse. Second, mutual cooperation between the two elites broke down, with both sides beginning to foreground issues of historical perception for their own political gain. The string of rash statements by various ruling party politicians in the mid-1990s was one example of this.

The collapse of the cooperative framework between the two ruling elites locked in a new trajectory. Significantly, of the two elements noted earlier—the generational shift and the reduced importance of the bilateral relationship—where the former was a temporary phenomenon, the impact of the latter continued and indeed grew stronger. In other words, South Korea's economic development, in tandem with economic globalization, led both countries to become increasingly less important to each other over time, to the point where even their respective leaders, the pinnacle of the ruling elite, were also actively highlighting issues of historical perception for their own political benefit. This fixed the historical perception discourse in both countries on an adversarial course that continues to this day.

2. The Slow Collapse of the Cold War Regime

What this reveals is that the intensification of the bilateral historical perception dispute has essentially been part of the collapse of an international relationship nurtured during the Cold War period.

The Japan-South Korea relationship was previously distorted by a strange power imbalance whereby Japan, despite having lost World War II, outweighed its former colony South Korea on both military and economic fronts. As a divided nation on the front lines of the Cold War, this left South Korea with no choice but to rely on Japan in various respects, which also necessitated containing its own dissatisfaction regarding colonial rule. Given the Cold War environment, Japan also needed South Korea to a degree, with repression of issues related to the past operating primarily to Japan's benefit.

Thus the ruling elites of both countries initially contained the historical issues that would lead to the present. However, the end of the Cold War created a new security environment, even as economic growth made South Korea more powerful and globalization reduced the country's economic dependence on Japan, so that South Korea no longer needed to contain its dissatisfaction over issues of historical perception. The ruling elite lost control over the discourse, and people began to raise issues as they saw fit. As the relationship with its neighbor declined in importance, the ruling elites in both countries chose to sacrifice that relationship in favor of manipulating issues of historical perception for their own benefit.

International relations in Northeast Asia that developed under Cold War conditions therefore underwent a gradual twenty-year collapse, as the dissolving legacy of the Cold War in the region exposed historical issues that had previously been suppressed. In this sense, the situation clearly has much in common with problems that have gradually emerged elsewhere in the world following the end of the Cold War, such as the breakup of Yugoslavia and the collapse of regimes in developing countries that were once supported by the Soviet Union (Syria and Iraq). In that sense, we are probably still living in a post-Cold War era.

Afterword

To essentially indulge in a little personal reminiscence, from April 2011 to March 2014 I wrote a series of articles for Minerva Shobō's PR magazine *Kiwameru* entitled "Nikkan rekishi ninshiki mondai ni dō mukiau ka" (How to approach the Japan-Korea historical perception issue). The initial request for the series came from Minerva Shobō's Horikawa Kentarō in June 2010 when I was on sabbatical as a visiting fellow at the University of Washington in Seattle—more than four years ago now.

Looking back, I remember vividly how tired I was then. Since Minerva Shobō published my first book in 2000—*Kankoku/Chosen nashonarizumu to shōkoku ishiki* (North and South Korean Nationalism as a Small Nation)—I had continued to publish at least one book every year, more in both 2007 and 2008. Given my inherently limited capacity, this was clearly overdoing things, the result of my inability to refuse a job. On reflection, I think my natural cowardice caused me to believe that turning down work equated to acknowledging the limits of my ability, so I threw myself into that work not so much for the sake of the publisher as to protect my own pride. Naturally, this foolish behavior simply placed me under ever-increasing psychological strain.

What finished me off was the second round of Japan-South Korea joint history research, which ran from June 2007 to March 2010. This project arose from an agreement between Koizumi Junichirō and Kim Dae-jung at their 2001 summit talks, and I was also part in the first round of research conducted from 2002 to 2005, but only as a cooperating researcher. It was during the second round of joint research, however, when I was upgraded to a research committee member, that things fell apart. In the subgroup on textbooks to which I was attached, the Japanese and South Korean researchers went head to head, refusing to budge on their own positions, with meetings descending into endless bickering. These meetings left me even more drained, as well as unnecessarily frazzled by my attempts to get the situation under control.

My year in Seattle that began in April 2010 was to some extent a way of fleeing unpalatable realities—essentially an escape from work. I was in such a poor state that I couldn't even maintain the concentration to read an academic text through to the end, let alone produce a decent paper myself. I decided to stop writing books and papers and devote my time in Seattle to recuperating until I recovered some mental poise.

A couple of months later, just when I was feeling a little better, the above request from Minerva Shobō arrived out of the blue. I had a decade-long relationship with Minerva dating back to my first book, and I had also written articles for newspapers and magazines before, so doing a series for a PR magazine seemed like an easy enough prospect. I agreed to take on the job—whether thoughtlessly or in a moment of particular brilliance, I can't decide even today. Anyhow, as soon as I started preparing the series, I realized that what Minerva was after was not a chatty diary of my South Korea research in Seattle, but rather rigorous academic content, and that the other contributors to the magazine alongside me were in fact Inoki Takenori, Tominaga Kenichi, and other major academic figures whom I had revered since my postgrad days.

In other words, I had somehow managed to take on the preposterous task of producing every month a 2,500-plus word article of the same quality as an academic paper. Moreover, because the plan was apparently to compile the series afterwards into a book, I would need to have an overall structure in mind and maintain the same tone throughout. Having broken down in Japan as a result of overwork and gone to the United States for a prolonged period of recuperation, I had to throw myself straight back into the deep end, just as a professional athlete might return to training as a form of rehabilitation. My convalescence in Seattle suddenly became a rehabilitation boot camp, requiring me to produce a regular 4,000-word monthly article under the long-distance guidance of my amazing "trainer" Horikawa Kentarō. Originally planned as a twenty-four-part series over two years, the articles were surprisingly well-received, so rather than winding up after the promised two years, I ended up writing thirty-six articles over three years. Along the way, my "trainer" changed from Horikawa to Tabiki Katsuji, who had edited several of my previous publications through

Minerva Shobō, such as *Kankoku ni okeru kenishugiteki taisei no seiritsu* [Establishment of an authoritarian regime in South Korea] and *Kōsō/Binhi* [King Gojong and Queen Min], so it was no coincidence that the change-over made me feel increasingly pressured to wind up at boot camp and return to professional life.

In addition, my Minerva Shobō boot camp made it difficult for me to take on any other work, so writing the series became the center of my academic life. I would like to take this opportunity to apologize to my various other publishers for the inconvenience over that time and hope they will forgive me for falling into Minerva Shobō's neatly laid trap!

The worth of the book resulting from my Seattle boot camp is of course something that I must leave readers to judge, but the fact is that the book does have some limitations. Dealing with a far more contemporary period than usual made it difficult to find objective and reliable resources for analysis purposes, and above all, the book was written in a limited period of time by a not particularly talented scholar! I look forward to taking on board any criticisms and reflecting them in my further research.

Finally, I would like to thank everyone who contributed to the production of this book. As noted above, Horikawa Kentarō and Tabiki Katsuji from Minerva Shobō lent various forms of assistance over the creation process. Just as no professional athlete succeeds without talented coaches and trainers, these four years have reminded me again just how vital a talented editor is to producing a good text. My return to professional life through the publication of this book is down to my two wonderful editors, and I look forward to working with them again in future.

Professional athletes also need talented managers to provide them with the right conditions. Minerva Shobō president Sugita Keizō, an outstanding business leader as well as editor, operates from Kansai rather than Tokyo, which is the heart of Japan's publishing culture, gifting authors with the chance to publish high-level academic works. My heartfelt gratitude goes to Mr. Sugita and all his staff for the invaluable opportunities they have offered to me right from my first forays into publishing.

I came up with the concept for the book and most of its content during my year in Seattle, and my troubled mind found enormous solace in the city's beautiful streets and the surrounding natural environment. I am grateful to Yong-Chool Ha and Clark Sorenson from the Center for Korea Studies, Jackson School of International Studies, University of Washington for giving me that precious opportunity. The University of Washington's fabulous East Asia Library was the reason that I was able to research the massive subject of Japan-South Korea relations while living in the United States. In particular, my thanks go to Yokota Keiko, who was then in charge of Japan-related works within the library's holdings. Yamashita Tatsuya and Kameda Naoko from the Kobe University Graduate School of International Cooperation Studies helped me with the proofreading. I look forward to repaying them one day for the many hours of time they so generously devoted to my project. Part of the book also uses results from "Oral History Survey of the Chun Doo-hwan Years," a project funded by a Grant-in-aid for Scientific Research (Basic Research B) from the Japan Society for the Promotion of Science (JSSP). This book could never have been completed without the support of Lee Do-hyung, Heo Mun-do, and the many other people who kindly took part in my survey, as well as the JSSP that backed my research.

Finally, this book holds for me many pleasant memories of the time that my family spent together in Seattle. I would like to close by expressing my deepest gratitude again to my daughters, Futaba and Shizuku, who came to the United States with me with only a smattering of English, and to my wonderful wife Tokiko, who has supported me through thick and thin.

Kimura Kan
September 7, 2014
From my lodgings at Korea University in Seoul,
quiet and empty over the Chuesok holiday
January 8, 2017
On a rainy day in winter

Chronology of the Japan-South Korea Historical Perceptions Issue

Year	Event
1905	Jan. 28: Japanese government reaffirms by cabinet decision its intention to claim territorial rights over Takeshima/Dokdo
	Nov. 17: Second Japan-Korea Treaty
1910	Aug. 29: Japan-Korea Annexation Treaty
1945	Aug. 15: Imperial Rescript on the Termination of the War
	Sept. 2: Signing ceremony for the formal surrender of Japan
	Sept. 11: US military occupation of the southern part of the Korean peninsula begins; first round of arrest warrants issued for war criminals
	Nov. 19: Second round of arrest warrants issued for war criminals
	Dec. 2: Third round of arrest warrants issued for war criminals
	Dec. 15: Shintō Directive; Yasukuni Shrine becomes a religious corporation
1946	April 17: Twenty-eight suspects indicted as Class A war criminals
	May 3: International Military Tribunal for the Far East (Tokyo War Crimes Trial) begins
1947	May 3: Japanese Constitution enters into force
	Aug. 15: Republic of Korea founded; Rhee Syngman becomes the first ROK president
	Nov. 12: Tokyo War Crimes Trial verdict announced; trial ends
1951	Sept. 8: San Francisco Peace Treaty signed with Japan
	Oct. 30: First round of Japan-South Korea talks begins
1952	Jan. 18: South Korean government establishes the Peace Line (Syngman Rhee Line)
1953	April 20: Dokdo Volunteer Guards land on Takeshima/Dokdo
	Oct. 6: Third round of Japan-South Korea talks complicated by comment from chief Japanese delegate Kubota Kanichirō
1956	April: Ulleungdo Security Force of North Gyeongsang Province stations police officers on Takeshima/Dokdo
1959	March 28: Chidorigafuchi National Cemetery construction completed (to house the remains of the unidentified war dead)

1960	April 19: April Revolution in South Korea brings down Rhee Syngman administration
1961	May 16: Coup d'état staged by Park Chung-hee
1962	Nov. 12: Kim-Ōhira memorandum created
1965	June 12: Ienaga Saburō launches his first textbook suit
	June 22: Conclusion of the Treaty on Basic Relations between Japan and the Republic of Korea
1971	Oct. 25: Republic of China (Taiwan) loses its United Nations membership
1972	Feb. 21: US President Richard Nixon visits China
	Sept. 29: Joint Communique of the Government of Japan and the Government of the People's Republic of China
1973	Jan. 27: Paris Peace Accords (ending the war and restoring peace in Vietnam)
	Aug. 8: Kim Dae-jung kidnapping
1974	Aug. 15: Mun Se-gwang attempts to assassinate Park Chung-hee
1975	April 30: Fall of Saigon and collapse of South Vietnam
	Aug. 15: Prime Minister Miki Takeo makes the first visit by a Japanese prime minister to Yasukuni Shrine on the anniversary of Japan's defeat
1978	Aug. 12: Treaty of Peace and Friendship between Japan and the People's Republic of China
	Oct. 17: Yasukuni Shrine enshrines Class A war criminals
1979	Jan. 1: Normalization of relations between the United States and China
	Oct. 26: Assassination of South Korean President Park Chung-hee
	Dec. 12: Coup d'état, Chun Doo-hwan and fellow members of the new military establishment seize power over the military
1980	May 17: Chun Doo-hwan and fellow members of the new military establishment seize political power through a de facto coup d'état
	May 18: Gwangju Incident
1981	Aug. 20: Japan-South Korea foreign ministers' talks; South Korean government asks Japanese side for a US$6 billion loan
1982	April 8: Japan's Supreme Court reverses the decision in the second textbook suit and returns it to the High Court for retrial (a loss for Ienaga)
	June 26: Textbook screening results are headlined by the Japanese media
	July 20: China's *People's Daily* launches official criticism of Japanese government over textbook screening
	Oct. 30: People's Conference to Protect Japan announces that it will create a new textbook
1983	Jan. 1: *Chosun ilbo* launches a series of articles under the slogan of "the road to overcoming Japan is to know Japan"
	Jan. 11: Nakasone Yasuhiro becomes the first Japanese prime minister to make an official visit to South Korea
1984	Jan. 19: Ienaga Saburō launches third textbook suit
	Sept. 6: Chun Doo-hwan becomes the first South Korean president to make an official visit to Japan
1985	Aug. 15: Prime Minister Nakasone makes an official visit to Yasukuni Shrine
1986	July 7: *New Version of Japanese History* finally passes screening
1987	June 29: Democratic Justice Party leader Roh Tae-woo announces his "Declaration for Democratization"
1988	Sept. 17: Seoul Olympics open; criticism of *gisaeng* tourism reaches its peak around this time

1990   Jan. 4: Yun Jeong-ok begins publishing a series of articles entitled "In the Footsteps of the Volunteer Labor Corps" in *The Hankyoreh*

Nov. 16: Formation of Chôngsindae-munje Taech'aek Hyôpuihoe

Dec. 18: Japanese government denies government involvement in the comfort women issue

1991   Jan. 9: Japan-South Korea summit talks (Kaifu Toshiki and Roh Tae-woo)

Aug. 14: Kim Hak-sun becomes the first former comfort woman to come out under her own name

Dec. 6: Kim Hak-sun and other former comfort women take the Japanese government to the Tokyo District Court; Chief Cabinet Secretary Katō Kōichi announces that no documentary materials indicating government involvement have been found

1992   Jan. 8: First "Wednesday demonstration" held outside Japanese embassy in Seoul

Jan. 11: *Asahi shimbun* reports materials indicating military involvement

Jan. 13: First Katō Statement

Jan. 16: Japan-South Korea summit talks (Miyazawa Kiichi and Roh Tae-woo)

Jan. 21: South Korea government officially seeks additional compensation in relation to the comfort women issue for the first time

July 6: Second Katō Statement

1993   June 16: Vote of no confidence in Miyazawa administration passes, LDP fractures

Aug. 4: Kōno Statement

1994   Dec. 24: METI Minister Hashimoto Ryūtarō suggests that it is a matter of "subtle definition" as to whether Japan had intended to wage a war of aggression against its Asian neighbors

1995   June 5: Former Deputy Prime Minister Watanabe Michio observes that the Treaty of Annexation was an "amicably concluded international agreement"

June 14: Chief Cabinet Secretary Igarashi Kōzō announces that the Japanese government will establish what subsequently becomes the Asian Women's Fund

July 19: Asian Women's Fund (AWF) inaugurated

Aug. 15: Murayama Statement

Oct. 5: Murayama Tomiichi states his belief that in the historical context of international relations at that time, Japan had signed and carried out the Treaty of Annexation legally

Nov. 14: South Korean President Kim Young-sam says at a South Korea-China summit that South Korea would "give Japan a licking and cure it of its bad habits"

1996   Feb. 6: Radhika Coomaraswamy submits a report to the United Nations Commission on Human Rights

Aug. 1: AWF atonement project launched in the Philippines

1997   Jan. 30: Inaugural general meeting of the Society for History Textbook Reform

Dec. 27: South Korean government applies for an IMF bailout

1998   Oct. 1: "A New Japan-Republic of Korea Partnership towards the Twenty-first Century"

2001   April 5: The screening council's suggested revisions are made to Fusōsha Publishing's *New History Textbook* and *New Civic Studies Textbook* and the textbooks are passed

April 26: Koizumi Junichirō becomes prime minister

Nov. 3: Third international conference in "A Reconsideration of the Annexation of Korea" series

2002   May 31: Japan and South Korea jointly host FIFA World Cup

Sept. 30: AWF atonement project ends

2004 April 3: South Korean actor Bae Yong-joon (known in Japan as "Yon-sama") visits Japan for the first time; "Korean Wave" reaches its peak

2005 Jan. 17: Roh Moo-hyun administration discloses diplomatic documents from the negotiation process for the Treaty on Basic Relations, decides to seek legal compensation in relation to comfort women, South Korean nationals in Sakhalin, and atomic bomb victims as issues outside the scope of the Treaty on Basic Relations

Feb. 22: Shimane Prefecture establishes "Takeshima Day"

July 26: Publication of Yamano Sharin's manga *Ken-Kanryū* (Hating "The Korean Wave")

2006 April 19: Japanese government plans to dispatch two Japanese Maritime Self-Defense Force vessels to the waters off Takeshima Island to conduct a hydrographic survey; Roh Moo-hyun instructs maritime police that if South Korea's territorial waters were invaded, they are to ram and destroy the Japanese vessels

Aug. 15: Prime Minister Koizumi Junichirō visits Yasukuni Shrine

2007 March 31: AWF dissolved

2010 Aug. 29: Centenary of the annexation of Korea

2011 Aug. 30: Korean Constitutional Court rules that the failure of the South Korean government to resolve the comfort women dispute is unconstitutional

Dec. 14: Statue of a young girl erected outside the Japanese Embassy in Seoul

2012 May 24: Korean Supreme Court overturns lower courts' rulings, determines that individual claims for compensation under the Treaty on Basic Relations have not been extinguished

Aug. 10: South Korean President Lee Myung-bak lands on Takeshima/Dokdo

2013 March 1: In a speech marking the thirty-first anniversary of March 1 Independence Movement Day, Park Geun-hye excoriates Japanese colonial rule

Dec. 26: Prime Minister Abe Shinzō visits Yasukuni Shrine

2014 June 25: 122 South Korean women forced to serve as comfort women for the US military file against the South Korean government for state compensation

Aug. 5: *Asahi shimbun* acknowledges that Yoshida Seiji's testimony was false and issues a retraction

Sept. 11: *Asahi shimbun* president Kimura Tadakazu holds a press conference to apologize for the paper's comfort women articles

Nov.: It emerges that a massive eight-year reinvestigation by the US government into alleged Japanese and German war crimes failed to uncover evidence of comfort women coercion by Japan

2015 July: Japan and South Korea wrangle at the UNESCO World Heritage committee over "sites of the Meiji Japan Industrial Revolution"; Japanese government uses the phrase "forced to work"

Nov.: First Japan-South Korea summit talks in three and a half years (Abe Shinzō and Park Geun-hye)

Dec.: Japanese and South Korean governments announce agreement on the comfort women issue, stating that, on the premise that the agreed measures are implemented, "this issue is resolved finally and irreversibly with this announcement"

Notes

INTRODUCTION

1. In Japan these islands are known as Takeshima, but in light of the territorial dispute, they are rendered here as Takeshima/Dokdo.

CHAPTER 1

1. *Chinilpa* in Korean—literally, "people friendly toward Japan." In its postwar context, this term refers negatively to Koreans who collaborated with the Japanese government during Japan's colonial rule.

2. Constraints of space limit my data coverage to *Chosun ilbo*, but I should add that all media data in both South Korea and Japan produce similar results.

3. For example, Chung Jae-jeong, "Symposium Seminar III: Perspective on modern Japan-South Korea relations—Learning the wisdom of coexistence from history," *Annals, Public Policy Studies* 8 (May 2014).

4. Ogura Kazuo, *Hiroku: Nikkan 1 chōenshikin* [Confidential notes: One trillion yen between Tokyo and Seoul], Kōdansha (2013) covers this in some detail.

5. *Yomiuri shimbun*, September 13, 1981.

6. Shigemura Toshimitsu and Iimura Tomoki (2010), "Nikkan sōgo orientalism no kokufuku: Gendaishi no kijutsuburi bunseki" [Japan and South Korea's mutual overcoming of Orientalism: Analysis of descriptions in contemporary history] in Second Japan-South Korea Joint History Research Committee Meeting (ed.), *Report on the Second Round of Japan-Korea Joint History Research (Textbook Group)* (2010).

7. For example, it was as of this period that the Society for the Bereaved Families of the Pacific War, comprising Korean war victims, became active. Interview with Yang Sun-im, January 24, 2017, Seoul.

8. Kim Do-hyung, "Hihyōbun" [Critical essay] in Second Japan-South Korea

Joint History Research Committee (ed.), *Report on the Second Round of Japan-South Korea Joint History Research (Textbook Group)* (2010), p. 321.

9. Jeong Na-mi and Kimura Kan, "'Rekishi ninshiki' mondai to daiichiji Nikkan rekishi kyōdō kenkyū o meguru ichikōsatsu: 1" [Reflections on the historical perception issues and the First Japan-South Korea Joint History Research Committee Meeting: 1] in *Kokusai kyōryoku ronshū* 16(1) (July 2008); "'Rekishi ninshiki' mondai to daiichiji Nikkan rekishi kyōdō kenkyū o meguru ichikōsatsu: 2" [Reflections on the historical perception issues and the First Japan-South Korea Joint History Research Committee Meeting: 2] in *Kokusai kyōryoku ronshū* [Journal of International Cooperation Studies] 16(2) (November 2008).

10. It should also be noted that this trend reversed as of 2005, after which the number of references to colonial rule decreased.

11. Shigemura and Iimura, *Nikkan sogō orientalism no kokufuku: Gendaishi no kijutsuburi bunseki.*

12. For example, Nakagawa Shōzō, "Kyōkasho e no kōgi to gohō: Dokusha to *Asahi shimbun*" [Opposition to and false reporting on textbooks: Readers and the *Asahi shimbun* newspaper], *Asahi shimbun*, September 19, 1982. In addition, unless noted otherwise, all references in this book to *Asahi shimbun* articles draw on Kikuzō II Visual, http://database.asahi.com/library2/main/top.php

13. Ezra F. Vogel, *Japan as Number One: Lessons for America*, Boston: Harvard University Press (1979).

14. Obviously, some Japan-related articles will not include the word "Japan," so this is no more than a provisional figure.

15. Analysis in this figure also draws on Kimura Kan, "Discovery of disputes: Collective memories on textbooks and Japanese-South Korean relations," *Journal of Korean Studies* 17(1) (Spring 2012).

16. In this analysis, the author was inspired by the following work: Kenneth E. Boulding, *Conflict and Defense: A General Theory*, New York: Harper & Row (1963).

CHAPTER 2

1. Yomiuri Shimbun Ōsaka Shakaibu (ed.), *Shimbun kisha ga kataritsugu sensō: 8) Sempan* [War as narrated by newspaper journalists: (8) War criminals], Kadokawa Shoten, Ōsaka (1986) deals with the social climate in relation to Class B and C war criminals in some detail.

2. The situation in South Korea immediately after liberation is examined in detail in Gang Jun-man, *Han'guk hyŏndaesa sanch'aek: 1940 nyŏndaep'yŏn* [Strolling through modern Korean history: 1940s], Inmulsa (2002). See also Kimura Kan, *Kankoku gendaishi* [Modern Korean history], Chūkō Shinsho (2008).

3. In Korea, the issue of pro-Japanese collaborators during the period of colonial rule is known as "the issue of punishing pro-Japanese collaborators." For details, see Jeong Un-hyeon, *Ch'inilp'aŭi han'guk hyŏndaesa* [Korean modern history of pro-Japanese collaborators], Inmunsŏwŏn (2016) and Panminjongmunjeyŏn'guso, ed., *Ch'inilp'a 99in: Punyabyŏl chuyo inmurŭi ch'iniriryŏksŏ* [99 pro-Japanese collaborators: Records of major characters, divided by fields], Inmunsŏwŏn (1993).

4. Dong-a ilbo (ed.), *Sŏlsan changdŏksu* [Solsan Chang Dok-soo], Dong-a

Ilbosa (1981), p. 329. These were the words of Shin Ik-hee, who became the first speaker of the National Assembly of South Korea.

5. For details on the Syngman Rhee Line, see works by Fujii Kenji including "Ri Shōban rain senpū e no katei ni kan suru kenkyū" [Research on the Syngman Rhee Line proclamation process], *Chōsen gakuhō* 185 (October 2002).

6. Hosoya Chihiro, *San Francisco kōwa e no michi*, [The road to the San Francisco Peace Treaty], Chūō Kōronsha (1984).

7. See, for example, "Kokumu daijin no enzetsu ni kan suru Suzuki-kun no shitsugi" [Question from Suzuki on the Minister of State's address] in *Kanpō gōgai* (October 16, 1951), p. 12.

8. Kim Deok-ryeon and Seo Eo-ri, "Chitpaphin han'guk, ilbon miguk tchamt-chamie to tanghaetta" [Trampled Korea: Betrayed by Japan and the US again], *Pressian* 15 (October 4, 2014). http://www.pressian.com/news/article.html?no=120624

9. Sogawa Takeo, "Nikkan kihon jōyaku" [Treaty on Basic Relations between Japan and the Republic of Korea] in *Kokusaihō gaikō zasshi* 64(4/5) (March 1966) and Sugiyama Shigeo, "Nikkan kihon jōyaku oyobi zaisan/seikyūken shori kyōtei nado no shomondai" [Issues in relation to the Treaty on Basic Relations between Japan and the Republic of Korea and the Agreement Between Japan and the Republic of Korea Concerning the Settlement of Problems in Regard to Property and Claims and Economic Coopcration] in *Juristo* 327 (August 1965).

10. Further details on this point can be found in Sin Dong-ho, *Onŭrŭi han'gukchŏngch'iwa 6.3 sedae* [Korean politics today and the 6.3 generation], Yemun (1966). See also Kimura Kan, *Minshuka no Kankoku seiji* [The preconditions for Korean democratization], Nagoya Daigaku Shuppankai (2007).

11. Manfred Hettling and Tino Schölz compare Japan to Germany in "Kako to no danzetsu to renzoku: 1945-nen irai no Doitsu to Nihon ni okeru kako to no torikumi" [Distance and continuity: Coming to terms with the past in Germany and Japan after 1945], trans. by Kawakita Atsuko in *Yōroppa kenkyū* 6 (March 2007).

12. See Kimura Kan, *Minshuka no Kankoku seiji* [The preconditions for Korean democratization] in regard to trends among the colonial generation during this period.

13. See Kimura Kan, *Gendai Kankoku seiji-shi* [A history of modern Korean politics] on Park Chung-hee's background.

14. Tatamiya Eitaro, *Hatoyama būmu no butai ura: Seijikisha no shuki* [Behind the scenes of the Hatoyama boom: A political reporter's notes], Jitsugyō no Sekaisha (1955).

15. Ōhinata Ichirō, *Kishi seiken 1241 nichi* [The Kishi administration: 1,241 days], Gyōsei mondai kenkyūjo shuppankyoku (1985).

16. For the background to this, see Kimura Kan, *Minshuka no Kankoku seiji* [The preconditions for Korean democratization].

17. See Kyech'ojŏn'giganhaenghoe (ed.), *Kyech'o pangŭngmojŏn [Biography of Kyecho Pang Ung-mo]*, Chosŏn Ilbosa (1980) on Bang Eung-mo.

18. In relation to Kim Seong-su, see Dong-a Ilbo (ed.), *P'yŏngjŏn inch'on kimsŏngsu: Chogukkwa kyŏree pach'in ilsaeng* [Biography of Inchon Kim Song-su: A life devoted to the nation], Dong-a Ilbosa (1991) and Gwon Seong-yeol (ed.), *Inch'on'gimsŏngsu: Inch'on kimsŏngsuŭi sasanggwa irhwa* [Inchon Kim Song-su: Thoughts and episodes], Dong-a Ilbosa (1985).

19. See Ch'inirinmyŏngsajŏn p'yŏnch'anwiwŏnhoe (ed.), *Ch'inirinmyŏngsajŏn* [List of pro-Japanese collaborators], Minjongmunjeyŏn'guso (2014) on the nature of their collaboration with Japanese colonial rule. The Presidential Committee for the Inspection of Collaborations with Japanese Imperialism, created by the government of the time, also designated them as pro-Japanese collaborators (Kim Minkyoung, "Kukkagigwan-do Kimsŏngsu Pangŭngmo 'ch'inil' injŏng'" [Governmental organization officially identifies the pro-Japanese behaviors of Kim Song-su and Pang Ung-mo], in *The Hankyoreh*, November 12, 2009). In addition, unless stated otherwise, all references to articles from South Korean newspapers other than *Chosun ilbo*, *Dong-a ilbo*, and *JoongAng ilbo* were sourced from KINDS http://www.kinds.or.kr (last accessed October 4, 2016).

20. Kawakami Jōtarō, Miwa Jusō, and many JSP members who were removed from public office had been affiliated with the former Japan Labor-Farmer Party. "'Nichirō' kei shidōsha no sengo to 'shakai shichō': Matsui Masakichi-shi ni kiku" [Postwar experience of the Japan Labor-Farmer Party leaders and social thought: Interview with Matsui Masakichi], *Ōhara shakaimondai kenkyūjo zasshi* 475 (June 1998).

21. Hashimoto Shinobu, "Watashi wa kai ni naritai: Chōhen terebi dorama" [I want to become a shellfish: Feature-length TV program], *Eiga hyōron* 15(11) (November 1958).

22. For example, *Mainichi shimbun* journalist Seki Chieko recalls that "War just wasn't a newsworthy topic—everyone knew everything that was to be known." (Seki Chieko interview, September 29, 2017, Tokyo).

23. Yun Jeong-ok, *Chōsenjosei ga mita ianfu mondai: Ashita o tomo ni tsukuru tame ni* [The comfort women issue seen from the perspective of Korean women: Opening the way for creating tomorrow together], San-ichi Shinsho (1992), and College of Liberal Arts, Ewha Womans University, *Yun Jeong-ok*, http://cms.ewha.ac.kr (last accessed October 1, 2016).

24. Based on searches in the databases Korean Studies Information Service System, http://kiss.kstudy.com (last accessed October 1, 2016) and DBpia, http://www.dbpia.co.kr (last accessed October 1, 2016).

25. Han'gukchŏngshindaeyŏn'guso, *Taeŭnggwa chŏnmang* [Response and Outlook], http://www.truetruth.org/know/know_04.htm (last accessed October 1, 2016).

26. Yun Jeong-ok, "Chŏngshindae wŏnhonŭi palchach'wi ch'wijaegi" [In the Footsteps of the Volunteer Labor Corps], *The Hankyoreh* (January 4, 12, 19, and 24, 1990).

27. It should be noted that at virtually the same time, Germany too was undergoing a process of rediscovering history—namely the historical facts of the Nazi regime. See Reinhard Rürup, "Vergangenheit und demokratische Gesellschaft: Erinnerungspolitik und Erinnerungskultur in Deutschland" (Japanese trans. by Asada Shinji), *Kōkyō kenkyū* 5(2), September 2008.

28. For example, Yun Jeong-ok knew no comfort women when she began her campaign, asking Matsui Yayori for introductions (Yun Jeong-ok, "Chŏngshindae Wŏnhonŭi Palchach'wi Ch'wijaegi," *The Hankyoreh*, January 12, 1990).

29. See Kimura Kan, "Kokusaifunsōka izen no Kankoku ni okeru ianfu mondai o meguru gensetsu jōkyō" [The comfort women discourse in South Korea prior to

the issue becoming an international dispute], *Kokusai kyōryoku ronshū* 22(2/3) (January 2015), on the perception of comfort women in South Korea prior to the 1980s.

30. For example, many former comfort women in South Korea are still afraid of people finding out about this. Interview with anonymous comfort women, Seoul, March 2016.

31. Ikei Masaru, *Orinpikku no seijigaku* [The political science of the Olympics], Maruzen (1992).

32. Park Seh-jik, *Dokyumento: Sōru gorin* [The Seoul Olympics: The inside story], Ushio Publishing (1991).

33. Korean Church Women United (ed.), *Kiisen kankō jittai hōkokusho* [Report on the actual state of *gisaeng* tourism], NCC Christian Church Center for Asian Materials (1984).

34. Han'gukchŏngshindaeyŏn'guso, *Taeŭnggwa chŏnmang* [Response and Outlook].

35. The decline in Japan's importance to South Korea was epitomized by the direct words of President Lee Myung-bak on August 2012: "Japan's influence is no longer what it was." An Hong-gi, "I taet'ongnyŏng: Ilbon yŏnghyangnyŏk, yejŏn katchi ant'a," OhmyNews, August 13, 2012.

36. For example, Japan Institute of International Affairs (ed.), *Shōrai no kokusai jōsei to Nihon no gaikō: 20 nen teido mirai no shinario puranningu* [The future international situation and Japan's diplomacy: Scenario planning for 20 years in the future], Japan Institute of International Affairs (2011).

37. Chapter 3, section 1: Trends in trade and investment in East Asia, *White Paper on International Economy and Trade 2014*, Ministry of Economy, Trade and Industry (2014).

38. EUROSTAT, "Intra-EU trade in goods—recent trends," http://ec.europa.eu/eurostat/statistics-explained/index.php/Intra-EU_trade_in_goods_-_recent_trends (last accessed October 1, 2016).

39. Trade Statistics of Japan, Ministry of Finance, http://www.customs.go.jp/toukei/suii/html/time.htm (last accessed October 1, 2016).

40. See Kimura Kan, "Shinseikenka no Nikkan kankei: Nikkan ryōkoku wa naze tairitsu suru ka" [Japan-South Korea relations under the new regime: Why do Japan and Korea collide?)], *Mondai to kenkyū* 42(4) (December 2013).

41. See Ko Yon-soo, *Kankoku no kigyō/kinyū kaikaku* [South Korean companies and financial reform], Tōyōkeizai shinpōsha (2009) on the string of currency crises and the response of the South Korean government.

42. Mukōyama Hidehiko, "Tsuyomaru Kankoku no tai-Chū keizai izon: Kenzaika suru jirenma" [South Korea's growing dependence on the Chinese economy: An emerging dilemma], *JRI Rebyū* 16(16) (2014).

43. See Abe Takeshi, *Tsūshōsangyō seisakushi 1980-2000 Dai 2 kan: Tsūshō bōeki seisaku* [The history of trade and industry policy 1980-2000 Vol. 2: Trade policy], Research Institute of Economy, Trade and Industry (2013).

44. Korean Economic Planning Board (ed.), *Chep8hoe han'gukt'onggyenyŏn'gam* [Eighth Korean Statistical Yearbook], National Bureau of Statistics, Economic Planning Board, Republic of Korea (1961).

45. In this regard Sano Kōji, "Kankoku no seichō moderu to Nikkan keizai kankei no henka; Nikkan kankei akka no keizaiteki haikei" [South Korea's growth

model and the change in economic relations between Japan and South Korea; Economic background to the deteriorating relations between Japan and South Korea], *Shōgaku ronshū* 83(2), provides a succinct summary.

CHAPTER 3

1. For a detailed analysis of the first history textbook dispute which broke out in 1982, see Kimura Kan, "Discovery of Disputes: Collective Memories on Textbooks and Japanese-South Korean Relations," *Journal of Korean Studies* 17(1) (Spring 2012), pp. 97–124.

2. Details of the Japan-South Korea Joint History Research Project and its results can be found on the Japan-Korea Cultural Foundation website http://www. jkcf.or.jp/projects/kaigi/history (Japanese only), as well as Kimura Kan, "How should we approach Japan-South Korea joint history research? Observations of a participant" in *The Journal of Contemporary Korean Studies* 10 (2011).

3. Shigemura and Iimura (2010), "Nikkan sōgo orientalism no kokufuku: Gendaishi no kijutsuburi bunseki" [Japan and South Korea's mutual overcoming of Orientalism: Analysis of descriptions in contemporary history].

4. See Ienaga Kyōkasho Soshō Bengodan (ed.), *Ienaga kyōkasho saiban: 32-nen ni wataru bengodan katsudō no sōkatsu* [The Ienaga textbook trials: Summary of the defense team's 32 years of activity], Nihon Hyōronsha (1998) for details of the trajectory of the Ienaga trials. Other references include Ōta Takashi, Oyama Hiroshi, and Nagahara Keiji (eds.), *Ienaga Saburō no nokoshita mono, hikitsugu mono* [What Ienaga Saburō left behind, what has been carried on], Nihon Hyōronsha (2003) and Ienaga Saburō, *kyōkasho saiban* [The textbook trials], Nihon Hyōronsha (1981).

5. For example, "Kaisetsu: 'Kentei' dō sabaku: Ienaga kyōkasho soshō, yōka ni saikōsaihanketsu, shidō yōryō ni tachiiru ka, kyōikuken ronsō no kakushin, gakushara chūmoku" [Editorial: How will screening be addressed? Supreme Court decision in Ienaga textbook trial to be handed down on the 8th; academics watch to see whether the court will address curriculum guidance as an issue at the core of the "right to education" debate], *Asahi shimbun*, April 4, 1982.

6. "Noshikakaru Ienaga soshō" [The looming Ienaga lawsuit decision], *Asahi shimbun*, August 20, 1982.

7. "*Kentei fugōkaku Nihonshi:* Ienaga kyōkasho ga besutoserā" [*Japanese History: The Version that Failed the Screening:* Ienaga textbook becomes a bestseller], *Mainichi shimbun*, June 11, 1974. Unless stated otherwise, all *Mainichi shimbun* articles drawn from the *Mainichi shimbun* database "Maisaku" (https://mainichi.jp/contents/edu/maisaku/login.html; last accessed October 3, 2016).

8. "Kyōkasho kentei mondai: Ienaga soshō ni hamon" [Textbook screening issue: Impact on Ienaga trial], *Mainichi shimbun*, August 27, 1982.

9. "Ilbon kyogwasŏ kŏmjŏngkanghwa, ch'imnyakyongŏ modusakche" [Reinforcement of official textbook screening: All words regarding invasion deleted], *Chosun ilbo*, June 27, 1982. Unless stated otherwise, all *Chosun ilbo* articles drawn from the *Chosun ilbo* database "Chosŏndatk'ŏm Kŏmsaek" (http://search.chosun.com/search/main.search; last accessed October 3, 2016).

10. "Ilbon saegyogwasŏ, 2ch'adaejŏnŭl chŏngdanghwa. 'Han'gukchibaegwŏn' dŭng moyokchŏkp'yohyŏn. Chunggongyŏksawaegokpinan" [New Japanese history

textbooks justify WWII, using insulting words such as "the right to rule Korea." Communist China also criticizes the textbooks], *Chosun ilbo*, June 29, 1982.

11. "Haegoehan ilbon'gyogwasŏ. Ch'immugŭi yŏksanŭn hododoelsu ŏpsŏ. Kyogwasŏmunjesowiuiwŏnyŏnetugi-ro" [A horrific Japanese textbook: History of silence returns], *Chosun ilbo*, July 8, 1982.

12. On this point, see Kim, Joo-un, *Han'gugŭi ŏllont'ongje: Ŏllont'ongjee taehan majimak kirogi-gil yŏmwŏnhamyŏ* [Korean media control: Will this be the last record on media control in this country?], Ribuk (2008), as well as Kim Min-jeong, *Kankoku no media kontorōru: Chun Doo-hwan seikenka ni okeru KOBACO no tanjō to media kontorōru no jisshōteki kenkyū* [Media control in South Korea: Empirical research on the birth of KOBACO and media control under the Chun Doo-hwan administration], V2 Solution, 2009.

13. "Shinryaku bokashi no kyōkasho kentei: Chūgoku ni tsuzuki Kankoku mo hihan, Jinmin nippō hajimete kōshiki ni, Chūgoku no kōgi" [Textbook screenings have shades of invasion: Korea follows China in criticizing Japan; People's Daily tenders China's first formal protest], *Asahi shimbun*, July 21, 1982. A Japanese translation of the short commentary was drawn from the following website ("Kono kyōkun wa shikkari to oboete okaneba naranai" [We must imprint this lesson on our memories]), *People's Daily*, July 20, 1982. Tanaka Akihiko, Institute for Advanced Studies on Asia, University of Tokyo, The World and Japan Database Project, *Documents Related to Japan-China Relations* (http://www.ioc.u-tokyo.ac.jp/~worldjpn/documents/indices/JPCH/index.html).

14. "Kyōkasho kentei de Shinka-sha ga hihan, Nicchū seimei ni hihan, shinryaku ni hansei wasureta kōi" [Xinhua criticizes textbook screening as contravening the Japan-China Declaration and behavior forgetting remorse over the invasion], *Asahi shimbun*, July 23, 1982.

15. "Ribenqinluezhong1guodilishiburongcuangai" [We will not allow the distortion of history], *People's Daily*, July 24, 1982. Tanaka Akihiko, Institute for Advanced Studies on Asia, University of Tokyo, The World and Japan Database Project, *Documents Related to Japan-China Relations* (http://www.ioc.u-tokyo.ac.jp/~worldjpn/documents/indices/JPCH/index.html).

16. "Seifu, taiōni kuryo" [Government struggles to respond], *Asahi shimbun*, July 27, 1982.

17. See Takahara Akio and Hattori Ryūji, *Nicchūkankeishi 1972–2012 (1): Seiji* [A History of Japan-China Relations, 1972–2012 (1): Politics], University of Tokyo Press (2012) on Japan-China relations at the time.

18. "Kyōkasho kijutsu henkō, gaikō mondai ni hatten, Chūgoku kōshiki ni kōgi" [Changes to textbook references escalate into a diplomatic issue, China makes a formal complaint], *Asahi shimbun*, July 27, 1982.

19. Ibid.

20. See I Seong-il, "1992 nyŏnhanjunggukkyojŏngsanghwa ŭiŭie kwanhan chaegoch'al: Hanbandowachunggukkwaŭi kwan'gye kujobyŏnhwarŭlchungshimŭ-ro" [Examination of the significance of normalization of China-Korea Relations in 1992: Focusing on changes in the structure of relations between China and the Korean Peninsula], *Chungguk'ak* 40 (December 2011) on South Korea-China relations during the Cold War.

21. A typical example of this argument is the article "Hitokawa mukeba igami

atte iru: Chūgoku, Kankoku, han-Nichirengō no jakuten" [At each other's throats just under the surface: The frailty of the anti-Japan alliance], *Shūkan shinchō*, July 17, 2014.

22. Chŏngbu, "Irŭi ch'imnyaksawaegukkongshik t'aeŭngyŏbukoshim" [Government struggles to form policies against distortions of history by Japanese government], *Chosun ilbo*, July 25, 1982.

23. Chŏngbu, "Onŭl kagŭisŏ taeŭngch'aek kyŏlchŏng, Ilbon'gyogwasŏ waegok; Kangnyo mangŏn'hyŏbŭi: Kyŏnghyŏpkwa pyŏl-do . . . Ŏmjungch'ŏrik'i-ro" [At today's cabinet meeting, government decides policies against Japanese government's distortion of history and reckless words], *Chosun ilbo*, July 27, 1982; "Gunkoku shugi e no gyakuryū: Chūgoku kaihōgunpō yori kibishii mikata" [Militarism backlash: Harsher outlook expressed in Liberation Army Daily], *Mainichi shimbun*, August 3, 1982.

24. "24 kaehangmok 167 kunde waegok. Kuksap'yŏnch'anwi, Ilbon kyogwasŏ 16 chong han'gukkwan'gye punsŏk" [167 items distorted in 24 places, National Institute of History analyzes 16 Japanese textbooks about parts of Korean history], *Chosun ilbo*, August 6, 1982.

25. "Pandaehisŭt'e-ri' Ilbonsahoe . . . Ibŏnenugyŏnghwa allŭregi. Ŏllonŭi 'panbokkyoyug' i kungmin senoe kaehŏndŭng hyŏnshillonen ilchehi 'Kŏbu'" ["Opposition hysteria" in Japanese society, allergy against right wing ideology: "Repeated education" by media brainwashes the people to resist all realistic policies such as constitutional amendment], *Chosun ilbo*, May 9, 1981.

26. "Yŏksaŭi choe' toep'uri haryŏna. Ilbon'gyogwasŏ 'Pyŏnshin' . . . Paegyŏnggwa teach'aek taedam" [Japanese textbook changes try to wash away the sins of history: Background and counterplans], *Chosun ilbo*, July 25, 1982.

27. Son Ki Sup, "Hanil anbogyŏnghyŏp oegyoŭi chŏngch'aekkyŏlchŏng: 1981–1983 NyŏnIlbonŭitaehan'guk chŏngbuch'agwan" [Japan's $4 billion Korean aid policy 1981–1983], *Kukchejŏngch'inonch'ong* 49(1) (2009).

28. Moon Chang-keuk, *Hanmi kaltŭngŭi haebu* [Anatomy of the US-ROK conflict], Nanam (1994); Hong Seuk-ryule, "K'at'ŏ haengjŏngbugi migugŭi taehanban-do chŏngch'aekkwa 3 chahoedam" [Korea's America policy and trilateral talks with the Carter administration], *Han'gukkwagukchejŏngch'i* 32(2) (2016); Kimura Kan, *Kankoku gendaishi* [History of modern Korea], Chūō Kōronsha (2008).

29. Frederic P. Miller, Agnes F. Vandome, and John McBrewster (eds.), *Koreagate: Political Scandal, South Korea, Richard Nixon, National Intelligence Service (South Korea), Tongsun Park, Unification Church, Sun Myung Moon*, Beau Bassin, Mauritius, Alphascript Pub. (2011).

30. In relation to Kim Hyung-wook, see Kim Hyung-wook, *Kimhyŏnguk'oegorok* [Memoir of Kim Hyung-wook], Ach'im (1985), Son Chung-mu, *Kimhyŏnguk: Ch'oehuŭi kŭŏlgul* [Kim Hyung-wook: The last face], Munhagyesulsa (1986), and Kim Hyung-wook, *Kenryoku to inbō: Moto KCIA buchō Kim Hyung-wook ga kataru* [Power and conspiracy: Former KCIA chief Kim Hyung-wook tells all], Gōdō Shuppan (1981).

31. Cho Gab-je, *Yugo!:Pumasat'aeesŏ 10.26 chŏngbyŏnkkaji yushinjŏnggwŏnŭl punggoeshik'in hamsŏng gwach'ongsŏngŭi hyŏnjang1-2* [The death of a president: From the Puma incident to the presidential assassination], Han'gilsa (1987) provides a vivid description of Park's frame of mind at the time.

32. Furuno Yoshimasa, *Kin Dai-chū jiken no seiji ketchaku: Shuken hōki shita Nihon seifu* [The political resolution of the Kim Dae-jung incident: The Japanese government renounces sovereignty], Tōhō shuppan (2007), Mainichi shimbunsha (ed.), *Kin Dai-chū jiken zenbō* [The full picture of the Kim Dae-jung incident], Mainichi Shimbunsha (1978).

33. Yu Sun-hee, *Boku Seiki no tai-Nichi, tai-Bei gaikō: Reisen henyōki Kankoku no seiji, 1968–1973* [Park Chung-hee's Japan and US diplomacy: Korean politics during the period of Cold War transformation], Minerva Shobō (2012).

34. Michael Hausenfleck, *The Reagan Doctrine: A Conceptual Analysis of the Democracy Imperative in U.S. Foreign Policy, 1981–1988*, UMI Dissertation Services (1995).

35. John Hackett, *The Third World War: The Untold Story* (Japanese translation by Aoki Eiichi, Futami Shobō) (1978). See also "John Hackett's The Third World War," *Mainichi shimbun*, August 12, 1978.

36. Fukunaga Fumio, *Ōhira Masayoshi: "Sengohoshu" to wa nani ka* [Ōhira Masayoshi: The thought and behavior of the postwar conservatives], Chūō Kōron Shinsha (2008).

37. Okada Ichirō, *Kakushin jichitai: Nekkyō to zasetsu ni nani o manabu ka* [Reformist local governments: What was learned from passion and setbacks], Chūō Kōron Shinsha (2016).

38. See Sugiyama Shōzō, *Yatōgaikō no shōgen* [Testimony on opposition party diplomacy], Minerva Shobō (1982) and Katsumata Seiichi, *Gaikō tōiinchō kokkai katsudō no sokuseki* [The footprints of diplomacy, party chairmanship and Diet activities], Nihon shakaitō chūō honbu kikanshikyoku (1987) on the JSP's foreign policy line.

39. "Nikkan mondai: Kankoku to no chokusetsu kōshō nozomu Shakaitō taisaku kettei" [The Japan-Korea issue: JSP decides on a policy of direct negotiations with South Korea], *Mainichi shimbun*, June 10, 1955, "Nikkan mondai: Ri Rain mondai, mondai kaiketsu ni Kankoku e Kagawa-shi o haken, Suzuki Shakaitō iinchō kataru" [The Japan-Korea issue: JSP Chairman Suzuki discusses the dispatch of Kagawa to Korea to try to resolve the Syngman Rhee Line issue], *Mainichi shimbun*, January 14, 1956.

40. "Kankoku no Nihon gyosen hokaku jiken: Sumiyaka na kaiketsu o yōbō, uha Shakaitō seimei" [Korean arrest of Japanese fishing vessels: Rightist JSP issues a statement calling for an early resolution], *Mainichi shimbun*, February 23, 1953, "Nihon Shakaitō uha: Takeshima mondai de Kankoku ni kōgi, seifu ni yōbō" [Right wing of JSP calls on government to complain to South Korea about the Takeshima issue], *Mainichi shimbun*, June 10, 1953.

41. "Taikankoku, Kitachōsen kankei, Nikkan kaidan, honkaidan, kaidan hantai ni kokumin undō, Shakaitō ketsugi" [Main talks get underway at Japan-South Korea talks on relations with North and South Korea, JSP adopts a resolution on a national protest against the talks], *Mainichi shimbun*, January 22, 1962.

42. "Shakaitō: Kitachōsen to no kokkō sokushin nado, tōmen no gaikō hōshin o kimeru" [JSP adopts an interim foreign policy line, including pursuing diplomatic relations with North Korea], *Mainichi shimbun*, February 21, 1966.

43. "Shakaitō no Kitachōsen hōmon: Pyonyan de daihyōdan no kangeikai" [JSP North Korea visit: Reception held in Pyongyang for delegation], *Mainichi shim-*

bun, August 16, 1970. See also Sugiyama Shōzō, *Yatōgaikō no shōgen* [Testimony on opposition party diplomacy].

44. "Nichibeikan taisei o keikai, Asukata-Kin Nissei talks" [Asukata-Kim Il-sung talks, concerns about the Japan-US-South Korea alliance], *Yomiuri shimbun*, March 15, 1981. Unless stated otherwise, all *Yomiuri shimbun* articles drawn from the *Yomiuri shimbun* database "Yomidasu rekishikan" (https://database.yomiuri.co.jp/rekishikan; last accessed October 3, 2016).

45. "Hikaku, heiwa chitai sōsetsu e, kaku tekkyo to gaikokugun tettai o, Shatō, Kitachōsen Rōdōtō ga kyōdō sengen" [JSP and North Korea's Labour Party release a joint declaration on establishing a nuclear-free peace zone, the elimination of nuclear weapons, and the withdrawal of foreign forces], *Yomiuri shimbun*, March 16, 1981, and "Asukata-Kin kaidan, ryōshi no hatsugen yōshi" [Summary of remarks by Asakata and Kim at talks], *Yomiuri shimbun*, March 15, 1981.

46. "Taikan kōshō tōketsu seyo, Shatō, gaishō ni mōshiire, Nikkan kankei" [JSP calls on foreign minister to freeze negotiations with South Korea, Japan-South Korea relations], *Asahi shimbun*, December 24, 1981, "Gunjijūshi no taikan keizai kyōryoku yameyo, Shatō fukuiinchō mōshiire" [JSP deputy chair calls for Japan to desist with military-oriented economic cooperation for South Korea], *Yomiuri shimbun*, August 8, 1981.

47. "Nikkan fuhai tettei kyūmei o sōhyo ya shakyō nado 70dantai daihyō ga apiiru Nikkan yuchaku" [Representatives of 70 organizations, including the General Council of Trade Unions of Japan, JSP, and JCP, call for thorough clarification of corruptions between Japan and South Korea, Japan-South Korea collusion] and "Beikan kankeisha no bakuro ni kitai shatō-daihyō-dan bei de kataru shatō-hōbei-dan" [JSP delegation says expecting disclosure by parties related to US and South Korea in US], *Asahi shimbun*, February 17, 1977.

CHAPTER 4

1. See Kimura Kan, "Daiichi rekishi kyōkasho funsō kara kokunichi undō e: Zentōkan seikenki no tai-Nichi-kan no henka ni tsuite no ichikōsatsu" [From the first history textbook dispute to the Kuk-il (Overcome Japan) movement: A few thoughts on the change in perceptions of Japan during the term of the Chun Doo-hwan administration], *Journal of International Cooperation* 22(1) (July 2014).

2. Yu Sun-hee, *Boku Seiki no tai-Nichi, tai-Bei gaikō* [Park Chung-hee's Japan and US diplomacy: Korean Politics During the Period of Cold War Transformation].

3. Murata Kōji, *Daitōryō no zasetsu: Kātā seiken no zai-Kan Beigun tettai seisaku* [President Carter's troop withdrawal policy from South Korea], Yūhikaku (1998).

4. "Minshutō yūi tamotsu: Beichūkan senkyo, Kātā daitōryō, fukuzatsu na shōri" [Democrats remain on top: US interim election sees a complicated victory for President Carter], *Yomiuri shimbun*, November 9, 1978.

5. "Kenedi shi nibai no ninki: Taikātā/beidaitōryō kōho shimei arasoi" [Kennedy twice as popular: Fight against Carter for the presidential nomination], *Yomiuri shimbun*, November 2, 1979.

6. Prior to the establishment of their regime, Chun and his military group executed two military coups. The first was on December 12, 1979, through which

they kicked out older military generals such as General Officer Jeong Seung-hwa, who was chief of general staff under Park Chun-hee, and established hegemony over South Korea's military forces. The second was a de facto coup on May 17, 1980, through which they expelled major politicians such as the three Kims (Kim Jong-pil, Kim Young-sam and Kim Dae-jung) to sweep clean the political arena.

7. Kimura Kan, "Shihai seitō ni miru Boku Seiki seiken kara Zen Tokan seiken e no renzoku to danzetsu" [Continuity and disruption in the shift from the Park Chung-hee administration to the Chun Doo-hwan administration within the ruling party], *Journal of International Cooperation Studies* 20(2–3) (January 2013). See also Tamura Tetsuo, *Gekidō Sōru 1500 nichi: Zen Tokan seiken e no michi* [1,500 dramatic days in Seoul: The road to the Chun Doo-hwan administration], Seikō Shobō (1984).

8. Hattori Ryūji, *Nakasone Yasuhiro: "Daitōryōteki shushō" no kiseki* [Nakasone Yasuhiro: The presidential prime minister], Chūō Kōron Shinsha (2015).

9. "Rēgan shi ga ichii: Furorida shū de ninki tōhyō, Kyōwatō daitōryō kōho, daitōryō senkyo" [Reagan takes the lead as Republican presidential candidate after winning the popular vote in Florida, presidential elections], *Asahi shimbun*, May 27, 1980.

10. Murata Kōji, *Rēgan: Ika ni shite "Amerika no gūzō" to natta ka* [How Reagan became an American idol], Chūō Kōron Shinsha (2011).

11. See Chi Tong-wook, *Kankoku daitōryō retsuden: Kenryokusha no eiga to tenraku* [The lives of Korea's presidents: The power, the glory, and the fall], Chūō Kōron Shinsha (2002), on the histories of these presidents.

12. A play on words using the similarity between the pronunciation of "Heo" and "four."

13. Kimura Kan, "Shihai seitō ni miru Boku Seiki seiken kara Zen Tokan seiken e no renzoku to danzetsu" [Continuity and disruption in the shift from the Park Chung-hee administration to the Chun Doo-hwan administration within the ruling party].

14. See Cheon Geum-seong, *Hwanggangesŏ pugakkkaji* [From Hwanggang River to Mount Puggak], Tongsŏmunhwasa (1981), on Chun Doo-hwan's early years.

15. Interview with Heo Hwa-pyeong in Seoul on March 25, 2012.

16. Cheon Geum-seong, *Hwanggangesŏ pugakkkaji* [From Hwanggang River to Mount Puggak].

17. Ogura Kazuo, *Hiroku: Nikkan icchōen shikin* [Confidential notes: One trillion yen between. Tokyo and Seoul].

18. Korean Economic Planning Board, *Han'gukt'onggyenyŏn'gam* [Korea statistical yearbook], Kyŏngjegihwawŏnt'onggyeguk (1967).

19. Ministry of Justice, *Shutsunyūkoku kanri tōkei tōkeihyō* [Immigration control statistics], http://www.moj.go.jp/housei/toukei/toukei_ichiran_nyukan.html (last accessed September 1, 2016).

20. For example, interview with Heo Mun-do on March 5, 2012, in Suwon, South Korea.

21. This section draws primarily on the above-cited interview with Heo Mun-do.

22. "Sae chuilt'ŭkp'awŏne hŏmundogija huim, Kimyunhwan'gukchang kwisa" [Heo Mun-do appointed new Tokyo correspondent, Kim Yun-hwan returns to Seoul], *Chosun ilbo*, July 16, 1974.

23. See "Hŏmundo chŏn kukt'ot'ongirwŏn changgwan pyŏlse" [Former unification minister Heo Mun-do dies], *Chosun ilbo*, March 5, 2016, on Heo Mun-do's career.

24. "3 Kimshidae p'ungmihaettŏn 'k'ingmeik'ŏ' kimyunhwan t'agye" [Kim Yun-hwan, "king-maker" of the Three Kim period, dies], *OhmyNews*, December 15, 2003.

25. "JAL ki napch'ibŏm ch'ep'o, sŭnggaek 76 myŏng chŏnwŏn musa" [JAL plane hijacker arrested, 76 passengers safe], *Chosun ilbo*, July 17, 1974.

26. "Munsaeganchipsŏ kwŏnch'ong-do 'pŏmhaeng kyehoek sugi' palgyŏn. Sŏurhaengttae kŏaeginch'ul sashil-do" [Pistol and assassination plan discovered at home of Mun Sae-gang. Mun also withdrew a large sum of money for his journey to Seoul], *Chosun ilbo*, August 18, 1974.

27. See Han Yang-myeong and Ahn Tae-hyun, "Ch'ukche chŏngch'iŭi tu p'unggyŏng: Kukp'ungp1kwa taehaktaedongje" [Two scenes of festival politics: Kukp'ung 81 and the Campus Festival], *Pigyominsok'ak* 26 (February 2004), and "Ŏjeŭi onŭl: 1981 nyŏn munhwadaech'ukche 'Kukp'ung 81'" [Yesterday and today: Kukpung 81, a major cultural festival in 1981], *Kyunghyang shinmuns*, May 27, 2009, on this event.

28. "Shinnyŏnt'ŭkchip: Kŭgirŭi-gil ilbonŭl alcha" [New Year special: Know Japan to overcome Japan], *Chosun ilbo*, January 1, 1983.

29. Interview with Lee Do-hyeong on December 8, 2012, in Seoul.

30. See Taehanmin'guk'ŏnjŏnghoe, *Taebyŏl hoewŏnjŏngbo* [Member information] (http://rokps.or.kr/profile; last accessed October 1, 2016), on Choi Byeong-ryeo's career.

31. See Kimura Kan, *Nihon ni okeru Kankoku/Chōsen kenkyū to sono kadai* [Research on South and North Korea in Japan and the challenges presented] and Shu Shing-ching (ed.), *Kindai Higashi-Ajia no aporia* [The aporia of modern East Asia], National Taiwan University Press (2014).

32. For example, Nikkan rekishikyōkasho kenkyūkai (ed.), *Kyōkasho o Nikkankyōryoku de kangaeru* [Japan-South Korea cooperation through the lens of textbooks], Ōtsuki Shoten (1993) and *Dai ikkai Nikkan gōdō rekishikyōkasho kenkyūkai: Kenkyū hōkokusho* [The first Japan-South Korea Joint History Research Project: Research report], Nikkan rekishikyōkasho kenkyūkai (1991). These works vividly depict the difference in attitude of the Japanese and South Korean researchers involved in the Japan-South Korea Joint History Research Project in the early 1990s.

33. Japan Conference website (http://www.nipponkaigi.org/about; last accessed October 1, 2016). See also Sugano Tamotsu, *Nippon kaigi no kenkyū* [Research on Japan Conference], Fusōsha (2016).

34. "Nihon o Mamoru Kokumin Kaigi kyōkasho no kiseki: Tanjō . . . ketchaku, irei zukume" [Trajectory and birth of the People's Conference to Protect Japan's textbook: An unusual conclusion], *Asahi shimbun*, July 10, 1986.

35. Labelled the "Miyazawa Textbook Statement." "Seifu kenkai (Kanbōchōkan danwa) zenbun: Seifu kenkai o happyō" [Entire text of the government's position

(Chief Cabinet Secretary Statement): Government announces its position], *Asahi shimbun*, August 27, 1982.

36. The following description draws primarily on Murao Jirō (ed.), *Shinpen Nihonshi no subete: Atarashii Nihonshi kyōkasho no sōzō e* [The story of "New Version of Japanese History": The creation of a new Japanese history textbook"], Hara Shobō (1987) and "Nihon o Mamoru Kokumin Kaigi kyōkasho no kiseki: Tanjō . . . ketchaku, irei zukume" [Trajectory and birth of the People's Conference to Protect Japan's textbook: An unusual conclusion], *Asahi shimbun*, July 10, 1986.

37. *Nihon no ibuki*, April 15, 1985.

38. "Kyōkasho mondai giin renmei ga hossoku" [Diet Members' Alliance for Considering the Textbook Issue launched], *Asahi shimbun*, October 26, 1985.

39. "Dai niji Nakasone dai 2 kai kaizō naikaku kakuryō no kaoburе" [Ministerial lineup in the second reorganized cabinet under the second Nakasone administration], *Asahi shimbun*, December 29, 1985.

40. "Nihon o Mamoru Kokumin Kaigi kyōkasho no kiseki: Tanjō . . . ketchaku, irei zukume" [Trajectory and birth of the Group for the Protection of Japan's textbook: An unusual conclusion].

41. "Nihon o Mamoru Kokumin Kaigi kyōkasho no kiseki: Tanjō . . . ketchaku, irei zukume" [Trajectory and birth of the Group for the Protection of Japan's textbook: An unusual conclusion].

42. "Nakasone shushō, mamoru kaigi no kyōkasho shūsei ni kitai" [PM Nakasone expects revisions to People's Conference textbook], *Asahi shimbun*, July 3, 1986.

43. "Nihon o Mamoru Kokumin Kaigi kyōkasho no kiseki: Tanjō . . . ketchaku, irei zukume" [Trajectory and birth of the People's Conference to Protect Japan's textbook: An unusual conclusion].

44. This is the same phrase as Emperor Hirohito used when he announced the unconditional surrender to the allied forces on August 15, 1945.

45. Nihon o Mamoru Kokumin Kaigi kyōkasho no kiseki: Tanjō . . . ketchaku, irei zukume" [Trajectory and birth of the Group for the Protection of Japan's textbook: An unusual conclusion].

46. "Nihon o Mamoru Kokumin Kaigi kyōkasho no kiseki: Tanjō . . . ketchaku, irei zukume" [Trajectory and birth of the Group for the Protection of Japan's textbook: An unusual conclusion].

47. The way in which it all developed is covered in "Kyōkasho kakikae kyohi: Nihon o Mamoru Kokumin Kaigi tsūkoku"[Warning issued over People's Conference refusal of textbook rewrite] and "Kyōkasho (Nihon o Mamoru Kokumin Kaigi) kakikaeneba, fugōkaku o kangaeru: Bunshō kyōchō" [Education Minister stresses that People's Conference textbook could be rejected if changes aren't made], *Yomiuri shimbun*, July 1, 1986; "Kyōkasho shūsei ōjiru: Nihon o mamoru Kokumin kaigi, kentei sagyō o saikai" [People's Conference accepts textbook changes, screening resumes] and "Kyōkasho kakikae konya ni mo seishiki kaitō: Nihon o Mamoru Kokumin Kaigi" [Official response to textbook revision request expected from People's Conference this evening], *Yomiuri shimbun*, July 3, 1986; "Kyōkasho kakikae ni kōgi seimei: Nihon o Mamoru Kokumin Kaigi" [People's Conference announces complaint about textbook revisions], *Yomiuri shimbun*, July 9, 1986.

48. "Shinpen Nihonshi saitaku wa 31 kō, yaku 8,300 bu" [31 schools adopt *New Version of Japanese History* (around 8,300 copies)], *Asahi shimbun*, September 6, 1986.

CHAPTER 5

1. See Yun Kŏn-chūa, *Gendai Kankoku no shisō: 1980–1990 nendai* [Modern Korean thought in the 1980s and 1990s], Iwanami Shoten (2000), on ideological tendencies from the 1980s to the 1990s in South Korea.

2. The Recruit scandal was an insider trading and corruption scandal that came to light in Japan in 1988. Shares in Recruit Cosmos, a then-unlisted real estate company, were handed out as bribes. Those Recruit personnel responsible for handing out the bribes and the politicians and bureaucrats who accepted them were arrested in a major scandal that shook the worlds of politics, bureaucracy, and mass media.

3. Hattori Ryūji, *Nakasone Yasuhiro: "Daitōryōteki shushō" no kiseki* [Nakasone Yasuhiro: The presidential prime minister].

4. See Gotō Kenji, *Takeshita seiken: 576 nichi* [The 576 days of the Takeshita administration], Gyōken Shuppankyoku (2000), on the Takeshita administration.

5. As the first female politician in Japan to lead a major party, Doi Takako's appointment attracted great interest, and her frank personality spurred a temporary boom in the JSP's popularity. For example, "2 oku kaseida otaka san: Watashi no CM uotchingu" [Takako earns 20 million yen: My TVCM viewing], *Asahi shimbun*, October 31, 1986.

6. "'Shushō taijin' kyō kyōgi, jiki ga shōten ni, 89 saninsen de jimin zanpai" [PM's exit discussed today; focus on timing; crushing loss for LDP in 1989 upper house election], *Asahi shimbun*, July 25, 1989.

7. The following description draws heavily on Sugiyama Shōzō, *Yatō gaikō no shōgen* [Testimony on opposition party diplomacy], as well as "Shakaitō no tai-Kanhōkan seisaku no suii" (1965 nen–1989 nen 11 gatsu)" [Trends in the JSP's South Korea policy: 1965–November 1989], *Asahi shimbun*, December 20, 1989.

8. "Kankoku yatō to sesshoku shitai shatō, Kita Chōsen ni hyōmei" [JSP tells North Korea that it wants to make contact with South Korea's opposition party], *Asahi shimbun*, May 23, 1985.

9. "Hansei, hantō zentai ni, shakyō ryōtō wa zen daitōryō kangeien de no tennō aisatsu ni hihanteki" [Expressions of remorse should be directed to a whole peninsula, JSP and the Communist Party both critical of Emperor's words at Chun Doo-hwan reception], *Asahi shimbun*, September 7, 1984.

10. "Tennō no o-kotoba de yatō jirenma, Kankoku no kokumin kanjō kizukai, seijiriyō o kenen" [Emperor's works pose dilemma for opposition parties; sensitivity to Korean public sentiment; concern at political exploitation], *Asahi shimbun*, September 3, 1984.

11. For example, "Kin Eisan shi, Ishibashi shi ni hō-Kan yōsei" [Kim Young-sam asks Ishibashi to visit South Korea], *Asahi shimbun*, October 4, 1985, "Shatōseikōken to Kin Eisan shi kaidan" [Talks between JSP Seikōken faction and Kim Young-sam], *Asahi shimbun*, October 9, 1985.

12. "Hō-Kan o gensoku jiyūka, minshuka no ugoki hyōka, Shakaitō hōshin"

[JSP decides to allow visits to South Korea, lauds democratization efforts], *Asahi shimbun*, February 11, 1988.

13. "Shakaitō no Ishibashi shi ga hō-Kan" [JSP's Ishibashi visits South Korea], *Asahi shimbun*, October 12, 1988.

14. However, South Korea was at that time concerned about JSP visits. "Shakaitō Hō-Kan daihyōdan ga irei no oboegaki, Kankoku taishikan ni biza shin-seiji" [JSP delegation to South Korea draws up unprecedented memo, applies to South Korean embassy for visas], *Asahi shimbun*, December 21, 1989.

15. "Kankoku to no kōryū, sekkyokuteki ni suishin, hō-Kan no shakai, Yama-guchi Shokichō kaiken" [JSP secretary-general Yamaguchi holds press briefing on Korea visits, notes that JSP will actively pursue exchange with South Korea], *Asahi shimbun*, December 22, 1989.

16. "Ro Kankoku daitōryō ga rainichi, shuppatsu seimei de, shin no yūkō kōchiku e" [Korean President Roh visits Japan, notes on departure that he aims to build true friendship], *Asahi shimbun*, May 24, 1990.

17. "Kyuchu bansankai de no Tenno Heika no o-kotoba" [Emperor's comment at Court banquet], *Asahi shimbun*, May 25, 1990.

18. "Sha, kō, min, shamin, kihonteki ni kōtei, kyōsan wa hihan, Tennō Heika no o-kotoba" [JSP, Komeitō, DPJ, SDP basically approve Emperor's comment, JCP critical], *Asahi shimbun*, May 25, 1990.

19. "Doi shi hō-Kan, gensoku de itchi, Ro daitōryō to shatō iinchō" [President Roh and JSP leader meet, agree in principle on Doi South Korea visit], *Asahi shimbun*, May 25, 1990.

20. "Sensō sekinin kokkai ketsugi, Yamaguchi shatō shokichō ga kyōryoku yōsei, tatō wa shōkyoku shisei" [JSP's Yamaguchi seeks cooperation on war respon-sibility Diet resolution, other parties reluctant], *Asahi shimbun*, May 16, 1990.

21. "Doi shi hō-Kan, gensoku de itchi, Ro daitōryō to shatō iinchō" [President Roh and JSP leader meet, agree in principle on Doi South Korea visit], *Asahi shimbun*, May 25, 1990.

22. See Kaifu Toshiki, *Seiji to kane: Kaifu Toshiki kaikoroku* [Politics and money: A memoir of Kaifu Toshiki], Shinchōsha (2010), on the Kaifu administration.

23. "Kin shuseki mo kokkō ni iyoku, tōitsu mondai wa kirihanasu, Kanemaru shi to Tanabe shira kaiken" [At talks with Kanemaru and Tanabe, President Kim also keen to establish diplomatic relations, prepared to exclude unification issue], *Asahi shimbun*, September 28, 1990; "Sakamoto kanbōchōkan, Kitachōsen ōkiku rosen tenkan, seifukan kōsho no kaishi gōi" [Chief Cabinet Secretary Sakamoto notes major shift in North Korean policy, agrees to launch intergovernmental negotitiations], *Asahi shimbun*, October 2, 1990.

24. Kanemaru's visit is covered in "Kanemaru hōchō o hyōsu" [Evaluating Kanemaru's visit to North Korea], *Gendai Koria* 36 (November 1990) and Shiota Ushio, "Kanemaru hō-Chōdan de nani ga hanasareta ka" [What was talked about with the Kanemaru delegation to North Korea?], *Bungei shunjū* 72(10) (August 1994).

25. "Kanemaru shi, chikaku hōkan, kitachōsen to no kyōdō sengen no shin'i o setsumei e" [Kanemaru to visit South Korea soon, explains true intentions behind joint declaration with North Korea], *Asahi shimbun*, October 3, 1990.

26. "Kaifu shushō, ichigatsu ni hō-Kan e, Nit-Chō kōsho mae ni chōsei" [PM

Kaifu to visit South Korea in January to liaise before Japan-North Korea negotiations], *Asahi shimbun*, November 14, 1990.

27. "Kaifu shushō no hō-Kan hantai undō aitsugu, kyōsei renkō no shinsō motome" [Series of protests against PM Kaifu's South Korea visit, calls to reveal truth about coercion], *Asahi shimbun*, January 9, 1991.

28. "Kankoku rikai e doryoku o kyōchō, Kaifu shushō, Ro daitōryō no yūshokukai de aisatsu" [PM Kaifu stresses efforts to gain South Korea's understanding in remarks at dinner meeting with President Roh], *Asahi shimbun*, January 10, 1991.

29. For example, the above article "Kaifu shushō no hō-Kan hantai undō aitsugu, kyōsei renkō no shinsō motome" [Series of protests against PM Kaifu's South Korea visit, calls to reveal truth about coercion] too describes the Korean Council, which was pursuing the issue of comfort women coercion, as a group "seeking the truth about the forced recruitment of comfort women."

30. Yun Jeong-ok, Chŏngshindae wŏnhonŭi palchach'wi ch'wijaegi [In the Footsteps of the Chôngsindae].

31. The Korean equivalent of *teishintai*, a wartime Japanese term meaning "volunteer labor corps" but actually referring to conscripted labor. The English translation of this is consequently frequently rendered as the "Women's Volunteer Labor Corps." Members of the *chôngsindae* were frequently conflated with comfort women in Korea, despite the fact that most performed only manual labor, not sexual services.

32. "Chŏngshindae chinsang kyumyŏng 'han mokso-ri'" [Request to find the facts about the comfort women], *Korea Jung-ang Daily*, October 20, 1990. Unless stated otherwise, all references to articles from this newspaper were sourced from the T'onghapkŏmsaek website (last accessed October 3, 2016).

33. The above conflation is apparent in the difference between the Chôngdaehyop's Korean title, which refers to the *chôngsindae*, or "volunteer" labor corps, and its English title, which points explicitly to women brought in to provide sexual services.

34. Han'gukchŏngshindaeyŏn'guso, *Taeŭnggwa chŏnmang* [Response and outlook].

35. "Tou, Nihon no kagai, wasuresarareta kako, shūsen 8/15" [August 15 war end anniversary, harm caused by Japan and the forgotten past come into question], *Asahi shimbun*, August 15, 1991.

36. Kimura Kan, *Kokusai funsōka izen no Kankoku ni okeru ianfu mondai o meguru gensetsu jōkyō* [Status of the discourse on the comfort women in South Korea prior to the issue becoming an international dispute].

37. "Kankoku no moto jūgun ianfura Nihon seifu o uttae, jindō e no tsumi tou" [Former South Korean comfort women sue Japanese government for crimes against humanity], *Asahi shimbun*, December 6, 1991.

38. "Jūgun ianfu hoshō mondai, jūrai no tachiba kaezu, gaimushō, seifukan de wa ketchaku" [Foreign Ministry says Japan will not change its position on comfort women compensation, issue to be resolved at intergovernmental level], *Asahi shimbun*, August 27, 1991.

39. "Jūgun inafu mondai de shisō kyūmei o yōsei" [Request for pursuit of truth in relation to comfort women issue], *Asahi shimbun*, December 11, 1991.

40. "Miyazawa shushō no hō-Kan, rainen 1 gatsu 16–18 nichi ni" [PM Miyazawa to visit South Korea January 16–18 next year], *Mainichi shimbun*, November 29, 1991. See also "Miyazawa shushō no hō-Kan, 1 gatsu chūjun ni, kanbōchōkan kaiken," *Asahi shimbun*, November 10, 1991.

41. Oh Byoung-sang, *Ch'ŏngwadae pisŏshil 4:6 kong not"aeu chŏnggwŏnŭi chŏngch'ibisarŭl t'onghae pon kwŏllyŏk kaltŭnggwa chŏngch'ibalchŏn* [The Blue House Secretarial Office 4:6: Power struggles and political developments in the Political Secretarial Office of the Roh Tae-woo government], Chungang Ilbosa (1985).

42. "Seifu, jūgun ianfu chōsa e" [Government to conduct comfort women investigation], *Asahi shimbun*, December 12, 1991.

43. *Dai 122 kai kokkai: Sangiin yosan iinkai giroku dai 2 gō* [122nd Diet Session: Upper House Budget Committee Minutes No. 2], Kokkai gijiroku kensaku shisutemu (http://kokkai.ndl.go.jp/cgi-bin/KENSAKU; last accessed September 13, 2016).

44. Lee Ok-sun was the subject of the first interviews, introduced by the Society for the Bereaved Families of Pacific War. See *Kuk'oehoeŭirok 13 tae 156 hoe 9 ch'a oemut'ongirwiwŏnhoe* [13th National Assembly minutes, 156th session: 9th Foreign Affairs and Unification Committee, December 13, 1991], Hoeŭirokshisŭt'em (http://likms.assembly.go.kr/record; last accessed September 13, 2016).

45. "Ianfu no hoshō o yōsei, shatō" [JSP calls for comfort women compensation], *Asahi shimbun*, December 17, 1991.

46. Hata Ikuhiko, *Ianfu to senjō no sei* [Comfort women and sex in the battlefield], Shinchōsha (1996).

47. "Chŏngshindae sagwa yo-gu/ Il taesagwanap shiwi" [Appealing for an apology: Demonstration in front of Japanese Embassy], *The Hankyoreh*, January 9, 1992. *Kukmin ilbo* reports that more than twenty people were involved in the protest. "Il ch'ong-ri panghan aptugo 'panil' kojo/ Kaktanch'eshiwi, t'psŏngmyŏng" [Escalation of anti-Japanese sentiment prior to Japanese minister's arrival: Protest group demonstrations and statements], *Kukmin ilbo*, January 9, 1992.

48. "Ianjo e no gun kanyo shimesu shiryō, bōeichō toshokan ni kyū Nihongun no tsūtatsu, nisshi" [Materials indicating military involvement in comfort women stations, Imperial Japanese Army notifications and diaries], *Asahi shimbun*, January 11, 1992.

49. Hata Ikuhiko, *Ianfu to senjō no sei* [Comfort women and sex in the battlefield].

50. "Gun no jūgun ianjo kanyo, Hokkaido de mo shiryō, Rikugunshō ga 'shōfu no yūchi'" [Materials showing military involvement in comfort women stations also emerge from Hokkaido, Ministry of War "solicited prostitutes"], *Asahi shimbun*, January 11, 1992.

51. "'Gun kanyo mitomezaru o enai,' jūgun ianfu mondai de Watanabe gaishō" [Foreign Minister Watanabe says military involvement with comfort women "must be admitted"] and "Ianfu mondai de kuni no sekinin ni hatsu no genkyū, 'gun kanyo hitei dekinu,' Katō kanbōchōkan" [Chief Cabinet Secretary Katō makes first reference to state responsibility in comfort women issue, says military involvement "cannot be denied"], both *Asahi shimbun*, January 12, 1992.

52. "Miyazawa shushō, hō-Kan-ji ni shazai, jūgun ianfu mondai de gun no kanyo mitomeru" [PM Miyazawa to apologize during South Korea visit and admit to military involvement in comfort woman issue], *Asahi shimbun*, January 13, 1992.

53. "Ianfu mondai no kanbōchōkan danwa" [Chief Cabinet Secretary makes statement on comfort women issue], *Asahi shimbun*, January 14, 1992.

54. *Katō naikaku kanbōchōkan happyō* [Statement by Chief Cabinet Secretary Katō], Ministry of Foreign Affairs website (http://www.mofa.go.jp/mofaj/area/taisen/kato.html; last accessed September 13, 2016).

55. *Dai 102 kai kokkai, sangiin gaimu iinkaigiroku dai 1 gō* [Minutes of first House of Councilors Foreign Affairs Committee meeting at 102nd Diet session], Kokkai gijiroku kensaku shisutemu (http://kokkai.ndl.go.jp/cgi-bin/KENSAKU; last checked September 13, 2016).

56. "Chŏngshindaenŭn morŭnŭn Il,' kangbyŏn/kwanbangjanggwan" [Cabinet Secretary says comfort women not being considered], *Seoul shinmun*, December 7, 1991.

57. Hata Ikuhiko, *Ianfu to senjō no sei* [Comfort women and sex in the battlefield].

58. For example, Senda Kakō, *Jūgun ianfu: "Koe naki onna" Hachiman nin no kokuhatsu* [Comfort women: 80,000 women finally find a voice].

59. Interview with former Deputy Chief Cabinet Secretary Ishihara Nobuo (April 21, 2014, in Tokyo). The interview was recorded for TBS Radio's "Ogiue Chiki Session 22" program, and is currently available on the following site: https://www.youtube.com/watch?v=CwW8HDwJvCg (last accessed September 13, 2016).

60. "Sōru de kōgi no demo" [Protest in Seoul], *Asahi shimbun*, January 14, 1992; "Miyazawa shushō hō-Kan o hikae, Sōru de demo, shūkai, jūgun ianfu mondai taiō ni kōgi" [Demo, rally in Seoul ahead of Miyazawa visit protesting handling of comfort women issue], *Mainichi shimbun*, January 16, 1992; "Panil taegyumo shiwi pisang/Kaktanch'e, 'posangŏmnŭn sajoe'panbal" [Large-scale anti-Japan demo emergency: Protest groups react to "apology without compensation"], *Kukmin ilbo*, January 14, 1992.

61. "Miyazawa shushō hō-Kan o hikae, Sōru de demo, shūkai, jūgun ianfu mondai taiō ni kōgi" [Demo, rally in Seoul ahead of Miyazawa visit protesting handling of comfort women issue], *Mainichi shimbun*, January 16, 1992.

62. For example, "Kukkyosaeng-do kŭllojŏngshindae kkŭrŏga/Pangsan, kyodonggyo hakchŏkpusŏ hwagin" [Japan mobilized elementary school students as labor corps: Confirmed from student registry list], *The Hankyoreh*, January 15, 1992, "Ilche, kukkyosaengkkaji chŏngshindae kkŭlgo-ga/Hakchŏkpusŏ hwagin" [Japanese empire mobilized even elementary school students as comfort women: Confirmed from students lists], *Korea Times*, January 15, 1992.

63. Hata Ikuhiko, *Ianfu to senjō no sei* [Comfort Women and Sex in the Battlefield]. See also Kimura Kan, *Kokusai funsōka izen no Kankoku ni okeru inafu mondai o meguru gensetsu jōkyō* [Status of the Discourse on the Comfort Women in Korea Prior to the Issue Becoming an International Dispute].

64. "Il, yŏkchoshijŏng 3 kaehang kŏbu" [Japan rejects three Korean government proposals on trade deficit dispute], *Chosun ilbo*, January 16, 1992.

65. Sano Kōji, "Kankoku no seichō moderu to Nikkan Keizai kankei no henka: Nikkan kankei akka no keizaiteki haikei" [South Korea's growth model and the change in Japan-Korea economic relations: The economic background to the deterioration in Japan-Korea relations], *Shōgaku ronshū* 83(2) (September 2014); Ko Yon-soo, *Kankoku no keizai shisutemu: Kokusai shihon idō no kakudai to kōzōkaikaku no*

shinten [South Korea's economic system: Greater international capital movement and the advance of structural reforms], Tōyō Keizai Shinpōsha (2000).

66. "Bōeki, gijutsu iten de Nihon no kyōryoku yōsei, Kankoku taishi, Miyazawa shushō ni" [Korean ambassador asks Miyazawa for Japan's cooperation on trade and technology transfer], *Asahi shimbun*, January 14, 1992; "Taeil muyŏkchŏkcha," *Chosun ilbo*, January 16, 1992.

67. "No taet'ongnyŏng yŏnduhoegyŏn ilmuniltap: Chŏnmun" [Q&A at President Roh's New Year press conference: Full text], *Seoul shinmun*, January 11, 1992; "Miyazawa shushō hō-Kan de wa, bōeki ga jūten, Ro daitōryō" [President Roh points to trade as focus of Miyazawa's Korea visit], *Asahi shimbun*, January 11, 1992.

68. "Hyŏnan pyŏrŭnŭn sŏul imong ŭi tonggyŏng" [Seoul and Tokyo have different dream on current issues], *Chosun ilbo*, January 16, 1992; "Il, yŏkchoshijŏng 3 kaehang kŏbu" [Japan rejects three Korean government proposals on trade deficit dispute], *Chosun ilbo*, January 16, 1992.

69. "Miyazawa shushō, Kankoku iri, kyō gogo shunō kaidan, Ajia shinchitsujo saguru" [Miyazawa in Korea, summit talks this afternoon to seek a new Asian order], *Asahi shimbun*, January 16, 1992; Kankoku daitōryō, higunji no kōken yōsei, bōeki wa jōho kitai, Nikkan shunō kaidan" [Korean president asks for a non-military contribution, expresses hopes for trade concessions], *Asahi shimbun*, January 17, 1992; "Nihon no jisscn o kitai suru Kankokugawa: Nikkan shunō kaidan" [Korea looks for action from Japan: Japan-Korea summit talks], *Mainichi shimbun*, January 18, 1992.

70. "Jūgun ianfu mondai, Miyazawa shushō ga shazai hyōmei, mune no tsumaru omoi, asu hō-Kan" [Miyazawa makes public apology on comfort women issue as "painful to the heart," Korea visit tomorrow], *Asahi shimbun*, January 15, 1992.

71. "Nikkan shunō kaidan: Yōshi" [Key points in Japan-Korea summit talks], *Asahi shimbun*, January 17, 1992.

72. "Hansei dodai ni kabekuzusu doryoku, Miyazawa shushō hō-Kan de Kankoku daitōryō aisatsu" [Miyazawa visit, Korean president calls for efforts to break down wall based on a foundation of remorse], *Asahi shimbun*, January 17, 1992.

73. "Mirai shikō no kankei nao tōku, rekishi, keizai de shukudai nokosu: Miyazawa shushō hō-Kan" [Miyazawa's Korea visit: Future-oriented relations even more distant, work remaining on history and economy], *Mainichi shimbun*, January 17, 1992.

74. Note again the confusion of comfort women and the volunteer corps.

75. "Miyazawa shushō to Ro Teu daitōryō no Nikkan shunō kyōdō kisha kaiken no naiyō" [Joint press briefing by PM Miyazawa and President Roh Tae-woo], *Mainichi shimbun*, January 17, 1992; "Nikkan shunō kyōdō kaiken: Yōshi" [Key points in joint press briefing by Japanese and Korean leaders], *Asahi shimbun*, January 17, 1992.

76. "Miyazawa shushō no seisaku enzetsu yōshi: Kankoku kokkai" [Key points in Miyazawa policy address in Korean legislature], *Mainichi shimbun*, January 18, 1992.

77. Calculated based on the various *Mainichi shimbun* reports.

78. "Tsurai tabi oe shinmiri, bukkokuji de hotokesama ni gasshō: Miyazawa shunō no hō-Kan" [Miyazawa glad to see end of draining trip to Korea, says a prayer at Bulguksa Temple], *Mainichi shimbun*, January 19, 1992.

79. "Ilche hŭisaengja paesang chŏngbu-ga sŏdurŭra" [Government should insist on compensation], *The Hankyoreh*, March 7, 1990.

80. It was apparently Deputy Chief Cabinet Secretary Ishihara Nobuo who suggested this strategy of profuse apology. See "Kōno danwa, Kankoku seifu mo naiyō hyōka" [Korean government approves Kōno Statement], *Asahi shimbun*, August 6, 2014.

81. *"Chŏngbu chŏngshindaebaesang yoguk'i-ro: Ire '65 nyŏn hyŏpchŏnggwa pyŏlgaemunje'"* [Government decides to appeal for compensation from Japan: Beyond the framework of the 1965 treaty], *Chosun ilbo*, January 22, 1992; "Chŏngshindaedaech"aek sewŏra no taet'ongnyŏng" [President Roh told to take measures on comfort women issue], *Chosun ilbo*, January 18, 1992.

82. See Park Yeong-kyu, *Kankoku daitōryō jitsuroku* [The true story of a South Korean president] (translated by Kim Jung-myeong), Kinema Junpōsha (2015), on the conditions leading up to the Roh Tae-woo administration.

83. See Oh Byoung-sang, "Ch'ŏngwadae pisŏshil 4" [The Blue House Secretarial Office 4] on the internal state of the Roh Tae-woo administration described in this section, as well as Yŏnsedaehakkyo kukkagwalliyŏn'guwŏnt'p (ed.), *Han'guktaet'ongnyŏng t'ongch'igusulsaryojip. 3, Not'aeu taet'ongnyŏng* [An aural history of Korea's presidents 3: President Roh Tae-woo], Sŏnin (2013) and Kim Young-sam, *Kimyŏngsam hoegorok: Minjujuŭirŭl wihan naŭi t'ujaeng 3* [Kim Young-sam memorandum: My struggle for democracy], Paeksansŏdang (2000).

84. Ikoma Tomokazu, "Kin Shōhitsu no seiji kenryoku tōsō katei bunseki: 1990 nen–1992 nen ni okeru minshu jiyūtō tōnai tōsō o chūshin ni" [Analysis of the process of Kim Jong-pil's fight for political power: The Democratic Liberal Party 1990–1992], *Ritsumeikan kokusai kankei ronshū* 12 (October 2012) describes the political situation during this period in some detail.

85. "Kankoku yotō, daitōryō kōho erabi kanetsu, Kim Eisan shi jiku ni kakushitsu" [Presidential candidate selection battle heats up within Korean ruling party, Kim Young-sam at center of feud], *Asahi shimbun*, January 10, 1992.

86. "Chŏngshindae sajoe paesanghaeya/Minjudangyŏsŏngt'ŭgwi sŏngmyŏng" [Japan should pay compensation for comfort women: Statement by Democratic Party Special Committee for Women], *Korea Times*, January 17, 1992.

87. "Ilbonsusang kuch'ejŏk paesangjoch'i mutcha ŏmultchŏk/ Miyajawa panghan imojŏmo" [Japanese Prime Minister had no clear answers on compensation: Episodes from Miyazawa's visit to Korea], *The Hankyoreh*, January 18, 1992; "2 Ch'ahoedam 75 punjung 22 pun'gan 'Chŏngshindae' ŏn'gŭp/No taet'ongnyŏng" [22 of 75 minutes was on comfort women issue: President Roh], *Seoul shinmun*, January 8, 1992.

88. "Chŏngshindae, kisurijŏn/ Minja, kashihwa ch'ok-gu" [Democratic Liberals ask Japan for concrete plans on comfort women and technology transfer], *Kukmin ilbo*, January 17, 1992.

89. "JPŭi myŏnp'ibarŏn" [Kim Jong-pil's statement evades his responsibility], *Dong-a ilbo*, January 17, 1992. Unless stated otherwise, all references to articles from this newspaper were sourced from the Midiak'ŏmgŏmsaek website at donga. com (http://news.donga.com/search?query=a&x=0&y=0; last accessed October 3, 2016). See also "Chidoja'-ŭi yŏksaŭishik/ JPparŏn mukkwahal su ŏpta" [A political leader's historical perception: We should not overlook Kim Jong-pil's state-

ment], *Segye ilbo*, January 19, 1982, and "Yŏ honam, ya yŏngnam, 'kyodubo' pisang/ Ch'ongsŏnch'wiyakchi kongnyaktaech'aek pushim" [Ruling party makes bridgehead in Yongnam area, opposition party in Heonam area: Trial and error process seeks to cover weakest areas ahead of general election], *Dong-a ilbo*, February 11, 1992.

90. See Park Chul-un, *Naŭi sam yŏksaŭi kwejŏk: Shirhyang 60 nyŏn, oeguk yurangŭi insaengŭl san p'alsun noinŭi hoego esei* [The path of my life: Story of an 80-year-old who lost his hometown 60 years ago to wander abroad], Handŭl (2005) for more on Park Chul-un.

91. See Sin Jung-seon, *Kangch'ŏrwang pakt'aejun* [Steel king Park Tae-joon], Munidang (2013) for more on Park Tae-joon.

92. Ikoma Tomokazu, "Kin Shōhitsu no seiji kenryoku tōsō katei bunseki: 1990 nen–1992 nen ni okeru minshu jiyūtō tōnai tōsō o chūshin ni" [Analysis of the process of Kim Jong-pil's fight for political power: The Democratic Liberal Party 1990–1992].

93. "Kimjongp'irwiwŏn chŏngshindaebosang yo-gu/ '65 nyŏn choyakch'egyŏlttaen charyoŏpsŏ haegyŏlmot'ae'" [Parliament member Kim Jong-pil requests compensation for comfort women: Impossible to settle the issue at the 1965 treaty negotiations because there were no reliable sources], *The Hankyoreh*, January 17, 1992.

94. "'Chŏngshindaebaesang' ire kongshikchegi/ chŏngbubangch'im" [Government official demands compensation for comfort women], *Segye ilbo*, January 19, 1992.

95. "Ianfu mondai de shazai arawasu sochi o kentō, hoshō wa konnan, futatabi kyōchō, kanbōchōkan" [Consideration given to means of expesssing an apology over the comfort women issue, Chief Cabinet Secretary reiterates that compensation difficult], *Asahi shimbun*, January 22, 1992.

96. "Kotoba dake o senkō saseru Nihon seifu, jūgun ianfu mondai (Repōto: Kankoku)" [Japanese government puts words before action over comfort women issue (Report: South Korea)], *Asahi shimbun*, January 28, 1992.

97. "Kako ni kugiri de icchi, Kaifu shushō, hibakusha shien ni 40 oku en, shunō kaidan" [PM Kaifu promises four billion yen support for atomic bomb victims at summit talks to draw a line under the past], *Asahi shimbun*, May 25, 1990.

98. For example, "Il, chŏngshindaebaesang kŏbu/ Chŏngbuch'awŏn nonŭibanbal" [Japan rejects compensation, reacts against Korean government demands], *Segye ilbo*, January 21, 1992.

99. "Ianfu mondai de shazai arawasu sochi o kentō, hoshō wa konnan, futatabi kyōchō, kanbōchōkan" [Consideration given to means of expesssing an apology over the comfort women issue, Chief Cabinet Secretary reiterates that compensation difficult], *Asahi shimbun*, January 22, 1992.

100. At the subsequent parliamentary elections, Kim Jong-pil's camp was roundly defeated, with Kim losing much of his political influence. Ikoma Tomokazu, "Kin Shōhitsu no seiji kenryoku tōsō katei bunseki: 1990 nen–1992 nen ni okeru minshu jiyūtō tōnai tōsō o chūshin ni" [Analysis of the process of Kim Jong-pil's fight for political power: The Democratic Liberal Party 1990–1992].

101. "Nihon ni busshitsuteki hoshō motomeru, jūgun ianfu de Kankoku daitōryō, shinsō kaimei jūshi" [Korean president says Korea will not ask Japan for material

compensation but will stress uncovering the truth over the comfort women issue], *Asahi shimbun*, March 14, 1992.

102. "Nikkan shinjidai e kōki, Kin Eisan jiki daitōryō tono kaiken o oete" [Interview with next president Kim Young-sam; an opportunity for a new era in Japan–South Korea relations], *Asahi shimbun*, January 10, 1993; "Ko Romei shi, Kankoku shin chūnichi taishi" [Gong Ro-myung, a new Korean Ambassador to Japan], *Asahi shimbun*, March 10, 1993.

103. Formally known as the "Report of the Special Rapporteur on violence against women, its causes and consequences, Ms. Radhika Coomaraswamy, submitted in accordance with Commission on Human Rights resolution 1995/85." The original text can be found at http://www.awf.or.jp/pdf/h0003.pdf (last accessed February 8, 2018).

104. "Masatsu saketa Kankoku no senjutsu, kokka baishō e fumikomazu, gaishō kaidan, moto ianfu ichijikin kyōgi" [Korea adopts strategy of avoiding friction, stops short of seeking state compensation, discusses lump-sum payments to former comfort women], *Mainichi shimbun*, January 16, 1996. However, just before bilateral foreign ministers' talks in January 1997, the South Korean government was investigating the possibility of making a claim to the Japanese government for state compensation pursuant to the Coomaraswamy Report. "Nikkan gaishō kaidan, Kankoku ga toriyame o kentō, moto ianfu ni ichijikin" [Korea looking at cancelling foreign ministers' talks, lump-sum payment to former comfort women], *Mainichi shimbun*, January 13, 1996.

105. "Moto jūgun ianfu shienkin, Kankoku seifu ga shikyū o kettei" [Korean government decides to pay support money to former comfort women], *Asahi shimbun*, April 21, 1998; "Kin Daichū Kankoku daitōryō no hatsugen yōshi: Nihon no hōdōkakusha to kaiken" [Summary of comments by Korean President Kim Daejung: Briefing for Japanese media], *Yomiuri shimbun*, April 30, 1998.

106. "Hoshō no yōkyū takamari mo, Nikkan kaidan no bunsho kōkai de Kankoku" [Korea showing increasing interest in seeking compensation, caused by release of diplomatic documents from bilateral talks], *Asahi shimbun*, January 17, 2005. Lee Jong-won et al., *Rekishi to shite no Nikkan kokkō seijōka 1–2* [Normalization of diplomatic relations between Japan and South Korea as history, Vols 1–2], University of Tokyo Press, offers further details on these diplomatic documents.

107. *Nikkan kokkō seijōka kōsho katei ni okeru Kankoku seifu no tai-Nichi seisaku kettei ni kan suru ichikōsatsu* [A study on the Korean government's policymaking in relation to Japan during the normalization of Japan-Korea relations], Lee Sangyeol, University of Tokyo Graduate School for Law and Politics, March 2002.

108. See, for example, the various judgments, including *Shazai nado seikyū kōso jiken, Tōkyō kōsai heisei 11 nen (ne) Dai 5333 gō, heisei 12 nen 11 gatsu 30 nichi min 16 bu hanketsu* [Appeal on claims for compensation, etc., Tokyo High Court 1999 (Ne), No. 5333, Judgment No. 16 on November 30, 2000] (https://www.gwu.edu/~memory/data/judicial/comfortwomen_japan/SongShindo%20-%20 11.30.00.pdf; last accessed September 25, 2016).

109. "Yunbyŏngse 'hanilch'ŏnggugwŏn hyŏpchŏnge taehan kibonipchang pyŏnhwaŏpta" [Yun Byŏng-se says no change in government stance on the Claims Settlement], *Yonhap News*, December 27, 2015.

110. Kubota Kanichirō, *Nikkan kōsho hōkoku (6) Seikyūken kankei bukai daiikkai*

kaigijōkyō [Report on Japan-Korea negotiations (6): First meeting of the Claims Subcommittee], May 11, 1953.

111. "Kimjongp'irwiwŏn chŏngshindaebosang yo-gu/ '65 nyŏnchoyakch'egyŏlttaen charyoŏpsŏ haegyŏlmot'ae" [Parliament Member Kim Jong-pil requests compensation for comfort women; impossible to settle the issue at the 1965 negotiations because of absence of reliable sources], *The Hankyoreh*, January 17, 1992.

112. "Taeilpaesangyo-gu kukchesosong/ Kwallyŏndanch'e yŏnhappon'gyŏk ch'aebi" [Civil society groups prepare to sue Japanese government], *Kyunghyang shinmun*, January 17, 1992.

113. "Jūgun ianfu mondai de hoshō no daitai sochi, kanbōchōkan ga kentō o yakusoku" [Chief Cabinet Secretary promises to find an alternative means of compensation on comfort women issue], *Mainichi shimbun*, January 15, 1992.

114. *Katō kanbōchōkan happyō* [Statement by Chief Cabinet Secretary Katō], Ministry of Foreign Affairs website (http://www.mofa.go.jp/mofaj/area/taisen/kato. html; last accessed September 13, 2016).

115. See Hata Ikuhiko, *Ianfu to senjō no sei* [Comfort women and sex in the battlefield], as well as "Jūgun ianfu mondai: Shushō, kyōseisei teigi tsukaiwake, kyōgi to kōgi, kaigai ni wa tsutawarazu" [Comfort women issue: PM on different definitions of coercion, difference between broad and narrow definitions not recognized abroad], *Mainichi shimbun*, March 6, 2007, on this debate over narrow and broad definitions.

116. *Katō kanbōchōkan happyō* [Statement by Chief Cabinet Secretary Katō], Ministry of Foreign Affairs website (http://www.mofa.go.jp/mofaj/area/taisen/kato. html; last accessed September 13, 2016).

117. For example, "Majimot'an chŏngshindae shin" [Impossible to put a period with this statement], *Chosun ilbo*, July 8, 1992.

118. "Jūgun ianfu no iatsuteki na boshū mo, Nihon ni tsuika chōsa seikyū, Kankoku ga hōkokusho" [Korean report suggests that comfort women were coercively recruited, calls for Japan to conduct another study], *Mainichi shimbun*, July 31, 1992.

119. "Jijitsujō no kyōsei renkō, Kankoku seifu chūkan hōkokusho, Nihon gawa happyō ni hanron, jūgunianfu mondai" [Korean government interim report on comfort women points to coercive recruitment of comfort women, contrary to the Japanese announcement], *Mainichi shimbun*, July 31, 1992.

120. "Jūgun ianfu mondai de Nihon ga shusshi, Kankoku ni zaidan, hoshō ni kawaru sochi to seifu kentō" [Government looks at setting up a comfort women foundation in Korea funded by Japan as an alternative to compensation], *Mainichi shimbun*, August 2, 1992. According to one South Korean government official, the Miyazawa administration's concession line served as the model for the agreement reached on December 28, 2015, between Japan and South Korea on the comfort women issue.

121. More details on the Asian Women's Fund can be found in Murayama Tomiichi et al. (eds.), *Dejitaru kinenkan, ianfu mondai to Ajia josei kikin* [Digital memorial: Comfort women and the Asian Women's Fund], Seitōsha (2014).

122. "Irŭi chŏngshindae saenghwalgigŭman pandae" [Opposed to Japanese proposal of living support foundation for comfort women], *Chosun ilbo*, September 1, 1992.

123. "Jūgun ianfu hoshō kikin anshō ni, kinsen ketchaku yūsen ni fuman, Kankoku seifu" [Comfort women compensation fund runs aground with Korean government unhappy at the priority on a cash solution], *Mainichi shimbun*, November 19, 1992.

124. "Kako no kaimei nao tōku, seifu no ianfu chōsa ni Ajia no koe" [Asia calls for comfort women studies, elucidation of past has a long way to go], *Asahi shimbun*, July 7, 1992.

125. "Jūgunianfu mondai de hoshō yōkyū, Kankoku to dōchō, taiō semarareru Nihon" [Other countries join Korea in calling for comfort women compensation, Japan forced to respond], *Mainichi shimbun*, January 31, 1992.

126. "Kokusai hōritsukai, kyō kara jūgunianfu chōsa, shiryō shūshū ya shōgen kikitori" [International legal committee starts comfort women investigation today, to collect materials and hear testimonies], *Mainichi shimbun*, April 23, 1993; "Ianfu mondai de, Ajia kankeikoku e hōmon chōsa o kibō, Chabesu hōkokukan" [Chavez wants to visit relevant Asian countries to investigate the comfort women issue], *Mainichi shimbun*, August 26, 1993.

127. "Jūgunianfu mondai de Nihon ni hoshō motomezu, Kim Eisan Kankoku daitōryō" [Korean President Kim Young-sam says Korea not to call on Japan for compensation over comfort women issue], *Mainichi shimbun*, March 14, 1993.

128. "Seifu, Kankokujin ianfu mondai sōki ketchaku e ugoku, daitōryō hatsugen wa shigunaru, kyōsei renkō mitomeru hōkō" [Government moves to find an early solution to the Korean comfort women issue, President's comment seen as a signal, government moving in direction of admitting forced labor], *Mainichi shimbun*, March 14, 1993. The official announcement was on March 23.

129. "Kankokujin ianfu mondai de, kyōsei renkō o mitomeru hōkō, seifu" [Government moves toward admitting coerced labor in relation to the Korean comfort women issue], *Mainichi shimbun*, March 24, 1993.

130. "Kankokujin jūgunianfu mondai, kyōsei renkō hiroku teigi, seishinteki appaku mo fukumeru, seifu ga shinkenkai" [Government adopts new view on Korean comfort women issue, definition of coercion broadened to include mental pressure], *Mainichi shimbun*, March 24, 1993.

131. "Kikitori chōsa jitchi e seifu hōshin o tenkan, kanbōchōkan ga seishiki hyōmei, jūgun ianfu mondai" [Chief Cabinet Secretary makes formal announcement of government's changed position on conducting interviews in relation to the comfort women issue], *Mainichi shimbun*, March 23, 1993.

132. "Moto jūgunianfu no hoshō mondai de, kojin no hoshō yōkyū haijo wa shinai, Kankoku gaishō" [Korean foreign minister says that Korea will not exclude individual claims for compensation in relation to the issue of compensation for former comfort women], *Mainichi shimbun*, March 24, 1993.

133. "Kankoku de jūgunianfu seikatsu shienhō ga seiritsu" [Korea passes law on living assistance for comfort women], *Mainichi shimbun*, May 19, 1993.

134. "Jūgun ianfu mondai no kikitori chōsa anshō ni, Kankoku no yūryoku dantai, shinsō kyūmei ga fujūbun to hanpatsu" [Interviews on comfort women issue run aground, major Korean group opposes because Japanese efforts to uncover truth "inadequate"], *Mainichi shimbun*, May 8, 1992.

135. See Hironaka Yoshimichi, *Miyazawa seiken 644 nichi* [The Miyazawa admin-

istration: 644 days], Gyōken shuppankyoku (1998) for more on the background to this.

136. "Ianfu mondai raigetsu ni mo chōsa kekka, kyōsei mitomeru hōkō, Mutō gaishō Kankoku de kyō shazai" [Results of comfort women investigation out next month, government moving toward admitting coercion, Foreign Minister Mutō apology in Korea today], *Mainichi shimbun*, June 29, 1993.

137. For example, "Dai 1 tō nara geya shinai, shushō renritsu seiken ni iyoku, 93 sōsenkyo, tōsho tōronkai" [Party leader debate for 93rd general elections, PM says leading party won't cross the floor, indicates coalition ambitions], *Mainichi shimbun*, July 4, 1993.

138. "Miyazawa shushō, kyō taijin hyōmei, jimin nobizu, seiken iji e ketsudan, 93 shūinsen kaihyō" [Miyazawa to announce resignation today, LDP fails to grow its vote, decides to hold on to administration, voting opens for 93rd lower house elections], *Mainichi shimbun*, July 19, 1993.

139. Immediately after the elections, Miyazawa himself thought there was a possibility that he might remain in power. "Miyazawa shushō kaiken no yōshi: Sōsenkyo go, 7 gatsu 19 nichi" [Key points in PM Miyazawa press briefing after general elections on July 19], *Mainichi shimbun*, July 19, 1993.

140. "Miyazawa shushō no taijin aisatsu yōshi: 22 nichi no jimintō ryōingiin sōkai" [Key points in PM Miyazawa exit speech: Joint meeting of LDP members from both houses on July 22], *Mainichi shimbun*, July 23, 1993.

141. "Kankokujin moto ianfu kikitori chōsa e, seifu, shūnai ni mo" [Government to conduct interviews with former Korean comfort women within the week], *Mainichi shimbun*, July 18, 1993.

142. "Kankokujin ianfu no kikitori kaishi, 26, 27 nichi ni 15 nin kara" [Interviews with Korean comfort women begin, 15 women to be interviewed on the 26th and 27th], *Mainichi shimbun*, July 24, 1993; "Kankoku no moto jūgun ianfu kara, genchi kikitori chōsa kaishi, 14 nin ga ōjiru" [Local interviews begin with Korea's former comfort women, 14 women take part], *Mainichi shimbun*, July 26, 1993.

143. "Hosokawa renritsu seiken tanjō e, tōshura nyūkaku, fukusōri ni Hata shi, 7 tōshu kaidan de kettei" [Hosokawa coalition government emerges from meeting of 7 party leaders who join the Cabinet, Hata appointed deputy PM], *Mainichi shimbun*, July 30, 1993.

144. "Jimin shinsōsai ni Kōno Yōhei shi, ryōingiin sōkai de senshutsu" [Joint meeting of LDP members from both houses elects Kōno Yōhei as new LDP leader], *Mainichi shimbun*, July 30, 1993.

145. "Jūgun ianfu seifu chōsa no kekka, seifu no kōshiki jijitsu nintei" [Results of government's comfort women investigation, government's formal recognition of the facts], *Mainichi shimbun*, August 5, 1993; "Jūgunianfu seifu chōsa no kekka, shiryō no yōshi" [Results of government's comfort women investigation: Summary of materials], *Mainichi shimbun*, August 5, 1993.

146. "Kōno kanbōchōkan ga danwa, ianfu chōsa kekka" [Chief Cabinet Secretary Kōno announces results of comfort women investigation], *Mainichi shimbun*, August 5, 1993.

147. *Ianfukankei chōsa kekka happyō ni kan suru Kōno naikakukanbōchōkan danwa* [Statement by Chief Cabinet Secretary Yōhei Kōno on the results of the study

on the comfort women issue], http://www.mofa.go.jp/mofaj/area/taisen/kono.html (last accessed September 29, 2016).

148. Interview with former Deputy Chief Cabinet Secretary Ishihara Nobuo, http://www.awf.or.jp/3/persons-03.html [Digital Memorial: Comfort women and the Asian Women's Fund] (last accessed September 29, 2016).

149. "Ianfu mondai, Miyazawa seiken de ketchaku, Nikkan no rigai itchi, seikyoku konmei o kini ugoki kasoku" [Comfort women issue to be "settled by Miyazawa administration," Japan-Korea interests aligned, political confusion accelerates moves], *Mainichi shimbun*, August 5, 1993.

150. "Jūgunianfu mondai no shazai o hyōka, NY taimuzu" [NY Times lauds comfort women apology], *Mainichi shimbun*, August 9, 1993.

151. "Jūgunianfu mondai, 'Nihon ga shazai,' to Shinkasha ga hōdō" [Xinhua reports that "Japan apologizes" in relation to comfort women issue], *Mainichi shimbun*, August 6, 1993.

152. "Kankoku no shimindantai, issō no kaimei o motomeru, Nihon no makuhiki shisei, hanpatsu mo: Ianfu chōsa hōkokusho" [Investigation report on comfort women; Korean civil groups call for greater elucidation, criticize Japan's effort to bring the curtain down on the issue], *Mainichi shimbun*, August 6, 1993.

153. "'Wagakuni no iken o hanei' to hyōka: Ianfu mondai, Nihon seifu chōsa kekka de Kankoku seifu" [Korean government lauds reflection of Korea's view in results of Japanese government's comfort women study], *Mainichi shimbun*, August 5, 1993.

154. "Ianfu mondai, Miyazawa seiken de ketchaku, Nikkan no rigai itchi, seikyoku konmei o kini ugoki kasoku" [Comfort women issue to be "settled by Miyazawa administration," Japan-Korea interests align, political confusion accelerates moves], *Mainichi shimbun*, August 5, 1993.

155. "Kankoku, tai-Nichi seisaku o tenkan, Hosokawa shinseiken tōjō o kini, kankei saikyōka o shikō" [Korea makes turnaround on Japan policy, wants to take opportunity of new Hosokawa administration to strengthen relations again], *Mainichi shimbun*, August 11, 1993.

156. "Taiheiyōsensō ninshiki, ippo fumikomu: Hatsukaiken de Hosokawa shushō" [PM Hosokawa goes further on Pacific War perception], *Mainichi shimbun*, August 11, 1993.

157. "Kinrin shokoku, kōiteki ni hyōka, hoshō mondai ni musubitsukeru ugoki mo: Hosokawa shushō 'shinryakusensō' hatsugen" [Japan's neighbors welcome PM Hosokawa's "war of aggression" comment, moves afoot to link it to compensation issue], *Mainichi shimbun*, August 14, 1993.

158. "Nikkan shunō kaidan no sōki jitsugen de itchi: Hosokawa shushō to Kin daitōryō" [Hosokawa and Kim agree to hold summit talks soon], *Mainichi shimbun*, August 10, 1993.

159. "11 gatsu, Nikkan shunō kaidan kaisai e" [Japan-Korea summit to be held in November], *Mainichi shimbun*, August 31, 1993.

160. "Shushō 'shokuminchi shihai' o shazai, sōshi kaimei, chōyō age, Kin daitōryō ni hatsuhyōmei: Nikkan shunō kaidan" [PM apologizes for colonial rule, raises forced name changes and conscription with President Kim for first time], *Mainichi shimbun*, November 7, 1993.

161. "Hosokawa Morihiro shushō, jinin o seishiki hyōmei, kōkeisha erabi, nankō

hisshi, saihen garami, Hata Tsutomu shi jiku ni" [PM Hosokawa Morihiro formally announces resignation, difficult successor selection ahead with possibility of reshuffle centered around Hata Tsutomu], *Mainichi shimbun*, April 9, 1994.

162. The actual Korean was "Pŏrŭjangmŏrirŭlkoch'yŏnok'etta." "Nosaka Kōken kanbōchōkan, Kankoku daitōryō no hyogen ni fukaikan, rekishininshiki hihan de 'porushanmori'" [Chief Cabinet Secretary Nosaka Koken unhappy with Korean President's "pŏrŭjang" historical perception criticism], *Mainichi shimbun*, November 17, 1995.

163. See Yakushiji Katsuyuki (ed.), *Murayama Tomiichi kaikoroku* [A memoir of Murayama Tomiichi], Iwanami Shoten (2012) and Murayama Tomiichi and Tsujimoto Kiyomi, *Sōjanō: Murayama Tomiichi 'Shushō taiken' no subete o kataru* [Murayama Tomiichi tells all about his experience as Prime Minister], Daisansho-kan (1998) on Murayama.

164. See Kōno Yōhei, *Nihon gaikō e no chokugen: Kaisō to teigen* [Plain speaking on Japan's diplomacy: Recollections and proposals], Iwanami Shoten (2015).

165. Murayama Tomiichi and Tsujimoto Kiyomi, *Sōjanō: Murayama Tomiichi 'Shushō taiken' no subete o kataru* [Murayama Tomiichi tells all about his experience as Prime Minister].

166. See Kawano Noriyuki (2001), "Kakuryō shitsugen no seijigaku" [The political science of ministerial gaffes], *Kokusai kyōryokushi* 7(1) (January 2001) on details of ministers' inappropriate remarks at this point in time.

167. Murayama Tomiichi and Tsujimoto Kiyomi, *Sōjanō: Murayama Tomiichi 'Shushō taiken' no subete o kataru* [Murayama Tomiichi tells all about his experience as Prime Minister].

168. See, for example, "'Dareka kawari ga oru kanō': Kyūshinryoku ushinau, Murayama seiken" ["Anyone to take over from me?" Murayama administration loses pull], *Mainichi shimbun*, February 22, 1995. See also Murayama Tomiichi, *Murayama Tomiichi no shōgenroku: Jishasa renritsu seiken no jissō* [Murayama Tomiichi's testimonies: The real facts of the LDP, JSP, and Sakigake coalition government], Shinseisha shuppan (2011).

169. "Jimin shinsōsai ni Hashimoto Ryūtarō shi, kanjichō ni Katō Kōichi shi o kiyō e: Koizumi shi ni taisa no 304 hyō" [Hashimoto Ryutaro becomes new LDP leader, Katō Kōichi to be appointed as LDP Chief Secretary: Major lead of 304 votes over Koizumi], *Mainichi shimbun*, September 23, 1995.

170. Kawano Noriyuki, "Kakuryō shitsugen no seijigaku" [The political science of ministerial gaffes]. See also "Hashimoto tsūsanshō no 'shinryakusensō' ni kan suru hatsugen, 24 ka no shūin zeisei kaikaku tokubetsui" [MITI Minister Hashimoto's remarks on Japan's "war of aggression," House of Representatives Special Committee on Tax Reform on 24th], *Asahi shimbun*, October 26, 1994.

171. "Kankoku ga ikan hyōmei, 'rekishiteki jijitsu waikyoku,' Hashimoto tsūsanshō no dai 2 jitaisen ninshiki" [Korea deplores "distortion of historical facts" in METI Minister Hashimoto's perception of WWII], *Asahi shimbun*, October 26, 1994.

172. "Ko Romei, Kankoku taishi ga ketchaku hyōmei, 'shinryaku' meguru Hashimoto tsūsanshō hatsugen" [Korean Ambassador Gong Ro-myung announces METI Minister Hashimoto's "war of aggression" comment settled], *Asahi shimbun*, October 26, 1994.

173. "Nikkan heigō jōyaku nado ni tsuite no Watanabe Michio moto fukusōri, gaishō hatsugen yōshi" [Summary of comments by Watanabe Michio, former Deputy Prime Minister and Foreign Minister, on the Treaty of Annexation], *Asahi shimbun*, June 5, 1995.

174. Kukkabŏmnyŏngjŏngbosent'ŏ, *Taehanmin'guk'ŏnbŏp* [The Constitution of Korea], http://www.law.go.kr/main.html (last accessed September 29, 2016).

175. Sung Nak-in, "Hŏnbŏpkwa kukkajŏngch'esŏng" [The constitution and state identity], *Sŏultaehakkyopŏp'ak* 52(1) (March 2011).

176. Tsukamoto Takashi, "Horon: Nikkan kihon jōyaku o meguru rongi" [Appendix: Debate over the Treaty on Basic Relations between Japan and the Republic of Korea] in Nikkan rekishi kyōdō kenkyū iinkai (ed.), *Nikkan rekishi kyōdō kenkyū hōkokusho (Dai 1 ki): Dai 3 bunka hōkokusho*, http://www.jkcf.or.jp/history_arch/first/3/09-02j_tsukamoto_j.pdf (last accessed September 29, 2016).

177. For details see Kimura Kan, "The Third International Conference for a Reconsideration of the Annexation of Korea."

178. "Shūshū e Fujio bunshō himen, jinin kobami, shushō ketsudan, kanbōchōkan danwa, ikan no i hyōmei, kōnin ni wa Shiokawashi" [PM decides to fire Education Minister Fujio in response to Fujio statement, Chief Cabinet Secretary issues statement expressing regret, Shiokawa appointed as successor], *Asahi shimbun*, September 9, 1986.

179. "Watanabe Michio shi, shazai no komento: Nikkan heigō jōyaku de no hatsugen" [Watanabe Michio apologizes for remarks about Annexation Treaty], *Mainichi shimbun*, June 6, 1995.

180. "Nikkan heigō jōyaku nado ni tsuite no Watanabe Michio moto fukusōri, gaishō hatsugen yōshi" [Summary of comments by Watanabe Michio, former Deputy Prime Minister and Foreign Minister, on the Treaty of Annexation].

181. "Jimin to shakai, kenkai de kuichigai, sengo 50 nen kokkai ketsugi" [Discrepancies between LDP and JSP views on Diet resolution on 50th anniversary of end of WWII], *Asahi shimbun*, February 4, 1995.

182. "Sengo ketsugian ni yotō ga gōi, 'shinryaku' to 'hansei' moru, konkokkaichū ni jitsugen e" [Ruling parties agree to include "war of aggression" and "remorse" references in postwar anniversary resolution and to get resolution through during current Diet session], *Asahi shimbun*, June 7, 1995.

183. "Sengo 50 nen no kokkai ketsugi, nanzan no yotōan, kakkai no hannō samazama" [Reception varied on ruling parties' troubled proposal on Diet resolution on 50th anniversary of end of WWII], *Asahi shimbun*, June 7, 1995.

184. "Yotō no sengo 50 nen kokkai ketsugian gōi de Ajia no hannō" [Asian responses to ruling parties' proposed Diet resolution on 50th anniversary of end of WWII], *Asahi shimbun*, June 7, 1995; "Shingapōru 'meikaku na shazai no kikai o isshita" [Singapore says that chance to make a clear apology was missed], "Kankoku, shuyō shimbun ga ichimen toppu de" [On front page of Korea's major papers], and "Filipin, 'shinryaku rongi' ni tomadoi no koe mo" [Confusion in Philippines over "war of aggression" question], all *Mainichi shimbun*, June 7, 1995.

185. "Yotō no sengo 50 nen kokkai ketsugian gōi de Ajiano hanō" [Asian responses to ruling party's proposed Diet resolution on 50th anniversary of end of WWII], *Asahi shimbun*, June 7, 1995.

186. "'Sekinin nogare' to Kankoku gaimushō ga 'ikan,' Nihon no sengo 50 nen ketsugi" [Korean foreign ministry deplores "evasion of responsibility" in Japan's Diet resolution on 50th anniversary of end of WWII], *Asahi shimbun*, June 11, 1995.

187. Ōnuma Yasuaki, *Ianfu mondai to wa nan datta no ka: Media, NGO, seifu no kōzai* [What was the comfort women issue about? The good and the bad of the media, NGOs and government], Chūō Kōron Shinsha (2006) details the background to this.

188. "Ianfukikin, seifu mo shien, fukushi/iryōmen ni kyoshutsu, 'tsugunai to hansei komete'" [Comfort women fund also to receive government support for welfare and medical costs in spirit of "atonement and remorse"], *Asahi shimbun*, June 15, 1995; Ōnuma Yasuaki, *Ianfu mondai to wa nan datta no ka* [What was the comfort women issue about?].

189. "Tōjisha yōkyū, aru teido hanei, Nihon no moto ianfu e no kikin kōsō de Kankoku hyōka" [Korea greets Japan's concept of a fund for former comfort women as reflecting the parties' demands to some extent], *Asahi shimbun*, June 15, 1996.

190. "Jūgun ianfu mondai de Nihon gawa ni chūmon, gaishō kaidan de Kankokugawa" [Korea has requests of Japan on comfort women issue at foreign ministers' talks], *Asahi shimbun*, June 24, 1996.

191. "Kankoku seifu ga 'ikan no i': Ajia heiwa kokumin kikin, moto jūgunianfu ni ichijikin nado shikyū" [Korean government deplores Asian Women's Fund lump-sum payments etc. to former comfort women], *Mainichi shimbun*, January 12, 1996.

192. Gong Ro-myung, *Naŭi oegyon not'ŭ: Anesŏ tŭtkopogo kyŏkkŭn han'gugoegyo 50nyŏn* [Diplomatic Notes: 50 years of Korean diplomacy from inside the government], Kip'arang (2014).

193. *Dai 134 kai kokkai honkaigi dai 4 gō, heisei 7 nen 10 gatsu itsuka (mokuyōbi)* [Agenda Item 4, 134th Diet plenary session, October 5, 1995], Kokkai kaigiroku kensaku shisutemu (http://kokkai.ndl.go.jp; last accessed September 29, 2016).

194. "Kankoku yoyatō, shazai o motomeru, Murayama shushō no Nikkan heigō jōyaku hatsugen" [Korean ruling and opposition parties seek apology over PM Murayama's remarks about Annexation Treaty], *Asahi shimbun*, October 11, 1995; "Chūnichi Kankoku taishi ga gaimushō e hanron, Nikkan heigō jōyaku ni kan suru Murayama shushō hatsugen" [Korean ambassador to Japan argues with MOFA over Murayama comment on Annexation Treaty], *Asahi shimbun*, October 12, 1995.

195. "Heigō jōyaku meguru hatsugen de, Murayama shushō o nazashi hinan, Kitachōsen tō kikānshi" [North Korea party organ specifically directs criticism at Murayama over Annexation Treaty comment], *Asahi shimbun*, October 10, 1995.

196. "Murayama shushō, 'gijiroku o yonde,' Kitachōsen no 'Nikkan heigō hatsugen e no hinan'" [Murayama responds to North Korean criticism on his Annexation Treaty comment by urging it to read the minutes], *Mainichi shimbun*, October 10, 1995.

197. Open Archives, *Murayama ilbonch'ong-ri mangŏn kyut'an daehoe* [Japanese Prime Minister Murayama condemnation contest], http://db.kdemocracy.or.kr/photo-archives/view/00755967 (last accessed September 29, 2016).

198. "Kin Eisan Kankoku daitōryō ga hanpatsu, kome kōshō de mo hinan,

Murayama shushō no Nikkan heigō hatsugen" [Korean President Kim Young-sam reacts to Murayama comment on Annexation Treaty, also criticizes rice negotiations], *Mainichi shimbun*, October 15, 1995.

199. "'Hohye-p'yŏngdŭngŭi tongbanja' chaehwagin" [Relationship as reciprocal and equal partners reconfirmed], *Chosun ilbo*, November 15, 1995.

CHAPTER 6

1. It was mostly from the 1990s onward that South Koreans started referring to Japanese who held a position similar to that of South Korea on the comfort women issue as "conscientious." A comparatively early example was "Ilchemanhaengŭn posangdwaeyahanda" [Japan must compensate for the brutal acts of the colonial period], *Chosun ilbo*, August 30, 1990.

2. More detail on the Textbook Reform Society can be found in Atarashii rekishi kyōkasho o tsukuru kai (ed.), *Atarashii rekishi kyōkasho o 'tsukuru kai' to iu undō ga aru* [There is a movement called the Society for History Textbook Reform], Fusōsha (1998).

3. "Kokuminkaigi ga hata age, gengō hōseika e hatarakikake" [People's Conference launched, pushes for era name law realization], *Asahi shimbun*, July 19, 1978.

4. "Atarashii rekishi kyōkasho o tsukuru kai hossoku, yūshikishara gurūpu ga setsuritsu sōkai" [Textbook Reform Society launched, group of key figures holds inaugural general meeting], *Yomiuri shimbun*, February 1, 1997.

5. "Watashi no iru fūkei, Tōkyō daigaku kyōju Fujioka Nobukatsu san, kyōkasho, Nihonjin to shite no hokori" [Tokyo University Professor Fujioka Nobukatsu talks about climate, calls textbooks a source of pride for himself as a Japanese citizen], *Yomiuri shimbun*, December 7, 1996.

6. "Rekishi ishiki hagukumu kyōkasho o, gakusha, bunkajinra ga yobikake, 'Tsukuru kai' ga hossoku" [Academics and cultural figures launch Textbook Reform Society, call for a textbook to foster historical consciousness], *Yomiuri shimbun*, December 11, 1996.

7. "Rekishi ishiki hagukumu kyōkasho o, gakusha, bunkajinra ga yobikake, 'Tsukuru kai' ga hossoku" [Academics and cultural figures launch Textbook Reform Society, call for a textbook to foster historical perceptions], *Yomiuri shimbun*, December 11, 1996. See also Atarashii rekishi kyōkasho o tsukuru kai (ed.), *Atarashii rekishi kyōkasho o 'tsukuru kai' to iu undō ga aru* [There is a movement called the Society for History Textbook Reform], Fusōsha (1998).

8. See "'Gōmanizumu sengen' Kobayashi Yoshinori cho; goseikon hōdō hihan mo fukkatsu" [Gōmanism Sengen by Kobayashi Yoshinori again criticizes media reporting on the royal wedding], *Yomiuri shimbun*, April 16, 1994, on Kobayashi's activities prior to Textbook Reform Society. Kobayashi Yoshinori's Gōmanism Sengen series, launched in *SPA! Magazine* in 1992 as an experimental "philosophical manga," was initially strongly liberal. In 1995, however, after an argument with the *SPA!* editorial section, Kobayashi moved his series to *Sapio*, where, in the wake of his comment about the comfort women issue, it took on a strongly nationalist tone. In that sense, the development of Kobayashi's thought was symbolic of the

state of ideology in Japan at the time. Kobayashi Yoshinori official website: http://yoshinori-kobayashi.com (last accessed October 18, 2016).

9. Atarashii rekishi kyōkasho o tsukuru kai (ed.), *Atarashii rekishi kyōkasho o 'tsukuru kai' to iu undō ga aru* [There is a movement called the Society for History Textbook Reform], Fusōsha (1998).

10. Tawara Yoshifumi, *Shiryō: Tsukurukai no naibukōsō no rekishi to konkai no naifun* [Representative documents: The history of Textbook Reform Society internal disputes and the current internal dispute], Kodomo to kyōkasho zenkoku netto 21. http://www.ne.jp/asahi/kyokasho/net21/ (last accessed September 30, 2016).

11. "Shasetsu: Kyōkasho kentei, kinrinshokoku jōkō no minaoshi shinchō ni" [Editorial: Cautious approach on review of neighboring country clause in textbook screening], *Yomiuri shimbun*, June 27, 2013.

12. Tawara Yoshifumi, *Shakaikamoku shunin chōsakan wa naze kainin saretanoka* [Why was the chief textbook examiner on social studies replaced?], Kodomo to kyōkasho zenkoku netto 21. http://www.ne.jp/asahi/kyokasho/net21/ (last accessed September 30, 2016).

13. "Jūgun ianfu mondai de kyōzai kenkyū e, Tōkyō to kyōikui" [Tokyo Metropolitan Board of Education to study educational materials on comfort women issue], *Asahi shimbun*, March 13, 1992.

14. "Kuni no kenkai jūshi medatsu, shakai issatsu atari no iken wa ōhaba gen, kōkō kyōkasho kentei" [High school textbook screening clearly following government position, major drop in comments per social studies textbook], *Asahi shimbun*, July 1, 1993.

15. "Subete no chūgaku kyōkasho ni kijutsu, jūgun ianfu nado no sengo hoshō" [References in all junior high textbooks to postwar compensation for comfort women, etc.], *Asahi shimbun*, May 29, 1996.

16. "Kyōin muke ni, 'kokka no hokori' o uttaeru zasshi sōkan, Ajia shokoku hanpatsu no kenen mo" [New magazine for teachers calls for "national pride," fears of Asian reaction], *Asahi shimbun*, November 16, 1995; "Fujioka Tōdai kyōju no jiyūshugi shikan kenkyūkai (sengo 51 nen no natsu kara)" [Tokyo University Professor Fujioka to set up Liberal View of History Study Group (from summer of the 51st year since WWII)], *Asahi shimbun*, August 17, 1996.

17. "Fujioka Tōdai kyōju no jiyūshugi shikan kenkyūkai (sengo 51 nen no natsu kara)" [Tokyo University Professor Fujioka to set up Liberal View of History Study Group (from summer of the 51st year since WWII)], *Asahi shimbun*, August 17, 1996.

18. For more on what Fujioka regarded as "masochistic" readings of history, see Fujioka Nobukatsu, *Jigyaku shikan no byōri* [Pathology of masochistic readings of history], Bungeishunjū (2000).

19. "Fujioka Tōdai kyōju no jiyūshugi shikan kenkyūkai (sengo 51 nen no natsu kara)" [Tokyo University Professor Fujioka to set up Liberal View of History Study Group (from summer of the 51st year since WWII)], *Asahi shimbun*, August 17, 1996.

20. "Ianfu kijutsu meguri ketsugi, akarui Nihon" ["Bright Japan" resolution on comfort women references], *Asahi shimbun*, September 14, 1996.

21. "Rekishi kyōkasho no ianfu kijutsu no teisei o, Shinshintō no kokkai giren

ga seimei" [New Frontier Party's Diet league calls for amendment of history textbook comfort women references], *Asahi shimbun*, December 21, 1996.

22. "Kahi dōsu, iinchō saiketsu de, ianfu kijutsu sakujo, kengikaii ga saitaku, Okayama" [Casting vote by Okayama Prefectural Assembly committee chair leads to adoption of resolution to remove comfort women references], *Asahi shimbun*, December 18, 1996.

23. This pattern emerged in the prefectures of Akita, Yamagata, Fukushima, Ibaraki, Tochigi, Niigata, Tottori, Yamanashi, Shizuoka, Kyōto, Ōsaka, Nara, Hiroshima, Kagawa, Tokushima, Ehime, Nagasaki, and Kumamoto. See, for example, "Chūgaku kyōkasho ianfu, Nankin gyakusatsu, 26 chihōgikai ga sakujo nado no ikensho" [Petitions in 26 local parliaments for removal of references to comfort women and the Nanking Incident in junior high school textbooks], *Asahi shimbun*, August 8, 1997; "Nichibenren, sakujo no seigan no fusaitaku o yōsei, kyōkasho no ianfu kijutsu" [Japan Federation of Bar Associations calls for rejection of petitions for removal of comfort women references in textbooks], *Asahi shimbun*, May 2, 1997.

24. "Rekishi kagai kōi no kijutsu, ōhaba gen, 2002 nendo ban chūgaku no rekishi kyōkasho" [References to historical harm well down in 2002 junior high history textbooks], *Asahi shimbun*, September 10, 2000.

25. "Kyōkasho kentei, nitchū, Nikkan kusuburu hidane, ryōdo, kuni no tachiba kyōchō" [Textbook screening a smoldering issue in Japan's relations with China and Korea, government position on national territory stressed], *Nihon keizai shimbun*, April 6, 2005. Unless otherwise stated, all *Nihon keizai shimbun* articles referenced in this book were drawn from the following database: http://telecom.nikkei.co.jp (last accessed October 3, 2016).

26. "Rekishi kyōkasho tsukuru kai kentei gōkaku e, monbukagakushō hōshin, hyakusūjukkasho shūsei de" [Textbook Reform Society's textbook passes after over 100 revisions in line with Ministry of Education policy], *Nihon keizai shimbun*, March 4, 2001.

27. "Seifu, seiji kainyū sezu, chūkan kenen no tsukuru kai kyōkasho" [Government will not intervene in Textbook Reform Society textbook issue despite Chinese and Korean concerns], *Asahi shimbun*, February 21, 2001.

28. "Chūgaku kyōkasho no saitaku shūryo, tsukuru kai hen wa 1% miman, Asahi shimbunsha chōsa" [Choice of junior high textbooks completed, *Asahi shimbunsha* survey shows Textbook Reform Society's textbook adopted by less than 1% of schools], *Asahi shimbun*, August 16, 2001; "Tsukuru kai kyōkasho saitaku, chūkō ikkankō de shiyō, tokyōi" [Textbook Reform Society textbook adopted, to be used in full high schools, says Metropolitan Education Board], *Asahi shimbun*, August 26, 2004.

29. "Tsukuru kai, jōshikiteki na saitaku kekka da" [Textbook Reform Society says textbook screening results "reasonable"], *Asahi shimbun*, October 7, 2005.

30. "Uha rondan, jingi naki tatakai, tsukuru kai bunretsu dake ja nai" [Ruthless battle within rightwing platform, more than just breakup of the Textbook Reform Society at issue], *Asahi shimbun*, December 4, 2006.

31. "Hoshukei, kyōkasho: Giron yobu, rainendo kara 4 nenkan no chūgaku shakaika kyōkasho o kakuchi de saitaku" [Conservative textbook sparks debate, to

be adopted as the junior high social studies textbook for the next four years around Japan], *Mainichi shimbun*, September 19, 2011.

32. Fujioka Nobukatsu, *Watashi wa naze kyōsantō o yameta ka* [Why I quit the JCP], Fujioka Nobukatsu netto hasshin kyoku, http://blog.so-net.ne.jp/fujioka-nobukatsu (last accessed April 30, 2006).

33. For example, Nishibe Susumu and Kobayashi Yoshinori, *Hanbei to iu sahō* [Anti-Americanism as a strategy], Shogakkan (2002).

34. Nishio Kanji, *Kokumin no rekishi* [History of the people of Japan], Sankei shimbun nyūsu sābisu (1999); Fujioka Nobukatsu, *Ojoku no kingendaishi: Ima, kokufuku no toki* [A contemporary history of humiliation: Enough is enough], Tokuma Shoten (1996).

35. "Nihon keizai wa sengo saiaku, sanini de Hashimoto Ryūtarō shushō ga ninshiki, daitan na sochi okonau" [PM Hashimoto recognizes in upper house committee that Japanese economy is at its worst in the postwar period, will take bold measures], *Mainichi shimbun*, April 6, 1998.

36. This section draws heavily on Kimura Kan, "Nationalistic Populism in Democratic Countries of East Asia," *Journal of Korean Politics* 16(2) (2007).

37. "98 nyūsu ripōto (Sono 1)" [98 news report: Part 1], *Mainichi shimbun*, December 30, 1998.

38. Katayama Chiaki, "Giin, kanryo, daikigyō, keisatsu nado no shinraikan chōsa kekka kara" [What survey results show about confidence in Diet members, bureaucrats, big companies, and the police, etc.], *Chūō chōsahō* 581 (July 2004).

39. "Kungminjŏngbu 6 kaewŏl sŏlmun/ IMF ch'eje: Ch'oeusŏn'gwaje kŭmyunggaehyŏk" [Six months of "government of the people"/ IMF regime: Financial reform the most urgent task], *Dong-a ilbo*, August 23, 1998.

40. Kimura Kan, "Nationalistic Populism in Democratic Countries of East Asia."

41. Kosuke Mizuno and Pasuk Phongpaichit (eds.), *Populism in Asia*, Singapore: NUS Press (2009).

42. Gotō Kenji, *Koizumi gekijō no jidai* [The era of Koizumi theater], Iwanami Shoten (2014); Yun Tae-yeong, *Taet'ongnyŏngŭi marhagi: Nomuhyŏntaet'ongnyŏngege paeunŭn sŏltŭkkwa sot'ongŭi pŏpch'ik* [The president's speech: President Roh Moo-hyun's technique of persuasion and communication], Wijŭdŏmhausŭ (2016); Kang Mun-gu, "Han'gugŭi minjujŏkkonggohwawa nomuhyŏnchŏngbu: Konghŏn'gwahan'gye" [Confirmation of South Korean democracy and the Roh Moo-hyun government], *Taehanjŏngch'ihak'oebo* 20(2) (2012).

43. Roh Moo-hyun, *Unmyŏngida: Nomuhyŏnchasŏjŏn* [My destiny: Autobiography of Roh Moo-hyun], Tolbegae (2010).

44. "Nomuhyŏnchŏntaet'ongnyŏng'Ilbonch'ŭngnyangsŏnŭl ch'immolshik'yŏra" [Former president ordered sinking of Japanese survey ships], *Chosun ilbo*, September 25, 2012.

45. "Jimin sōsai sen kakujinei no sōdatsusen, gyōkai hyō ni ihen, Koizumi ninki de soshiki hyō ni yurumi" [LDP presidency election develops into harsh competition for each faction; Koizumi's popularity frays organized vote, spurring unusual business voting behavior], *Yomiuri shimbun*, April 18, 2001.

46. "Sōshi kaimei chōsen no hito ga myōji o kure to itta jimintō, Asō Tarō shi

ga hatsugen" [LDP's Asō Tarō says that Koreans asked to be given Japanese surnames], *Mainichi shimbun*, June 1, 2003; "Sōshi kaimei wa chōsenjin ga nozonda, Asō Tarō shi hatsugen o Kankokushi hihan hōdō" [Korean papers critical of Asō Tarō suggestion that Koreans wanted to change their names], *Asahi shimbun*, June 2, 2003; "Ro daitōryō hōnichi, sanjūku, gunjin tomurau hi, Asō shi no hatsugen, yūjihōsei seiritsu?" [President Roh's visit to Japan faces triple trouble: Day mourning fallen soldiders, Asō comment, and passing of bill on military emergencies?], *Asahi shimbun*, June 4, 2003.

47. "Kako yori mirai tsuranuku, Nikkan shunō kaidan" [Japan-Korea summit talks focus on the future, not the past], *Asahi shimbun*, June 8, 2003; "Nodaet'ongnyŏngpangil: T'ŭkp'awŏnkandamhoeilmuniltap" [President Roh's visit to Japan: Full text of press conference Q&A], *Chosun ilbo*, June 8, 2003.

48. "Nikkan shunō kaidan, kyōdō kaiken: Yōshi" [Main points of joint press briefing after Japan-Korea summit talks], *Asahi shimbun*, July 22, 2004.

49. Kimura Kan, "Nationalistic Populism in Democratic Countries of East Asia."

50. See also Kimura Kan, "Shidōryoku no kiki ni chokumen suru Kankoku seiji: Chōsōki reimudakkuka wa saigen suru ka" [Korean politics facing a leadership crisis: Another super-early transition to lame duck status?], *Kokusai mondai* 614 (September 2012).

51. Kimura Kan, "Shidōryoku no kiki ni chokumen suru Kankoku seiji: Chōsōki reimudakkuka wa saigen suru ka" [Korean politics facing a leadership crisis: Another super-early transition to lame duck status?], *Kokusai mondai* 614 (September 2012).

52. See Kobayashi Yoshiaki, *Seiken kōtai: Minshutō seiken to wa nan de atta no ka* [A change of government: What was the DPJ administration?], Chūō Kōronsha (2012) for more on the DPJ's period in power.

53. For example, "Nikkan sakkā W-hai, yume no kaimaku, yūkō no shinjidai e kitai, Kin daitōryō sengen" [President Kim declares hopes that the fulfilment of the Japan-Korea World Cup will open the way for a new era of friendship], *Asahi shimbun*, June 1, 2002; *W-hai sakkā no nekkyō to isan" 2002 nen Nikkan wārudo kappu o megutte* [The passion and legacy of the World Cup: Reflecting on the 2002 Japan-Korea World Cup], Sekaishisōsha (2003).

54. "Hatsurainichi ni 4 sennin, Pe Yonjun san, 'Fuyuno sonata' fan to kōryū" [Bae Yong-joon's first Japan visit attracts 4,000 people, actor engages with *Fuyu no Sonata* fans], *Asahi shimbun*, April 5, 2004.

55. See Kimura Kan, "Būmu wa nani o nokoshita ka: Nashonarizumu no naka no Kanryū" [What was the legacy of the boom? The Korean boom and nationalism] in Ishita Saeko et al. (eds.), *Posuto Kanryū no media shakaigaku* [Post Korean Wave media sociology], Minerva shobō (2007) on the discourse in South Korea at the time.

56. Ishihara Shintarō and Morita Akio, *The Japan That Can Say No*, Kōbunsha (1989).

57. "Chūgoku wa hakenshugi, Ishihara tochiji ga hihan, Senkaku mondai" [Governor Ishihara criticizes China's hegemonism over Senkaku Islands issue], *Asahi shimbun*, September 20, 2012; "'Nihon no shokuminchi tōchi, kōhei to kiita,' Ishihara tochiji, kaiken de hatsugen, IOC hyōkai shisatsu" [Governor Ishihara says

at press briefing that he has heard that Japan's colonial rule was fair, IOC Evaluation Commission tour], *Asahi shimbun*, April 17, 2009.

58. The same result appears in public opinion surveys. Cabinet Office, *Gaikō ni kansuru yoron chōsa* [Public opinion survey on foreign policy], http://survey.gov-online.go.jp/index-gai.html (last accessed on October 1, 2016).

59. Kimura Kan, "Will the 'Comfort Women' Agreement Reduce Japan-ROK Mutual Distrust?," publication pending.

60. "Shasetsu: Kankoku daitōryōsen, Higashi Ajia renkei no kōki ni" [Editorial: Korean presidential election could be a golden opportunity for East Asian cooperation], "Ōsaka umare daitōryō, takamaru kitai, zainichi korianra, Kankoku shindaitōryō kimaru" [New Korean president chosen, Korean nationals living in Japan have high hopes in relation to Ōsaka-born president], both *Asahi shimbun*, December 20, 2007; "Kankoku daitōryōsen: Ri Mei hakushi tōsen, Nikkan kankei o saikōchiku, Nihon seifu, kaizen ni kitai" [Korean presidential election: Lee Myung-bak elected, may rebuild Japan-Korean relations? Japanese government hopeful of improvement], *Mainichi shimbun*, December 20, 2007.

61. "Kankoku shuyōshi, sōsenkyo kekka o ichimen toppu ni, Nikkan kankei kōten ni kitai" [Main Korean papers put Japanese election results of front page, hopeful of change for the better in Japan-Korea relations], *Asahi shimbun*, August 31, 2009.

62. "Nikkan shunō kaidan: 'Shinjidai' o kōchiku, sōgo hōmon o saikai de gōi" [Japan-Korea summit talks: Building a "new era," agreement to resume mutual visits], *Mainichi shimbun*, February 26, 2008; "Nikkan kankei, tairitsu yori keizai kōryu yūsen, Ri Meihaku jiki Kankoku daitōryo to kaiken" [Press briefing with incoming Korean president Lee Myung-bak, priority in Japan-Korea relations to be placed on economic exchange rather than friction], *Asahi shimbun*, February 2, 2008.

63. See Kimura Kan, "Hatoyama's Legacy and ROK-Japan-China Trilateral Cooperation: The Japanese Perspective," *JPI Peace Net* 2011(7) (April 2011) for more detail on the South Korean response to Hatoyama's East Asian Community concept.

64. "Moto ianfu no seikyūken mondai, Kankoku seifu no fusakui shiteki, kenpōsai" [Constitutional Court points to Korean government omission on former comfort women claim rights issue], *Asahi shimbun*, August 31, 2011; "Moto ianfu no kojin seikyūken, Nikkan kyōtei fukumazu, Kankoku seifu ga kenkai" [Korean government takes position that claim rights of former comfort women not included in bilateral treaty], *Asahi shimbun*, September 2, 2011; "Kankoku: Gaikōtsūshōshō, moto ianfu mondai de kyōgi teian, chikaku Nihon seifu ni" [Korean foreign ministry plans to propose to Japanese government soon that consultations are held on former comfort women issue], *Mainichi shimbun*, September 9, 2011.

65. Lee Myung-bak also didn't raise the comfort women issue at the September 2011 summit talks when his political foundation was still relatively firm. However, following the scandal involving Lee Sang-deuk, the president's elder brother and a key player in orchestrating the Japan-South Korea relationship, in November 2011, Lee Myung-bak's political pull rapidly declined. "Kankoku daitōryō jikkei no hisho kōsoku, assen shūzai yōgi, gigoku jiken ni hatten mo" [Secretary of Korean president's elder brother Lee Sang-deuk arrested on suspicion of accepting cash payments, escalates into bribery scandal], *Asahi shimbun*, December 11, 2011.

66. "Nikkan shunō kaidan: 'Ianfu, yūsen kaiketsu o' Ri daitōryō ga yōsei, Noda shushō 'Shōjozō tekkyo o'" [Japan-Korea summit talks: President Lee calls for resolution of comfort women issue to be prioritized, PM Noda wants statue of young girl removed], *Mainichi shimbun*, December 19, 2011.

67. "Kankoku daitōryō, Takeshima ni jōriku, Nihon, chūkan taishi ga kikoku" [Korean president lands on Takeshima, Japanese ambassador in Korea comes home], *Mainichi shimbun*, August 11, 2012.

68. "'Tennō ga kokoro kara ayamaru nara kinasai,' hō-Kan meguri Ri daitōryō hatsugen" [President Lee says on Emperor's Korea visit that he will be welcomed if he will apologize from the bottom of his heart], *Asahi shimbun*, August 15, 2012.

69. Kimura Kan, "Will the 'Comfort Women' Agreement Reduce Japan-ROK Mutual Distrust?"

Bibliography

WORKS CITED

Abe, Takeshi. *Tsūshōsangyō seisakushi 1980–2000 Dai 2 kan: Tsūshō bōeki seisaku* [History of Japan's trade and industry policy 1980–2000 Vol. 2: International trade policy]. Tokyo: Research Institute of Economy, Trade and Industry, 2013.

Boulding, Kenneth E. *Conflict and Defense: A General Theory*. New York: Harper & Row, 1963. Japanese translation by Uchida Tadao and Etō Shinkichi as *Funsō no ippan riron*. Tokyo: Diamond, Inc., 1971.

Cabinet Office, Government of Japan. *Gaikō ni kansuru yoron chōsa* [Public opinion survey on foreign policy]. Online. Available at http://survey.gov-online.go.jp/index-gai.html

Cheon, Geum-seong. *Hwanggangesŏ pugakkkaji* [From Hwanggang River to Mount Puggak]. Seoul: Tongsŏmunhwasa, 1981.

Chi, Tong-wook. *Kankoku daitōryō retsuden: Kenryokusha no eiga to tenraku* [The lives of Korea's presidents: The power, the glory, and the fall]. Tokyo: Chūō Kōron Shinsha, 2002.

Ch'inirinmyŏngsajŏn p'yŏnch'anwiwŏnhoe, ed. *Ch'inirinmyŏngsajŏn* [List of pro-Japanese collaborators]. Seoul: Minjongmunjeyŏn'guso, 2014.

Cho, Gab-je. *Yugo!:Pumasat'aeesŏ 10.26 chŏngbyŏnkkaji yushinjŏnggwŏnŭl punggoeshik'in hamsŏng gwach'ongsŏngŭi hyŏnjang1-2* [The death of a president: From the Puma incident to the presidential assassination]. Seoul: Han'gilsa, 1987.

Chung, Jae-jeong. "Symposium Seminar III: Perspective on Modern Japan-South Korea Relations—Learning the Wisdom of Coexistence from History." *Annals, Public Policy Studies* 8 (May 2014): 21–31.

Dong-a Ilbo, ed. *P'yŏngjŏn inch'on kimsŏngsu: Chogukkwa kyŏree pach'in ilsaeng* [Biography of Inchon Kim Song-su: A life devoted to the nation]. Seoul: Dong-a Ilbosa, 1991.

Dong-a Ilbo, ed. *Sŏlsan changdŏksu* [Solsan Chang Dok-soo]. Seoul: Dong-a Ilbosa, 1981.

Eurostat. "Intra-EU Trade in Goods—Recent Trends." Online. Available at http://ec.europa.eu/eurostat/statistics-explained/index.php/Intra-EU_trade_in_goods_-_recent_trends

Fujii, Kenji. "*Ri Shōban* Rain senpū e no katei ni kan suru kenkyū" [Research on the Syngman Rhee Line proclamation process]. *Chōsen gakuhō* 185 (October 2002).

Fujioka, Nobukatsu. *Jigyaku shikan no byōri* [Pathology of masochistic readings of history]. Tokyo: Bungeishunjū, 2000.

Fujioka, Nobukatsu. *Ojoku no kingendaishi: Ima, kokufuku no toki* [A contemporary history of humiliation: Enough is enough]. Tokyo: Tokuma Shoten, 1996.

Fujioka, Nobukatsu. *Watashi wa naze Kyōsantō o yameta ka* [Why I quit the JCP]. Fujioka Nobukatsu netto hasshin kyoku. Online. Available at http://blog.so-net.ne.jp/fujioka-nobukatsu

Fukunaga, Fumio. *Ōhira Masayoshi: "Sengohoshu" to wa nani ka* [Ōhira Masayoshi: The thought and behavior of the postwar conservatives]. Tokyo: Chūō Kōron Shinsha, 2008.

Furuno, Yoshimasa. *Kin Dai-chū jiken no seiji ketchaku: Shuken hōki shita Nihon seifu* [The political resolution of the Kim Dae-jung incident: The Japanese government renounces sovereignty]. Tokyo: Tōhō Publishing Co., Ltd., 2007.

Gang, Jun-man. *Han'guk hyŏndaesa sanch'aek: 1940 nyŏndaep'yŏn* [Strolling through modern Korean history: 1940s]. Seoul: Inmulsa, 2002.

Gong, Ro-myung. *Naŭi oegyon not'ŭ: Anesŏ tŭtkopogo kyŏkkŭn han'gugoegyo 50onyŏn* [Diplomatic Notes: 50 years of Korean diplomacy from inside the government]. Seoul: Kip'arang, 2014.

Gotō, Kenji. *Koizumi gekijō no jidai* [The era of Koizumi theater]. Tokyo: Iwanami Shoten, 2014.

Gotō, Kenji. *Takeshita seiken: 576 nichi* [The 576 days of the Takeshita administration]. Tokyo: Gyōken Shuppankyoku, 2000.

Gwon, Seong-yeol, ed. *Inch'on'gimsŏngsu : Inch'on kimsŏngsuŭi sasanggwa irhwa* [Inchon Kim Song-su: Thoughts and episodes]. Seoul: Dong-a Ilbosa, 1985.

Hackett, John. *The Third World War: A Future History*. London: Sidgwick & Jackson, 1978. Japanese translation by Aoki Eiichi as *Dai sanji sekaitaisen*. Tokyo: Futami Shobō, 1978.

Han, Yang-myeong, and Tae-hyun Ahn. "Ch'ukche chŏngch'iŭi tu p'unggyŏng: Kukp'ungp1kwa taehaktaedongje" [Two scenes of festival politics: Kukp'ung 81 and the Campus Festival]. *Pigyominsok'ak* 26 (February 2004).

Han'gukchŏngshindaeyŏn'guso. *Taeŭnggwa chŏnmang* [Response and outlook]. Online. Available at http://www.truetruth.org/know/know_04.html

Hashimoto, Shinobu. "Watashi wa kai ni naritai: Chōhen terebi dorama" [I want to become a shellfish: Feature-length TV program]. *Eiga hyōron* 15:11 (November 1958).

Hata, Ikuhiko. *Ianfu to senjō no sei* [Comfort women and sex in the battlefield]. Tokyo: Shinchōsha, 1996.

Hattori, Ryūji. *Nakasone Yasuhiro: "Daitōryōteki shushō" no kiseki* [Nakasone Yasuhiro: The presidential prime minister]. Tokyo: Chūō Kōron Shinsha, 2015.

Hausenfleck, Michael. "The Reagan Doctrine: A Conceptual Analysis of the Democracy Imperative in U.S. Foreign Policy, 1981–1988." PhD diss., Brandeis University, 1995.

Hettling, Manfred, and Tino Schölz. "Kako to no danzetsu to renzoku: 1945-nen irai no Doitsu to Nihon ni okeru kako to no torikumi" [Distance and continuity: Coming to terms with the past in Germany and Japan after 1945]. Tranlated by Kawakita Atsuko. *Yōroppa Kenkyū* 6 (March 2007).

Hironaka, Yoshimichi. *Miyazawa seiken 644 nichi* [The Miyazawa administration: 644 days]. Tokyo: Gyōken Shuppankyoku, 1998.

Hitokawa mukeba igami atte iru: Chūgoku, Kankoku, han-Nichirengō no jakuten [At each other's throats just under the surface: The frailty of the anti-Japan alliance]. *Shūkan shinchō* (July 17, 2014).

Hong, Seuk-ryule. "K'at'ŏhaengjŏngbugi migugŭi taehanban-do chŏngch'aekkwa 3 chahoedam" [Korea's America policy and trilateral talks with the Carter administration]. *Han'gukkwagukchejŏngch'i* 32:2 (2016).

Hosoya, Chihiro. *San Furanshisuko kōwa e no michi* [The road to the San Francisco Peace Treaty]. Tokyo: Chūō Kōron Sha, 1984.

I, Seong-il. "1992 nyŏnhanjunggukkyojŏngsanghwa ŭiŭie kwanhan chaegoch'al: Hanbandowachunggukkwaŭi kwan'gye kujobyŏnhwarŭlchungshimŭ-ro" [Examination of the significance of normalization of China-Korea Relations in 1992: Focusing on changes in the structure of relations between China and the Korean Peninsula]. *Chunggguk'ak* 40 (December 2011).

Ienaga, Saburō. *Kyōkasho saiban* [The textbook trials]. Tokyo: Nippon Hyōronsha, 1981.

Ienaga Kyōkasho Soshō Bengodan, ed. *Ienaga kyōkasho saiban: 32-nen ni wataru bengodan katsudō no sōkatsu* [The Ienaga textbook trials: Summary of the defense team's 32 years of activity]. Tokyo: Nippon Hyōronsha, 1998.

Ikei, Masaru. *Orinpikku no seijigaku* [The political science of the Olympics]. Tokyo: Maruzen, 1992.

Ikoma, Tomokazu. "Kin Shōhitsu no seiji kenryoku tōsō katei bunseki: 1990 nen–1992 nen ni okeru minshu jiyūtō tōnai tōsō o chūshin ni" [Analysis of the process of Kim Jong-pil's fight for political power: The Democratic Liberal Party 1990–1992]. *Ritsumeikan Daigaku kokusai kankei ronshū* 12 (October 2012).

Ishihara, Shintarō, and Akio Morita. *"No" to ieru Nihon* [The Japan that can say no]. Tokyo: Kōbunsha, 1989.

Japan Institute of International Affairs, ed. *Shōrai no kokusai jōsei to Nihon no gaikō: 20 nen teido mirai no shinario puranningu* [The future international situation and Japan's diplomacy: Scenario planning for 20 years in the future]. Tokyo: Japan Institute of International Affairs, 2011.

Jeong, Na-mi, and Kan Kimura. "'Rekishi ninshiki' mondai to daiichiji Nikkan rekishi kyōdō kenkyū o meguru ichikōan: 1" [Some thoughts in relation to historical perception issues and the First Japan-Korea Joint History Research Committee Meeting: 1]. *Kokusai kyōryoku ronshū* 16:1 (July 2008).

Jeong, Un-hyeon. *Ch'inilp'aŭi han'guk hyŏndaesa* [Korean modern history of pro-Japanese collaborators]. Seoul: Inmunsŏwŏn, 2016.

Kaifu, Toshiki. *Seiji to kane: Kaifu Toshiki kaikoroku* [Politics and money: A memoir of Kaifu Toshiki]. Tokyo: Shinchōsha, 2010.

Kanemaru hōchō o hyōsu [Evaluating Kanemaru's visit to North Korea]. *Gendai Koria* 36 (November 1990).

Kang, Mun-gu. "Han'gugŭi minjujŏkkonggohwawa nomuhyŏnchŏngbu: Konghŏn'gwahan'gye" [Confirmation of South Korean democracy and the Roh Moo-hyun government]. *Taehanjŏngch'ihak'oebo* 20:2 (2012).

Katayama, Chiaki. "Giin, kanryo, daikigyō, keisatsu nado no shinrai kankei chōsa kekka kara" [What survey results show about confidence in Diet members, bureaucrats, big companies, and the police, etc.]. *Chūō chōsahō* 581 (July 2004).

Katō kanbōchōkan happyō [Statement by Chief Cabinet Secretary Katō]. Ministry of Foreign Affairs. Online. Available at http://www.mofa.go.jp/mofaj/area/taisen/kato.html

Katsumata, Seiichi. *Gaikō tō iinchō kokkai katsudō no sokuseki* [The footprints of diplomacy, party chairmanship and Diet activities]. Tokyo: Nihon Shakaitō Chūō Honbu Kikanshikyoku, 1987.

Kawano, Noriyuki. "Kakuryō shitsugen no seijigaku" [Politics of Ministers' Slips of the Tongue]. *Kokusai kyōryoku kenkyūshi* 7:1, January 2001.

Kim, Deok-ryeon, and Eo-ei Seo. "Chitpaphin han'guk, ilbon miguk tchamtchamie to tanghaetta" [Trampled Korea: Betrayed by Japan and the US again]. October 4, 2014. Online. Available at http://www.pressian.com/news/article.html?no=120624

Kim, Do-hyung. "Hihyōbun" [Critical essay]. In *Report on the Second Round of Japan-Korea Joint History Research (Textbook Group)*, edited by Second Japan-South Korea Joint History Research Committee. Tokyo: The Japan-Korea Cultural Foundation, 2010.

Kim, Hyung-wook. *Kenryoku to inbō: Moto KCIA buchō Kim Hyung-wook ga kataru* [Power and conspiracy: Former KCIA chief Kim Hyung-wook tells all]. Tokyo: Gōdō shuppan, 1982.

Kim, Hyung-wook. *Kimhyŏnguk'oegorok* [Memoir of Kim Hyung-wook]. Seoul: Ach'im, 1985.

Kim, Joo-un. *Han'gugŭi ŏllont'ongje: Ŏllont'ongjee taehan majimak kirogi-gil yŏmwŏnhamyŏ* [Korean media control: Will this be the last record on media control in this country?]. Seoul: Ribuk, 2008.

Kim, Min-jeong. *Kankoku no media kontorōru: Chun Doo-hwan seikenka ni okeru KOBACO no tanjō to media kontorōru no jisshōteki kenkyū* [Media control in South Korea: Empirical research on the birth of KOBACO and media control under the Chun Doo-hwan administration]. Tokyo: V2 Solution, 2009.

Kim, Min-kyoung. "Kukkagigwan-do Kimsŏngsu Pangŭngmo 'ch'inil' injŏng" [Governmental organization officially identifies the pro-Japanese behaviors of Kim Song-su and Pang Ung-mo]. *The Hankyoreh* (November 12, 2009).

Kim, Young-sam. *Kimyŏngsam hoegorok: Minjujuŭirŭl wihan naŭi t'ujaeng 3* [Kim Young-sam memorandum: My struggle for democracy]. Seoul: Paeksansŏdang, 2000.

Kimura, Kan. "Būmu wa nani o nokoshita ka: Nashonarizumu no naka no Kanryū" [What was the legacy of the boom? The Korean boom and nationalism]. In *Pōsuto Kanryū no media shakaigaku* [Post Korean Wave media sociology], edited by Saeko Ishita et al. Kyoto: Minerva Shobō, 2007.

Kimura, Kan. *Chōsen hantō o dō miru ka* [How should we read the Korean peninsula?]. Tokyo: Shūeisha, 2004.

Kimura, Kan. "Daiichiji rekishi kyōkasho funsō kara kokunichi undō e: Zen Tokan seikenki no tai-Nichikan no henkan ni tsuite no ichikōsatsu" [From the first textbook dispute to the Kuk-il (Overcome Japan) movement: Some thoughts on the change in South Korea's view of Japan during the Chun Doo-hwan era]. *Kokusai kyōryoku ronshū* 22:1 (July 2014).

Kimura, Kan. "Discovery of Disputes: Collective Memories on Textbooks and Japanese-South Korean Relations." *Journal of Korean Studies* 17:1 (Spring 2012).

Kimura, Kan. "Gendai Kankoku seiji-shi" [A history of modern Korean politics]. Tokyo: Chūō Kōron Shinsha, 2008.

Kimura, Kan. "Hatoyama's Legacy and ROK-Japan-China Trilateral Cooperation: The Japanese Perspective." *JPI Peace Net* 7 (April 2011).

Kimura, Kan. "How Should We Approach Japan-Korea Joint History Research? Observations of a Participant." *The Journal of Contemporary Korean Studies* 10 (2011).

Kimura, Kan. *Kankoku gendaishi* [Modern Korean history]. Tokyo: Chūō shinsho, 2008.

Kimura, Kan. "Kokusaifunsōka izen no Kankoku ni okeru ianfu mondai o meguru gensetsu jōkyō" [The comfort women discourse in South Korea prior to the issue becoming an international dispute]. *Kokusai kyōryoku ronshū* 22 (January 2015).

Kimura, Kan. *Minshūka no Kankoku seiji* [The preconditions for Korean democratization]. Nagoya: Nagoya daigaku shuppankai, 2007.

Kimura, Kan. "Nationalistic Populism in Democratic Countries of East Asia." *Journal of Korean Politics* 16:2 (2007): 2.

Kimura, Kan. *Nihon ni okeru Kankoku/Chōsen kenkyū to sono kadai* [Research on South and North Korea in Japan and issues faced]. Tokyo: Nakanishiyama shuppan, 2009.

Kimura, Kan. "'Rekishi ninshiki' mondai to daiichiji Nikkan rekishi kyōdō kenkyū o meguru ichikōan: 2" [Some thoughts on the historical perceptions dispute and the First Japan-Korea Joint History Research Committee Meeting: 2]. *Kokusai kyōryoku ronshū* [Journal of International Cooperation Studies] 6:2 (November 2008).

Kimura, Kan. "Shidōryoku no kiki ni chokumen suru Kankoku seiji: Chōsōki reimudakkuka wa saigen suru ka" [Korean politics facing a leadership crisis: Another super-early transition to lame duck status?]. *Kokusai mondai* 614 (September 2012).

Kimura, Kan. "Shihai seitō ni miru Boku Seiki seiken kara Zen Tokan seiken e no renzoku to danzetsu" [Continuity and disruption in the shift from Park Chung-hee to Chun Doo-hwan within the ruling party]. *Journal of International Cooperation Studies* 20 (January 2013).

Kimura, Kan. "Shinseikenka no Nikkan kankei: Nikkan ryōkoku wa naze tairitsu suru ka" [Japan-South Korea relations under the new regime: Why do Japan and Korea collide?]. *Mondai to kenkyū* (December 2013).

Kimura, Kan. "Will the 'Comfort Women' Agreement Reduce Japan-ROK Mutual Distrust?" In *Joint U.S.-Korea Academic Studies 2016*. Washington, DC: Korea Economic Institute of America.

Ko, Yon-soo. *Kankoku no keizai shisutemu: Kokusai shihon idō no kakudai to kōzō kaikaku no shinten* [South Korea's economic system: Greater international capital movement and the advance of structural reforms]. Tokyo: Tōyō Keizai Shinpōsha, 2000.

Ko, Yon-soo. *Kankoku no kigyō/kinyū kaikaku* [Korean companies and financial reform]. Tokyo: Tōyō Keizai Shinpōsha, 2009.

Kobayashi, Yoshiaki. *Minshutōseiken to wa nan de atta no ka* [What was the DPJ administration?]. Tokyo: Chūō Kōron Sha, 2012.

Kobayashi, Yoshinori, ed. *Atarashii rekishi kyōkasho o 'tsukuru kai' to iu undō ga aru* [There is a movement called the Society for History Textbook Reform]. Tokyo: Fusōsha, 1998.

"Kokumu daijin no enzetsu ni kan suru Suzuki-kun no shitsugi" [Question from Suzuki on the Minister of State's address]. *Kanpō gōgai* (October 16, 1951).

Kōno, Yōhei. *Nihon gaikō e no chokugen: Kaisō to teigen* [Plain speaking on Japan's diplomacy: Recollections and proposals]. Tokyo: Iwanami Shoten, 2015.

Korean Economic Planning Board, ed. *Chep 8hoe han'gukt'onggyenyŏn'gam* [Eighth Korean statistical yearbook]. Seoul: National Bureau of Statistics, Economic Planning Board, Republic of Korea, 1961.

Korean Economic Planning Board, ed. *Han'gukt'onggyenyŏn'gam* [Korean statistical yearbook]. Seoul: National Bureau of Statistics, Economic Planning Board, Republic of Korea, 1967.

Kubota, Kanichirō. *Nikkan kōshō hōkoku (6) Seikyūken kankei bukai daiikkai kaigijōkyō* [Report on Japan-Korea negotiations (6): First meeting of the Claims Subcommittee]. May 11, 1953.

Kukkabŏmnyŏngjŏngbosent'ŏ. *Taehanmin'guk'ŏnbŏp* [The Constitution of Korea]. Online. Available at http://www.law.go.kr/main.html

Kyech'ojŏn'giganhaenghoe, ed. *Kyech'o pangŭngmojŏn* [Biography of Kyecho Pang Ung-mo]. Seoul: Chosŏn Ilbosa, 1980.

Lee, Jong-won, et al. *Rekishi to shite no Nikkan kokkō seijōka 1–2* [Japan-Korea Normalization from a Historical Perspective, vols 1–2]. Tokyo: University of Tokyo Press, 2011.

Lee, Sang-yeol. *Nikkan kokkō seijōka kōshō katei ni okeru Kankoku seifu no tai-Nichi seisaku kettei ni kan suru ichikōsatsu* [A study on the Korean government's policymaking in relation to Japan during the normalization of Japan-Korea relations]. Tokyo: University of Tokyo Graduate School for Law and Politics, March 2002.

Mainichi Shimbunsha. *Kin Dai-chū jiken zenbō* [The full picture of the Kim Daejung incident]. Tokyo: Mainichi Shimbunsha, 1978.

Miller, Frederic P., Agnes F. Vandome, and John McBrewster, eds. *Koreagate: Political Scandal, South Korea, Richard Nixon, National Intelligence Service (South Korea), Park Tong-sun, Unification Church, Sun Myung Moon.* Beau Bassin, Mauritius: Alphascript Publishing, 2011.

Ministry of Economy, Trade and Industry. *White Paper on International Economy and Trade 2014.* Tokyo: Ministry of Economy, Trade and Industry, 2014.

Ministry of Justice. *Shutsunyūkoku kanri tōkei tōkeihyō* [Immigration control statistics]. Online. Available at http://www.moi.go.jp/housei/toukei_ichiran_nyukan.html

Mizuno, Kōsuke, and Pasuk Phongpaichit, eds. *Populism in Asia.* Singapore: NUS Press, 2009.

Moon, Chang-keuk. *Hanmi kaltŭngŭi haebu* [Anatomy of the US-ROK conflict]. Seoul: Nanam Publishing, 1994.

Mukōyama. Hidehiko. "Tsuyomaru Kankoku no tai-Chū keizai izon: Kenzaika suru jirenma" [Korea's growing dependence on the Chinese economy: An emerging dilemma]. *JRI Rebyū* 16:16 (2014).

Murao, Jirō, ed. *Shinpen Nihonshi no subete: Atarashii Nihonshi kyōkasho no sōzō e* [The story of "New Version of Japanese History": The creation of a new Japanese history textbook]. Tokyo: Hara Shobō, 1987.

Murata, Kōji. *Daitōryō no zasetsu: Kātā seiken no zai-Kan Beigun tettai seisaku* [President Carter's troop withdrawal policy from South Korea]. Tokyo: Yūhikaku, 1998.

Murata, Kōji. *Rēgan: Ika ni shite "Amerika no gūzō" to natta ka* [How Reagan became an American idol]. Tokyo: Chūō Kōron Shinsha, 2011.

Murayama, Tomiichi, et al. *Dejitaru kinenkan, ianfu mondai to Ajia josei kikin* [Digital memorial: Comfort women and the Asian Women's Fund]. Tokyo: Seitōsha, 2014.

Murayama, Tomiichi. *Murayama Tomiichi no shōgenroku: Jishasa renritsu Seiken no jissō* [Murayama Tomiichi's testimonies: The real facts of the LDP, JSP, and Sakigake coalition government]. Tokyo: Shinseisha Shuppan, 2011.

Murayama, Tomiichi, and Kiyomi Tsujimoto. *Sōjanō: Murayama Tomiichi 'Shushō taiken' no subete o kataru* [Murayama Tomiichi tells all about his experience as Prime Minister]. Tokyo: Daisan Shokan, 1998.

Nakagawa, Shōzō. "Kyōkasho e no kōgi to gōhō: Dokusha to *Asahi shimbun*" [Opposition to and false reporting on textbooks: Readers and the *Asahi Shimbun* newspaper]. *Asahi shimbun* (September 19, 1982).

National Church Women's Association, The Korean Christian Church in Japan, ed. *Kiisen kankō jittai hōkokusho* [Report on the actual state of *gisaeng* tourism]. Tokyo: NCC Christian Church Center for Asian Materials, 1984.

"Nikkan heigō jōyaku nado ni tsuite no Watanabe Michio moto fukusōri, gaishō hatsugen yōshi" [Summary of comments by Watanabe Michio, former Deputy Prime Minister and Foreign Minister, on the Treaty of Annexation]. *Asahi shimbun* (June 5, 1995).

Nikkan rekishi kyōkasho kenkyūkai. *Dai ikkai Nikkan gōdō rekishi kyōkasho kenkyūkai: Kenkyū hōkokusho* [The first Japan-Korea Joint History Research Project: Research report]. Tokyo: The Japan-Korea Cultural Foundation, 1991.

Nikkan rekishi kyōkasho kenkyūkai. *Kyōkasho wo Nikkan kyōryoku de kangaeru* [Japan-Korea cooperation through the lens of textbooks]. Tokyo: Ōtsuki Shoten, 1993.

Nishibe, Susumu, and Yoshinori Kobayashi. *Hanbei to iu sahō* [Anti-Americanism as a strategy]. Tokyo: Shōgakukan, 2002.

Nishio, Kanji. *Kokumin no rekishi* [History of the people of Japan]. Tokyo: Sankei Shimbun Nyūsu Sābisu, 1999.

Ogura, Kazuo. *Hiroku: Nikkan 1 chōenshikin* [Confidential notes: One trillion yen between Tokyo and Seoul]. Tokyo: Kōdansha, 2013.

Oh, Byoung-sang. *Ch'ŏngwadae pisŏshil 4:6 kong not'aeu chŏnggwŏnŭi chŏngch'ibisarŭl t'onghae pon kwŏllyŏk kaltŭnggwa chŏngch'ibalchŏn* [The Blue House Secretarial Office 4.6: Power struggles and political developments in the Political Secretarial Office of the Roh Tae-woo government]. Seoul: Chungang Ilbosa, 1985.

Ōhara shakaimondai kenkyūjo. *Nichirō kei shidōsha no sengo to 'shakai shichō': Matsui Masakichi-shi ni kiku* [Postwar experience of the Japan Labor-Farmer Party leaders and social thought: Talking to Matsui Masakichi]. *Ōhara shakaimondai kenkyūjo zasshi* 475 (June 1998).

Ohinata, Ichirō. *Kishi seiken 1241 nichi* [The Kishi administration: 1,241 days]. Tokyo: Gyōsei mondai kenkyūjo, 1985.

Okada, Ichirō. *Kakushin jichitai: Nekkyō to zasetsu ni nani o manabu ka* [Innovative local governments: What was learned from passion and setbacks]. Tokyo: Chūō Kōron Shinsha, 2016.

Ōnuma, Yasuaki. *Ianfu mondai wa nan datta no ka: Media, NGO, seifu no kōzai* [What was the comfort women issue about? The good and the bad of the media, NGOs and government]. Tokyo: Chūō Kōron Shinsha, 2006.

Open Archives. *Murayama ilbonch'ong-ri mangŏn kyut'an daehoe* [Japanese Prime Minister Murayama condemnation contest]. Online. Available at http://db.kdemocracy.or.kr/photo-archives/view/00755967

Ōta, Takashi, Hiroshi Ōyama, and Keiji Nagahara. *Ienaga Saburō no nokoshita mono, hikitsugu mono* [What Ienaga Saburō left behind, what has been carried on]. Tokyo: Nippon Hyōronsha, 2003.

Panminjongmunjeyŏn'guso, ed. *Ch'inilp'a 99in: Punyabyŏl chuyo inmurŭi ch'iniriryŏksŏ* [99 pro-Japanese collaborators: Records of major characters, divided by fields]. Seoul: Inmunsŏwŏn, 1993.

Park, Chul-un. *Naŭi sam yŏksaŭi kwejŏk: Shirhyang 60 nyŏn, oeguk yurangŭi insaengŭl san p'alsun noinŭi hoego esei* [The path of my life: Story of an 80-year-old who lost his hometown 60 years ago to wander abroad]. Seoul: Handŭl, 2005.

Park, Seh-jik. *Dokyumento: Sōru gorin* [The Seoul Olympics: The inside story]. Tokyo: Ushio Publishing, 1991.

Park, Yeong-kyu. *Kankoku daitōryō jitsuroku* [The true story of a South Korean president]. Translated by Kim Jung-myeong. Tokyo: Kinema-Junpōsha, 2015.

"'Rekishi ninshiki' mondai to daiichiji Nikkan rekishi kyōdō kenkyū o meguru ichikōsatsu: 2" [Reflections on the historical perception issues and the First Japan-South Korea Joint History Research Committee Meeting: 2]. *Kokusai kyōryoku ronshū* [Journal of International Cooperation Studies] 16:2 (November 2008).

Roh, Moo-hyun. *Unmyŏngida: Nomuhyŏnchasŏjŏn* [My destiny: Autobiography Roh Moo-hyun]. Seoul: Tolbegae, 2010.

Rürup, Reinhard. "Vergangenheit und demokratische Gesellschaft: Erinnerungspolitik und Erinnerungskultur in Deutschland." Japanese translation by Asada Shinji. *Kōkyō kenkyū* 5:2 (September 2008).

Sano, Kōji. "Kankoku no seichō moderu to Nikkan keizai kankei no henka: Nikkan kankei akka no keizaiteki haikei" [South Korea's growth model and the change in Japan-Korea economic relations: The economic background to the deterioration in Japan-Korea relations]. *Shōgaku ronshū* 83:2 (September 2014).

Senda, Kako. *Jūgun inanfu: "Koe naki onna" Hachiman nin no kokuhatsu* [Comfort women: 80,000 women finally find a voice]. Tokyo: Fusōsha, 1973.

Shigemura, Toshimitsu, and Tomoki Iimura. "Nikkan sogō orientalism no kokufuku: Gendaishi no kijutsuburi bunseki" [Japan and South Korea's mutual overcoming of Orientalism: Analysis of descriptions in contemporary history]. In *Report on the Second Round of Japan-Korea Joint History Research (Textbook Group)*, edited by Second Japan-South Korea Joint History Research Committee. Tokyo: The Japan-Korea Cultural Foundation, 2010.

Shiota, Ushio. "Kanemaru hō-Chōdan de nani ga hanasareta ka" [What was talked about with the Kanemaru delegation to North Korea?]. *Bungei shunjū* 72:10 (August 1994).

Shu, Shing-ching. *Kindai Higashi Ajia no aporia* [The aporia of modern East Asia]. Taipei: National Taiwan University Press, 2014.

Sin, Dong-ho. *Onŭrŭi han'gukchŏngch'iwa 6.3 sedae* [Korean politics today and the 6.3 generation]. Seoul: Yemun, 1966.

Sin, Jung-seon. *Kangch'ŏrwang pakt'aejun* [Steel king Park Tae-joon]. Seoul: Munidang, 2013.

Sogawa, Takeo. "Nikkan kihon jōyaku" [Treaty on Basic Relations between Japan and the Republic of Korea]. *Kokusaihō gaikō zasshi* 64 (March 1966).

Son, Chung-mu. *Kimhyŏnguk: Ch'oehuŭi kŭŏlgul* [Kim Hyung-wook: The last face]. Seoul: Munhagyesulsa, 1986.

Son, Ki-Sup. "Hanil anbogyŏnghyŏp oegyoŭi chŏngch'aekkyŏlchŏng: 1981–1983 Nyŏn Ilbonŭitaehan'guk chŏngbuch'agwan" [Japan's $4 billion Korean aid policy 1981–1983]. *Kukchejŏngch'inonch'ong* 49.1 (2009).

Sugano, Tamotsu. *Nippon kaigi no kenkyū* [Research on Japan Conference]. Tokyo: Fusōsha, 2016.

Sugiyama, Shigeo. "Nikkan kihon jōyaku oyobi zaisan/seikyūken shori kyōtei nado no shomondai" [Issues in relation to the Treaty on Basic Relations between Japan and the Republic of Korea and the Agreement Between Japan and the Republic of Korea Concerning the Settlement of Problems in Regard to Property and Claims and Economic Cooperation]. *Juristo* 327 (August 1965).

Sugiyama, Shōzō. *Yatōgaikō no shōgen* [Testimony on opposition party diplomacy]. Tokyo: Minerva shobō, 1982.

Sung, Nak-in. "Hŏnbŏpkwa kukkajŏngch'esŏng" [The constitution and state identity]. *Sŏultaehakkyopŏp'ak* 52:1 (March 2011).

Takahara, Akio, and Ryūji Hattori. *Nicchūkankeishi 1972–2012: Seiji* [A History of Japan-China Relations, 1972–2012: Politics]. Tokyo: University of Tokyo Press, 2012.

Tamura, Tetsuo. *Gekidō Sōru 1500 nichi: Zen Tokan seiken e no michi* [1,500 dramatic days in Seoul: The road to the Chun Doo-hwan administration]. Tokyo: Seikō Shobō, 1984.

Tanaka, Akihiko. Institute for Advanced Studies on Asia, University of Tokyo, The World and Japan Database Project, *Documents Related to Japan-China Relations*. Online. Available at http://www.ioc.u-tokyo.ac.jp/~worldjpn/documents/indices/JPCH/index.html

Tatamiya, Eitarō. *Hatoyama būmu no butai ura: Seijikisha no shūki* [Behind the scenes of the Hatoyama boom: A political reporter's notes]. Tokyo: Jitsugyō no Sekaisha, 1955.

Tawara, Yoshifumi. *Shiryō: Tsukurukai no naibukōsō no rekishi to konkai no naifun* [Representative documents: The history of Textbook Reform Society internal disputes and the current internal dispute]. Kodomo to kyōkasho zenkoku netto 21. Online. Available at http://www.ne.jp/asahi/kyokasho/net21/siryou20060314.html

Tsukamoto, Takashi. "Horon: Nikkan kihon jōyaku o meguru rongi" [Addendum: Debate over the Treaty on Basic Relations between Japan and the Republic of Korea]. In *Nikkan rekishi kyōdō kenkyū hōkokusho (Dai 1 ki): Dai 3 bunka hōkokusho*, edited by Nikkan rekishi kyōdō kenkyū iinkai. Online. Available at http://www.jkcf.or.jp/history_arch/first/3/09-02j_tsukamoto_j.pdf

Vogel, Ezra F. *Japan as Number One: Lessons for America*. Cambridge, MA: Harvard University Press, 1979.

Whang, Soon-hee. *W-haisakka no nekkyo to isan: 2002 nen Nikkan wārudo kappu o megutte* [The passion and legacy of the World Cup: Reflecting on the 2002 Japan-Korea World Cup]. Tokyo: Sekaishisōsha, 2003.

Yakushiji, Katsuyuki, ed. *Murayama Tomiichi kaikoroku* [A memoir of Murayama Tomiichi]. Tokyo: Iwanami Shoten, 2012.

Yomiuri Shimbun Ōsaka Shakaibu, ed. *Shimbun kisha ga kataritsugu sensō: 8) Sempan* [War as narrated by newspaper journalists: (8) War crimes]. Ōsaka: Kadokawa Shoten, 1986.

Yŏnsedaehakkyo kukkagwalliyŏn'guwŏnt'p, ed. *Han'guktaet'ongnyŏng t'ongch'igusulsaryojip. 3, Not'aeu taet'ongnyŏng* [An oral history of Korea's presidents 3: President Roh Tae-woo]. Seoul: Sŏnin, 2013.

Yu, Sun-hee. *Paku Seiki no tai-Nichi, tai-Beigaikō: Reisen henyōki Kankoku no seiji,*

1968–1973 [Park Chung-hee's Japan and US diplomacy: Korean politics during the period of Cold War transformation]. Kyoto: Minerva Shobō, 2012.

Yun, Jeong-ok. "Chŏngshindae wŏnhonŭi palchach'wi ch'wijaegi" [In the Footsteps of the Volunteer Labor Corps]. *The Hankyoreh* (January 4, 12, 19, and 24, 1990).

Yun, Jeong-ok. "Chŏngshindae Wŏnhonŭi Palchach'wi Ch'wijaegi." *The Hankyoreh*, January 12, 1990.

Yun, Jeong-ok. *Chōsenjosei ga mita ianfu mondai: Ashita o tomo ni tsukuru tame ni* [The comfort women issue seen from the perspective of Korean women: Opening the way for creating tomorrow together]. Tokyo: San-ichi Shinsho, 1992.

Yun, Kŏn-ch'a. *Gendai Kankoku no shisō: 1980–1990 nendai* [Modern Korean thought in the 1980s and 1990s]. Tokyo: Iwanami Shoten, 2000.

Yun, Tae-yeongc. *Taet'ongnyŏngŭi marhagi: Nomuhyŏntaet'ongnyŏngege paeunŭn sŏltŭkkwa sot'ongŭi pŏpch'ik* [The president's speech: President Roh Moo-hyun's technique of persuasion and communication]. Seoul: Wijŭdŏmhausŭ, 2016.

2. OTHER RELATED WORKS BY KIMURA KAN

Asaba, Yūki, Kan Kimura, and Daisuke Satō. *Tettei kenshō: Kankokuron no tsūsetsu, zokusetsu—Nikkan tairitsu no kanjō vs. ronri* [Investigation: Popular perceptions of Korea—Emotions vs logic in the tension between Japan and Korea]. Tokyo: Chūkō Shinsho Rakure, 2012.

Ishita, Saeko, Kan Kimura, and Chie Yamanaka, eds. *Posuto Kanryū no media shakaigaku* [Post Korean Wave media sociology]. Kyoto: Minerva Shobō, 2007.

Kagotani, Koji, Kan Kimura, and Jeff Weaver. "Democracy and Diversionary Incentives in Japan-South Korea Disputes." *International Relations of the Asia-Pacific* 13:3 (September 2013).

Kimura, Kan. "Kankoku ni okeru rekishi ronsō to Nikkan kankei" [The history debate in South Korea and Japan-South Korea relations]. *Gendai kankoku chōsen kenkyū* 9 (November 2009).

Kimura, Kan. "Popurizumu no naka no rekishi ninshiki: Nikkan no jirei o chūshin ni" [The historical perceptions issue in the context of populism: With a focus on the Japan-Korea case]. *Leviathan* (Spring 2008).

Kimura, Kan. "Northeast Asian Trilateral Cooperation in the Globalizing World: How to Reestablish Mutual Importance." *Kokusai kyōryokuronshū* 22:1 (July 2014).

Kimura, Kan. "Why Are the Issues of 'Historical Perceptions' between Japan and South Korea Persisting?" *Kokusai kyōryokuronshū* 19:1 (July 2011).

3. FURTHER READING

Chosun ilbo, ed. *Kankokujin ga mita Nihon: Nihon o ugokashite iru mono* [Japan as seen by Koreans: What is influencing Japan]. Tokyo: Saimaru Shuppankai, 1984.

Dudden, Alexis. *Troubled Apologies among Japan, Korea, and the United States.* New York: Columbia University Press, 2008.

Funahashi, Shigeyuki. *Shōgen: Sengo hanseiki no seiji katei—Konmei no ima, 21 seiki e no messēji* [Testimony: Political process in the 50 years since the war—Message to the 21st century from amidst the current confusion]. Tokyo: Akashi Shoten, 2001.

Jeong, Dae-sun. *Nihongun no seidorei: Nihongun ianfu mondai no jitsuzō to sono kaiketsu no tame no undō.* Translated into Japanese by Jeong Chin-sung and Iwakata Hisahiko. Tokyo: Ronsōsha, 2008.

Josei no tame no Ajia heiwa kokumin kikin. *Oraru hisutorii: Ajia josei kikin* [Oral history: The Asian Women's Fund]. 2007. Online. Available at http://www.awf.or.jp/pdf/0w12-1.pdf

Kawakami, Tamio. *Shakaitō no gaikō: Atarashii jidaizukuri no tame ni* [Shakaitō's diplomacy for a new era: The political chronicle of a social democrat]. Tokyo: Saimaru Shuppankai, 1994.

Kenmochi, Hisaki, Nobuko Kosuge, and Lionel Babicz. *Rekishi ninshiki kyōyū no chihei: Doku-Futsu kyōtsū kyōkasho to Nitchū-Kan no kokoromi* [In search of a shared historical awareness: The Joint German-French textbook and the Japan-China-Korea attempts]. Tokyo: Akashi Shoten, 2009.

Kim, Unyong. *Idai naru Orinpikku: Badenbaden kara Sōru e* [The Greatest Olympics: From Baden-Baden to Seoul]. Tokyo: Baseball Magazine Sha, 1989.

Kobayashi, Yoshinori. *Gōmanism sengen* [Arrogance manifesto], vols. 1–8 (1993–1996). Tokyo: Gentōsha.

Kōno danwa sakusei katei nado ni kan suru kentō chiimu, ed. *Ianfu mondai o meguru Nikkankan no yaritori no keii: Kōno danwa sakusei kara Ajia josei kikin made* [The course of Japan-Korea exchange over the comfort women issue: From the creation of the Kōno Statement to the Asian Women's Fund]. Online. Available at http://www.mofa.go.jp/files/000042173.pdf

Kosuge, Nobuko. *Sengo wakai: Nihon wa kako kara tokihanatareru no ka* [Paths to reconciliation in East Asia: An investigation of Japan's postwar/postcolonial reconciliation with its Asian neighbors]. Tokyo: Iwanami Shoten, 2005.

Lee, Jon-wuon, Tadashi Kimiya, and Toyomi Asano. *Rekishi to shite no Nikkan kokkō seijōka I-II* [Korea-Japan normalization as history I-II]. Tokyo: Hōsei Daigaku Shuppankyoku, 2011.

Lind, Jennifer. *Sorry States: Apologies in International Politics*. Ithaca: Cornell University Press, 2010.

Miyazawa, Kiichi, Takashi Mikuriya, and Takafusa Nakamura, eds. *Kikigaki Miyazawa Kiichi kaikoroku* [Interviews: Miyazawa Kiichi Memoirs]. Tokyo: Iwanami Shoten, 2005.

Murayama, Tomiichi, and Makoto Sakata. *Murayama danwa to wa nani ka* [What is the Murayama Statement?]. Tokyo: Kadokawa Shoten, 2009.

Nikkan rekishi kyōdō kenkyū iinkai, ed. *Nikkan rekishi kyōdō kenkyū hōkokusho (Dai 2 ki): Kyōkasho shō gurūpu hen* [Japan-Korea Joint History Research Report (Phase 2): Textbook subgroup]. Tokyo: The Japan-Korea Cultural Foundation, 2010.

Sakai, Toshiki. *Gendai Kankoku ni okeru rekishi kyōiku no seiritsu to kattō* [Establishment and issues in history education in modern Korea]. Tokyo: Ochanomizu Shobō, 2003.

Sawada, Katsumi. *Datsunichi suru Kankoku: Rinkoku ga Nihon o suteru hi* [South Korea's separation from Japan: The day when Japan is abandoned by its neighbor]. Tokyo: Ubikita Studio, 2006.

Soderberg, Marie, ed. *Changing Power Relations in Northeast Asia*. New York: Routledge, 2010.

Takahashi, Shiro. "Shinpen Nihonshi kentei: Zenkiroku" [Looking at *A New Version of Japanese History*: The full record]. *Shokun!* 18:9 (September 1986).

Takahashi, Tetsuya. *Yasukuni mondai* [The national politics of the Yasukuni Shrine]. Tokyo: Chikuma Shobō, 2005.

Weber, Max. *Ist die Geschichte eine Wissenschaft?* Translated into Japanese by Morioka Hiromichi as *Rekishi wa kagaku ka*. Tokyo: Misuzu Shobō, 1965.

Yamano, Sharin. *Ken-Kanryū* [Hating "The Korean Wave"]. Tokyo: Shinyūsha, 2005.

Yi, Suk-cha. *Kyōkasho ni egakareta Chōsen to Nihon: Chōsen ni okeru shotō kyōkasho no suii 1895–1979* [Korea and Japan as painted in textbooks: Trends in elementary school textbooks in Korea 1895–1979]. Tokyo: Horupu Shuppan, 1985.

Yoshimi, Yoshiaki. *Jūgun ianfu shiryōshū* [Documents on military comfort women]. Tokyo: Ōtsuki Shoten, 1992.

4. DATABASE REFERENCES

(a) Newspaper Databases

Asahi shimbun, *Kikuzō II Visual*, http://database.asahi.com/library2

Chosun ilbo, http://srchdbl.chosun.com/pdf/i_archive

Dong-a ilbo, *donga.com*, http://news.donga.com

Hankook ilbo, http://search.hankooki.com
JoongAng ilbo, http://koreajoongangdaily.joins.com
KINDS, http://www.kinds.or.kr
Mainichi shimbun, *Maisaku*, https://dbs.g-search.or.jp/WMAI/IPCU/WMAI_
    ipcu_menu.html
Nifty, *Shimbun/Zasshi kiji odan deetaabeesu*, http://business.nifty.com/gsh/RXCN
Nihon keizai shimbun, *Nikkei Telekon*, http://t21.nikkei.co.jp/g3/CMN0F12.do
Yomiuri shimbun, *Yomidasu rekishikan*, https://database.yomiuri.co.jp/rekishikan

(b) Diet and Election Databases

Diet Proceedings Record Search System, http://kokkai.ndl.go.jp
ROK Ministry of Foreign Affairs, http://ww.mofa.go.kr/main/index.jsp
ROK National Assembly Minutes, http://likms.assembly.go.kr/record/index.html

(c) Biographic Information Databases

Chosun.com, http://db.chosun.com/people/index.html
dongA.com, http://www.donga.com/immul
JOINS, http://people.joins.com

(d) Statistical Databases

Korean Statistical Information Service, http://kosis.kr
Statistics Japan, http://www.stat.go.jp/data/index.htm
Trade Statistics of Japan, Ministry of Finance, http://www.customs.go.jp/toukei/
    suii/html/time.htm
World Databank, http://databank.worldbank.org/data/home.aspx

(e) Public Opinion Surveys

Cabinet Office, http://www.stat.go.jp/data/index.htm
EAI, http://eai.or.kr
Jiji Press, http://www.jiji.com/service/yoron/result
Realmeter, http://realmeter.net

(f) Document and Paper Databases

DBpia, http://www.dbpia.co.kr
Japan Center for Asian Historical Records, http://www.jacar.go.jp
Korean Studies Information Service System, http://kiss.kstudy.com

(g) Public Institution Websites

Asian Women's Fund, http://www.ajw.or.jp
Human Rights Museum, https://www.womenandwar.net/contents/home/home.nx
Korea Chongshindae's Institute, http://www.truetruth.org
Korean Council for the Women Drafted for Military Sexual Slavery by Japan War
    & Women's Office of the President, http://www.president.go.kr
ROK Ministry of Foreign Affairs, http://www.mofa.go.kr/main/index.jsp

(h) Textbooks

Asahina, Masayuki, et al. *Shinpen kokumin Nihonshi* [A new edition of national Japanese history]. Tokyo: Hara Shobō, 1987.
Ienaga, Saburō. *Kentei fugōkaku Nihonshi* [Japanese history: The version that failed the screening]. Tokyo: Sanichi Shobō, 1974.
Inoue, Muneo, Kazuo Kasahara, and Kōta Kodama. *Shosetsu Nihonshi (Shinban)* [Detailed explanation of Japanese history: New edition]. Tokyo: Yamakawa Shuppansha, 1984.
Nihonshi [Japanese history]. Tokyo: Jikkyō Shuppan, 1983.
Nishio, Kanji, et al. *Atarashii rekishi kyōkasho: Shihanbon* [New Version of Japanese History: Trade Copy]. Tokyo: Fusōsha, 2001.

Index

Abe Shinzō, 164–165, 173

Agawa Sawako, 152

Akihito, Emperor, 100–101, 123

Aoki Ihei, 98

"apology diplomacy," 114–115, 119, 122–123, 130

Asahi shimbun, 29
  comfort women issue and, 107–108, 111, 130, 186
  historical perception and, 25–26

Asian currency crisis of 1997, 42, 158, 160–161, 164

Asian Women's Fund, 131, 135, 146, 148, 185

Asō Tarō, 163–166

Association of Pacific War Victims and Bereaved Families, 133–134

The Association of Pacific War Victims and Bereaved Families in South Korea, 136

Asukata Ichio, 67–68

Atsumi Jirō, 33

Bae Yong-joon, 168, 186

Bang Eung-mo, 29

Bush, George H. W., 74

Carter, Jimmy, 65, 72–74

Chen Shui-bian, 161, 164

China
  diplomatic relations with South Korea, 33, 44, 57
  invasion of Vietnam, 73
  Japan and, 56, 170, 184
  Japanese history textbooks and, 55–58
  trade dependency ratio (TDR) of, 41–42
  trade with South Korea, 35–36, 44
  United States and, 64, 72, 170–171, 184

Choi Byeong-ryeo, 83

Chôngdaehyop/Chôngsindae-munje Taech'aek Hyôpuihoe (Korean Council for the Women Drafted for Military Sexual Slavery by Japan), 103–104, 107, 127, 132–133, 136, 185, 202n33

Chosun ilbo, 29, 60
  articles about Japan in, 5–6, 14–15, 184
  Heo Mun-do and, 80, 83

Chosun ilbo (*continued*)
  Japanese history textbooks and,
    53–54, 82
  Japanese "shift to the right" and,
    59–62, 67
  Kuk-il movement and, 82–83
Cho Yong-pil, 33
Chun Doo-hwan, 75
  attempted assassination of, 33
  brought to power through coup
    d'état, 9, 33, 69, 73, 75, 81, 102,
    184, 196n6
  contrasted with Park, 74–76
  democratization and, 8, 96, 102
  fact-finding process and, 120
  historical perception and, 9
  legitimacy of Chun administration,
    9, 63
  media control and, 53
  Olympics and, 33
  South Korea/China relations and,
    57
  South Korea/Japan relations and,
    8–9, 63, 69, 76–77, 80, 85, 99–
    100, 184
  South Korea/USA relations and,
    63, 76
  visit to Japan of, 99–100
Claims Settlement Agreement, 104–
    105, 114–115, 118–119, 127–128,
    132, 171
Cold War, 43–45, 63–65, 70
  détente period of, 71–74
  end of, 98, 149, 156–157, 177
  Japanese foreign policy and, 170
  new Cold War, 171
  South Korea/Japan relations and,
    97–98, 177
comfort women issue, 17, 30–32, 34,
    96–97, 103–105, 113–137, 148
  addressed in South Korean publica-
    tions, 6, 15, 25
  alternatives to compensation for,
    128–129, 131–132
  Asahi report on, 107–108, 117, 122,
    128, 186
  Asian Women's Fund and, 131, 135,
    146, 148
  chronology of, 184–186
  compensation for South Koreans,
    104–106, 115, 118–119, 121–127,
    132, 146, 208n104
  contemporary women's issues and, 97
  fact-finding investigations into,
    128–132, 133–134
  historical backdrop of, 129
  as international issue, 131–132
  Japanese domestic politics and, 122–
    130, 132–136
  in Japanese history textbooks, 152,
    154–155
  Katō statements on, 108–110, 122,
    123, 125, 128–129, 128–130
  Kōno Statement on, 134–137
  legal structure of, 126–127, 129
  Miyazawa's visit to South Korea
    and, 105–107, 111, 113–115, 117–
    119, 121, 123
  Seoul Olympics and, 34
  South Korea/Japan relations and,
    30–32, 34, 96–97, 103–110,
    113–119, 122, 124–125, 128, 132,
    136–137, 146, 148, 151, 171–173,
    176, 185
  South Korean domestic politics and,
    117–122, 130, 132, 146, 148
  statue commemorating, 172, 186
  terminology of, 111
Coomaraswamy Report, 125, 185,
    208n104

Democratic Liberal Party (DLP) of Japan, 116–120
Democratic Party (Korean), 117–118
Democratic Party (of Japan), 164–165
Deng Xiopeng, 57, 64
Diet Members' Alliance for a Bright Japan, 155
Diet Members' League for the Transmission of a Correct History, 155
Doi Takako, 99, 101, 200n5
Dokdo. *See* Takeshima Island issue
Dong-a ilbo, 29
    comfort women issue and, 119
    Japanese history textbooks and, 53

East Germany, 33
Estrada, Joseph, 161
Etō Takami, 141

FIFA World Cup, 39, 168, 185
forced transport/labor issue, 17, 53, 103–104, 112, 129, 132
    addressed in South Korean newspapers, 6, 25
    See also comfort women issue
Fujioka Nobukatsu, 152, 154–158
Fujio Masayuki, 141, 144
Fujita Kimio, 90
Fukuda Takeo, 65
Fukuda Yasuo, 164–166
Fukuda Yūsuke, 152

gisaeng (courtesan) tourism, 34, 96–97, 184
globalization, 37, 39–43, 159–160, 176–177
Gōmanism Sengen, 153, 216n8
Gong Ro-myung, 146
Gorbachev, Mikhail, 98
Gulf War, 102

Gwangju incident, 9, 33, 53, 57, 63, 73
    fact-finding and, 120
    protests over, 81

Hackett, John, 65
Hallyu, 168–169
Han Sang-il, 62
Hara Shobō, 88, 90
Hashimoto Ryūtarō, 142–143, 163, 185
    "irresponsible statements" made by, 141, 143
Hata Ikuhiko, 107, 109, 129
Hata Tsutomu, 133, 138
Hatoyama Ichirō, 27–28
Hatoyama Yukio, 164–166, 171
Hattori Tamio, 86
Hayashi Kentarō, 88
Hayashi Mariko, 152
Heo Hwa-pyeong, 75
Heo Mun-do, 75, 80–81, 83
Heo Sam-soo, 75
Hirohito, Emperor, 99–100, 123
historical perception, 17–19, 21, 45, 91, 138–140, 158, 175–176
    chronology of, 183–186
    comfort women issue and, 122–123, 130–131, 175–176
    contemporary significance of, 95–96
    control of by ruling elites, 91, 97, 101, 174, 177
    democratization of South Korea and, 8–9
    framed in South Korean publications, 5–7, 13–15, 25–26
    historical trajectory of, 13–16
    "irresponsible statements" of Japanese officials and, 140–142
    Japanese government and, 97, 137–140, 142

historical perception (*continued*)
  Japanese history textbooks and, 10–
    13, 49–50, 91, 97, 151, 175–176
  Japanese nationalism and, 9–11, 151
  Japanese Socialist Party and, 99–101
  measuring impact of factors affect-
    ing, 175–176
  in Murayama administration, 144–
    145
  political destabilization and, 165,
    167
  postwar closure (first phase), 22–26
  postwar generation (third phase),
    30–32
  rise of populist nationalism and,
    162–163, 173–174
  Second World War and, 137–138,
    145
  silent era (second phase), 26–30
  South Korea/Japan relations and,
    34, 45, 97–98, 99–101, 122–123,
    138–139, 151, 167–168, 173,
    175–176
  theoretical framework for analysis,
    16–17
  three phases of, 14–18, 21–22
history textbooks. *See* Japanese history
  textbooks
Horikawa Kentarō, 179, 180
Hosokawa Morihiro, 134, 137–138

Ibuka Masaru, 88
Ienaga Saburō, 51–52, 184
Igarashi Kōzō, 185
independence movement
  addressed in South Korean newspa-
    pers, 6, 15
International Military Tribunal for the
  Far East, 22, 28, 154, 183
"In the Footsteps of the Volunteer

Labor Corps" (Yun, 1990), 31,
  185
Iran, 73
Iraq, 177
Ishibashi Masashi, 100
Ishida Kazuto, 152
Ishihara Nobuo, 135
Ishihara Shintarō, 170
Islamic Revolution, 73
Itohisa Yaeko, 106–107

Japan
  China and, 55–56, 64, 71–72
  comfort women and (*See* comfort
    women issue)
  emergence of postwar generation
    in, 30–32
  end of Cold War and, 156–157
  history textbooks in. *See* Japanese
    history textbooks
  influence of elites in, 159–160
  international trade and, 35–37,
    39–43
  "irresponsible statements" made by
    Japanese officials, 140–142
  during Kaifu administration, 101–
    102
  limits of populism in, 164–165
  media moguls in, 29–30
  new "Korean cognoscenti" in, 86
  1980 elections in, 73–74
  North Korea and, 66–69, 102
  political fluidity in, 65–66
  political turmoil of late 1980s, 98–
    101
  during postwar era, 22–23, 27–28
  recession of 1990s and, 158, 160–
    161
  rise of nationalism in, 9–11, 58–59,
    87–88, 163–164, 170, 173

rise of populism in, 161–164

San Francisco Peace Treaty and, 24, 26, 183

Socialist Party of. *See* Japanese Socialist Party (JSP)

South Korea and. *See* South Korea/Japan relations

South Korean visitors to, 77–80

"tilt to the right" in, 9–11, 13, 59–62, 67

Tokyo War Crimes Trial, 22, 28, 154, 183

trade dependency ratio (TDR) of, 41–42

United States and, 157–158, 170

See also South Korea/Japan relations

Japan as Number One (Vogel, 1979), 13

Japan-China Joint Communiqué, 72

Japan Communist Party (JCP), 66

Japanese history textbooks, 9–13, 49–59, 82–85, 87–91, 151–158

Chinese response to, 55–58, 87, 89

chronology of, 184–185

comfort women issue in, 132, 152, 154–155

Ienaga lawsuits and, 50–53

Japanese nationalism and, 88, 91, 95

"neighboring country clause" and, 153–154, 155

New Version of Japanese History, 88–91, 97, 152

1982 history textbook controversy, 50–55, 83–84, 87

1987 textbook controversy, 85–86

in 1990s, 151–158

South Korea/Japan relations in, 153

South Korean response to, 53–55, 57–59, 87, 89

Textbook Reform Society and, 152–158

Japan Labor-Farmer Party, 190n20

Japan Renewal Party, 133–134

Japan Socialist Party (JSP), 65–70, 99–101, 133, 142

decline of, 156

historical perception and, 142

purge of party members, 29

Japan-South Korea Joint History Research Project, 49, 179–180

Japan/South Korea relations. *See* South Korea/Japan relations

The Japan That Can Say No (Ishihara/Morita), 170

Jeong Seung-hwa, 197n6

Jikkyō Shuppan publishing company, 12, 50

Joint Private-Government Committee on Measures Pursuant to the Publication of Documents on South Korea-Japan Talks, 125

Kaifu Toshiki, 88–89, 101–104

Kameda Naoko, 182

Kanemaru Shin, 102

Kan Naoto, 164–166

Katō Kōichi, 105, 107

Katō Statements, 108–110, 122, 123, 125, 128–130, 185

Kawakami Jōtarō, 29, 190n20

Kaya Okinori, 28

Ken-Kanryū (Hating "The Korean Wave"), 169, 186

Kennedy, Edward, 73

Kentei fugōkaku Nihonshi (Ienaga, 1982), 52

Kim Dae-jung, 64, 69, 75, 85, 100, 116–117, 179, 197n6

comfort women issue and, 125

kidnapping of, 80, 184

Kim Hak-sun, 104–105, 185
Kim Hyung-wook, 64
Kim Il-sung, 67, 99
Kim Jae-gyu, 75
Kim Jong-pil, 116, 121, 197n6,
    207n100
  comfort women issue and, 118–119,
    121, 124
Kim Seong-su, 29
Kim Yoon-hwan, 80
Kim Young-jak, 81
Kim Young-sam, 75, 100, 105–106,
    116–117, 197n6
  comfort women issue and, 125, 132
  elections of 1992 and, 120
  recession of 1990s and, 160
  South Korea/Japan relations and,
    137–138, 147–148, 185
Kishi Nobusuke, 28
Kissinger, Henry, 63
Kobayashi Yoshinori, 152, 153, 216n8
Koga Tadashi, 153
Koizumi Junichirō, 158, 161–164,
    168, 173, 179, 185
  rise of nationalism and, 163–164
Kōno Statement, 134–137, 154,
    185
Kōno Yōhei, 134–136, 138, 142
"Koreagate" scandal, 63–64, 69
Korean Council for the Women
    Drafted for Military Sexual Slav-
    ery by Japan, 111
Korean Military Academy (KMA),
    75–76
Korean War, 43, 66, 76
Kuk-il movement, 82–83, 91
Kukp'ung 81, 81
Kuroda Katsuhiro, 86
Kyōkasho Mondai o Kangaeru Giin
    Renmei (Diet Members' Alliance
    for Considering the Textbook
    Issue), 88

League of Parliamentarians on the
    Fiftieth Anniversary of the End of
    World War II, 145–146
Lee Do-hyung, 60, 82–83
Lee Dong-won, 27
Lee Hu-rak, 75
Lee Myung-bak, 166, 170, 191n35,
    221n65
Lee Sang-deuk, 221n65
Liberal Democratic Party (LDP) of
    Japan, 65, 73–74, 133–134, 142
  following 1986 elections, 98–100
  history textbooks and, 155
  21st century populism and, 164–
    165
Liberal View of History Study Group,
    154

Mahathir Mohamad, 161
Marxism, 96
Ma Ying-jeou, 166
Miki Takeo, 184
Minerva Shobō, 179–181
Miwa Jusō, 190n20
Miyazawa Kiichi, 74, 88, 103, 109,
    133
  no-confidence vote and, 133, 185
  visit to South Korea by, 105–107,
    111–115, 117–119, 121, 123, 128,
    130
Miyazawa Statement, 88–89
Moriyama Kinji, 88
Mun Se-gwang, 64, 80–81, 184
Murao Jirō, 88
Murayama Nagataka, 29
Murayama Statement, 138, 140, 145,
    185

Murayama Tomiichi, 138–139
  historical perception and, 138–140,
    148
  "irresponsible statements" and,
    140–143, 146–147
  Japanese annexation of Korea and,
    146–147, 185
  resolution regarding WWII, 145

Nagano Shigeto, 141
Nakasone Yasuhiro, 74, 89–90, 98,
    102, 144
  Japan's rightward shift and, 13
Narita Tomomi, 67
Naruse Masato, 90
New Frontier Party (Japan), 142, 155
Newly Industrializing Economies
    (NIEs), 37
New Party Sakigake (Japan), 133–134,
    142
New Version of Japanese History, 88–91,
    97, 152
Nihon o Mamoru Kokumin Kaigi
    (People's Conference to Protect
    Japan), 87–90, 152
Nippon Kaigi (Japan Conference), 87
Nippon Kyōiku Saisei Kikō (Japan
    Educational Revival Organiza-
    tion), 156
Nishio Kanji, 152, 154–155, 157–
    158
Nishizaki Kiyohisa, 90
Nixon, Richard, 72, 184
Noda Yoshihiko, 164–166
North Korea, 33
  Cold War and, 44
  comfort women issue and, 131, 136
  globalization and, 41
  Japan and, 66–69, 99–100, 102, 131,
    147, 170

  nuclear program of, 45
  South Korea and, 33

Ōhira Masayoshi, 65, 73
Okonogi Masao, 86
Okuno Seisuke, 141
Ozawa Ichirō, 133

Paris Peace Accords, 72, 184
Park Chul-un, 120–121
Park Chung-hee, 8, 184
  assassination of, 9, 13, 63, 72–73,
    81
  attempted assassination of, 64, 80–
    81, 184
  contrasted with Chun, 74–75
  coup staged by, 28–29
  criticism of, 81
  economic strategy of, 44
  Japanese language and, 85
Park Geun-hye, 166, 173
Park Tae-joon, 116–117, 120
People's Conference for Realization of
    an Era Name Law, 152–153
populism, global rise of, 161–162, 164
  leading to nationalism, 164
Presidential Secretariat, 75
pro-Japanese collaboration, 23–24, 28,
    187n1, 188n3
  addressed in South Korean newspa-
    pers, 6, 15

Reagan, Ronald, 63, 74
Recruit stock scandal, 98, 200n2
reparations (from Japan), 14, 22–23,
    26, 115, 118, 121–123
  discussed in South Korean publica-
    tions, 6
Reunification Democratic Party,
    116–117

Rhee Syngman, 28, 76–77, 79, 183–184

Roh Moo-hyun, 161–163, 163–164, 166, 173

Roh Tae-woo, 100–102, 105–106, 112, 120
   comfort women issue and, 113, 124–125
   election of, 116–117

Saikawa Eita, 153

Sakamoto Takao, 152

Sakurai Shin, 141

San Francisco Peace Treaty, 24, 26, 183

Satō Eisaku, 27

Semarang incident, 135

Senda Kakō, 30

Senkaku Islands issue, 56, 165

Seoul 1988 Olympics, 32–33

Shigemitsu Mamoru, 28

Shigemura Toshimitsu, 12, 86

Shimamura Yoshinobu, 141

Shimizu Sumiko, 104

Shin Yong-ha, 62

Shōriki Matsutarō, 29

Sino-Vietnamese War, 73

Sixth Republic, 8

Society for History Textbook Reform (Textbook Reform Society), 151–158, 163, 185

Society for the Bereaved Families of the Pacific War, 187n7

Sorenson, Clark, 181

South Korea, 143–144
   China and, 170–171
   Cold War and, 43–45, 63–64, 72
   comfort women issue in domestic politics, 117–122
   constitution of, 143
   democratization in, 8–9, 100, 105
   détente period of Cold War and, 71–74
   economic growth of, 40–41
   elections of 1988 in, 116–117
   elections of 1992 in, 120–122
   emergence of postwar generation in, 30–32, 74–76
   globalization and, 43
   impact of Chun administration in, 75–76
   influence of elites in, 159–160
   international trade and, 35–36, 41–44
   Japan and. *See* South Korea/Japan relations
   Japanese history textbooks and, 53–55, 57–59
   Marxism in, 96
   media moguls in, 29–30
   new "Japan cognoscenti" in, 77–81, 91
   North Korea and, 102
   Olympics of 1988 in, 32–33
   postwar era in, 23–24
   Presidential Secretariat of, 75
   "pro-Japanese collaborators" in, 23–24, 28
   recession of 1990s and, 42, 160–161
   rise of populism in, 161–164
   trade deficits of, 112
   trade dependency ratio (TDR) of, 41–42
   use of Japanese language in, 84–86
   See also South Korea/Japan relations

South Korea/Japan relations, 7–8, 167–168, 171, 175–177
   during twenty-first century, 171–174, 191n35
   academic cooperation and, 86

arrogance of Japanese in, 85–86

bilateral trade and, 35–37, 39–41, 43, 45, 112, 148–149, 176

chronology of, 183–186

Chun Doo-hwan administration and, 8

during colonial era, 26, 29–30, 143–144

comfort women issue and, 30–32, 34, 96–97, 103–110, 113–119, 122, 124–125, 128, 132, 136–137, 146, 148, 151, 171–173, 176, 185

democratization of South Korea and, 8–9

during détente era, 76

effect of Cold War on, 44–45, 64, 70, 97–98, 149, 177

emergence of postwar generation and, 30–32, 74–77, 79–80

FIFA World Cup and, 39, 168

following resolution of comfort women issue, 137–138

forced transport/labor issue and, 103–104

gisaeng (courtesan) tourism and, 34

globalization and, 39, 41, 159, 176–177

historical perception and, 34, 45, 97–98, 99–101, 122–123, 138–139, 151, 167–168, 173, 175–176

horizontally-based, 85–87

in immediate postwar era, 22–24, 29

"irresponsible statements" of Japanese officials and, 140–143

Japan/China relations and, 71–72, 170

Japanese annexation of Korea, 143–147, 171, 183

Japanese elections of 1980 and, 73–74

Japanese history textbooks and, 10–11, 13, 49, 53–55, 57–59, 70, 82–85, 87, 91, 153, 176

Japanese journalists in South Korea, 85–86

Japanese nationalism and, 9–11, 58–59, 170

Japanese prosperity and, 96

Japanese "shift to the right" and, 9–11, 59–62

Japanese Socialist Party and, 67, 69–70, 72, 99–101

Japan/North Korea relations and, 102

Kim Dae-jung incident and, 64

Kuk-il movement and, 82–83

lack of diplomatic relations, 77

Marxist view of, 96

Mun Se-gwang incident and, 64, 80–81

Murayama incident, 146–148

new "Japan cognoscenti" and, 77–85, 91

normalization of diplomatic relations, 16, 24, 27, 66–67, 77, 80

official diplomatic visits, 102–103, 105–106, 110–115, 117–119, 123

Olympics of 1988 and, 33

"pro-Japanese collaborators" and, 23–24, 28, 187n1, 188n3

reparations issue, 14, 22–23, 26, 115, 118, 121–123

San Francisco Peace Treaty, 24, 26, 183

South Korean Marxism and, 96

South Korea's economic development and, 40–41

Syngman Rhee Line, 22, 23–24, 26, 66, 183

tourism and, 37–40

South Korea/Japan relations
(*continued*)
travel between nations, 37–39,
77–80
use of Japanese language, 84–86
Yasukuni Shrine issue, 23, 59–60,
67, 125, 163–164, 183–186
See also historical perception
Soviet Union (USSR)
boycott of 1984 Olympics, 32
invasion of Afghanistan, 65, 73
Japan and, 170
South Korea and, 33, 44
United States and, 63
Sugita Keizō, 181
Suzuki Zenkō, 74
Syngman Rhee Line, 22, 23–24, 26,
66, 183
Syria, 177

Tabiki Katsuji, 180–181
Taiwan (Republic of China), 64, 184
Takahashi Shirō, 152
Takemura Masayoshi, 133
"Takeshima Day" ordinance, 163, 186
Takeshima Island issue, 26, 163, 167,
169, 187n1
addressed in South Korean newspa-
pers, 6, 15, 25
chronology of, 183, 186
Lee's visit to Takeshima, 171
Takeshita Noboru, 98–99
Tanabe Makoto, 99, 102
textbook issue. *See* Japanese history
textbooks
Textbook Reform Society. *See* Society
for History Textbook Reform
Thaksin Shinawatra, 161
The Third World War: The Untold Story
(Hackett, 1978), 65

Tokyo War Crimes Trial, 22, 28, 154,
183
addressed in South Korean publications, 25
trade dependency ratio (TDR), 41–42
Treaty of Annexation, 143–144, 146,
185
Treaty on Basic Relations between
Japan and the Republic of Korea,
8, 16, 26–27, 66, 100
chronology of, 183–186
Claims Settlement Agreement of,
104–105, 114–115, 118–119, 127–
128, 132, 171
comfort women issue and, 104–105,
118–119, 125–127
Japanese annexation of Korea and,
144

United States
boycott of 1980 Olympics, 32, 65
Cold War and, 43–44, 63–65, 72
détente period of Cold War and,
72–73
diplomatic relationship with South
Korea, 44, 63–64, 74, 76–77
economic influence of, 37
election of 1980 in, 74
Japan and, 157–158, 170
trade dependency ratio (TDR) of,
41–42
trade with South Korea, 35–36, 43
USSR and, 63
Uno Seiichi, 88
Uno Sōsuke, 99

Vietnam War, 44, 63, 72, 184
Vogel, Ezra, 13
volunteer labor corps issue, 111, 121,
202n31, 202n33

addressed in South Korean newspapers, 15, 31, 185
See also comfort women issue

Watanabe Michio, 108, 185
"irresponsible statements" made by, 141, 143, 145
Watashi wa kai ni naritai [I want to become a shellfish] (TV show), 29–30
Winter Sonata, 168
World Cup, 39, 168, 185

Yagi Noboru, 100
Yamaguchi Tsuruo, 100
Yamamoto Natsuhiko, 152
Yamano Sharin, 169, 186

Yamashita Tatsuya, 182
Yasukuni Shrine issue, 23, 67, 125, 163–164, 183–186
addressed in South Korean newspapers, 14–15, 25, 59–60
Yokota Keiko, 182
Yomiuri shimbun, 29
Yong-Chool Ha, 181
Yoshida Mitsuo, 86
Yoshida Seiji, 186
Yoshimi Yoshiaki, 129
Yugoslavia, 177
Yuk Young-soo, 64
Yun Jeong-ok, 31, 103–104, 185

Zhou Enlai, 56